GERMANY
1945–1990

GERMANY
1945–1990
A Parallel History

BY

JÜRGEN WEBER

CEU PRESS

Central European University Press
Budapest New York

First published in German as Kleine Geschichte Deutschlands seit 1945
by Deutscher Taschenbuch Verlag GmbH & Co. KG, München in 2002

English edition published in 2004 by
Central European University Press

An imprint of the
Central European University Share Company
Nádor utca 11, H-1051 Budapest, Hungary
Tel: +36-1-327-3138 or 327-3000
Fax: +36-1-327-3183
E-mail: ceupress@ceu.hu
Website: www.ceupress.com

400 West 59th Street, New York NY 10019, USA
Tel: +1-212-547-6932
Fax: +1-212-548-4607
E-mail: mgreenwald@sorosny.org

Translated by Nicholas T. Parsons

ISBN 963 9241 70 9 cloth

Library of Congress Cataloging-in-Publication Data

Weber, Jürgen, 1944–
    [Kleine Geschichte Deutschlands seit 1945. English]
    Germany, 1945–1990: a parallel history / by Jürgen Weber;
    translated by Nicholas T. Parsons.
        p. cm.
    Includes bibliographical references.
    ISBN 963 9241 70 9
    1. Germany—History—1945-1990. I. Title.
DD257.W399 2004p
943.087—dc22
                                                        2003015670

Preprint by Attributum Stúdió, Budapest
Printed in Hungary by Akaprint, Budapest

Contents

1. Into the Abyss:
Germany under Allied Occupation, 1945–46

The "total war", to which Joseph Goebbels, Hitler's propaganda minister, had exhorted the German people in February 1944, led to a military, political and moral catastrophe that was unique in German history, and which ended in May 1945 in the complete defeat of the Third Reich. As state, as a nation, as a people and as a functioning economy, Germany appeared to be at an end.

By an enormous effort of will and the huge application of resources the United States of America, the Soviet Union and Great Britain had overcome Hitler's totalitarian regime, which latterly was facing fifty-one states that had declared war against it. For six years the world had been a conflagration, acts of cruelty had been done in the name of duty, the primary aim of the state had become the destruction of the enemy, modern war technology had developed an unprecedented capacity for destruction affecting the civil population even more harshly than the military, and the life of the individual had counted for little.

THE AUDIT OF HORROR

Large swathes of Europe had been devastated and Germany lay in ruins. The loss of human life was unimaginable. Realistic estimates of the victims of Hitler's policies that led to the Second World War put the figure at more than 55 million dead over the whole world. More than half of these were accounted for by the Soviet Union.

Six million people were killed under Nazi rule solely because of their Jewish origin. This monstrous policy, carried out by special commando groups and in vast liquidation camps, shocked the entire world. The name of Germany was uttered only with contempt.

During the war, nearly six million Poles lost their lives and about seven million Germans, of which half a million were the victims of air raids, one million were soldiers who died in Soviet prison camps and an estimated two million died as refugees when driven from their homeland. The dead also included hundreds of thousands of Americans, French and British. To this may be added around 35 million people worldwide who were disabled by the war—in Germany alone, there were two and a half million seriously disabled. Finally the lamentable figure for war victims should include millions of people who disappeared or went missing, widows, orphans, refugees and the victims of expulsion.

Last but not least one should also recall that imprisonment was the bleak experience of millions of people—35 million worldwide, of which about 11 million were Germans. Of the twenty lands that took German prisoners, the greatest numbers were captured by the victorious powers: 3.2 million soldiers were captured by the Russians, 3.8 million by the Americans, 3.7 million by the British and 245,000 by the French. The English and the Americans handed over 700,000 prisoners to the French for "work contributing to the reconstruction of the country". By 1948 all prisoners of war had returned from the western countries, but not until 1956 did the last prisoners return from the Soviet Union. Among the terrible consequences of the Second World War was that 20 million people in Europe were obliged to leave their homeland, among them Poles, Czechs, Ukrainians and above all Germans. For about 12 million of these, expulsion and flight was to be their bitter fate. In the last months of the conflict, over five million people fled westwards from East Germany to escape the advancing Red Army; shortly afterwards began the brutal expulsion of Germans from Czechoslovakia.

THE DEFEATED ENEMY STATE

The unconditional surrender of the German army on the 8th of May 1945 ended the war in Europe. The ordinary Germans, who wanted the war no more than the other nations, but who had for the most part adulated Hitler, had tolerated the Nazi regime and had not dislodged this regime by their own efforts, now found themselves thrown on the mercy of the victorious nations. They had thereby removed themselves from the community of civilised nations and their future lay entirely in the hands of the victorious powers.

The German attempt to "conquer the world", as well as the Nazi policies of oppression and extermination in their own country and in the occupied territories, had discredited the German name and aroused demands among the victorious powers for punishment of those guilty of war crimes, as well as for compensation for damage caused by the war and for extremely severe measures to be taken so that such events could not reoccur. Unpredictability and aggression were seen as the salient characteristics of German politics. For this reason the coalition formed against Hitler demanded the right to dispose over Germany and the Germans, which in practice meant a temporary military occupation of the vanquished country, as well as more permanent political and economic control.

The Allies left Germany in no doubt that she was not occupied in order to facilitate her liberation, but as a conquered enemy state. As had been agreed between them some months previously, they set up their occupation regime in Germany in the summer of 1945 and applied the "Berlin Declaration" of 5th June 1945, by which Germany was obliged to accept and follow "all the requirements which now or later should be placed upon her". The Allies now exercised the "paramount administrative power", which encompassed all matters of state down to details concerning the smallest village.

OCCUPATION ZONES

The dictatorship, with which the Germans had been so ready to identify, was now without its dictator. The country was administered by military governors and their military and civil officials in four occupation zones. The American zone, governed by General Eisenhower with 12,000 American soldiers, had its headquarters in Frankfurt am Main; the British zone, under General Montgomery with 25,000 British troops, was based at Bad Oeynhausen; General Lattre de Tassigny, with 11,000 French troops, was based at Baden-Baden; and 60,000 Soviet troops were under the command of Marshal Zhukov, who presided over the Soviet military administration from his headquarters in Berlin-Karlshorst. In Berlin, in place of the government of the Reich, the Allied Control Council met to take all necessary administrative decisions concerning "Germany as a whole". As the representatives of their respective governments, the four commanders were supposed to make all important decisions on a unanimous basis, which should then be implemented in their own way by the individual military administrations of the respective occupation zones. However, this actually happened only in the case of comparatively few decisions. Increasing conflicts of interest between the Allies hindered the operation of a joint occupation policy. Each of the victorious powers ruled and administered its own zone in the manner it thought fit. This isolationist policy naturally hindered economic exchange between the different parts of Germany and arbitrarily fragmented the traditional centres of economic activity.

MISERY AND LIBERATION

Whether Germany still existed at all was now a moot point, although the ordinary citizen had other worries. For him or her, the most pressing problem was survival itself. Millions of homes, above all in the towns, had been bombed and often completely destroyed. Many sought shelter in ruins, cellars or Nissen huts. Families were torn apart and millions of people deracinated. Most of the population were on the edge of starvation. Yet the collapse of the structures of the state and of society also represented for many the hour of liberation. This was the case for hundreds of thousands of inmates of concentration camps and prisons, for resistance fighters and opponents of the regime who had survived, for prisoners of war and those in forced labour camps; and finally also for those Germans who, simply as passive victims of the regime, had yearned for an end to state-organised terror and war. Many shared the feeling expressed by Theodor Heuss of being "simultaneously saved and annihilated". A collective sigh of relief went through the land, but at the same time there was fear for the future—"at least we have survived" gave way to "what will become of us?" Few anticipated that the new masters in military uniform would so soon sit down to negotiate with the Germans at the same table, especially since the pictures and reports of mass murder in the death camps were emerging to shock world opinion. How, they wondered, would the victors react to such horrors?

However, the coalition of victorious powers rested on a fragile base. Now that the German aggressor had been defeated, it appeared that, although all could agree on the broad, abstract aims regarding the future of Germany—the destruction of German militarism and Nazism as a pre-condition for a return to "an honourable existence and a place in the community of naions"—the concrete measures required to achieve this were a matter for dispute.

PUNISHMENT OF THE NAZI ELITE AND NAZI WAR CRIMINALS BY THE ALLIED COURTS

An exception to this rule was the unanimous agreement among the Allies to set up a military court in Nürnberg to try the main war criminals. Trials were held for symbolic reasons in the city of the Nazi rallies and 22 leading Nazis were tried from 20th November 1945 onwards, among them leading Nazis such as Göring, Hess, von Ribbentrop, Speer, Streicher, Dönitz and Keitel. The Allies charged them with the preparation and conduct of a war of aggression, war crimes and genocide. At the beginning of October 1946, the Allied judges handed down twelve death sentences, seven long prison sentences, of which three were for life, and three acquittals. The NSDAP, the SS, the Gestapo and the SS (SD) were declared to be criminal organisations, although the prosecution of their members, if there was no evidence of personal guilt, was not pursued.

In Nürnberg, for the first time, the full extent of the criminality of the

Nazi leadership emerged. The press and the radio reported it in detail, as also the attempts of those charged to justify their actions or evade responsibility for them. Once powerful Nazi functionaries refused to admit responsibility for the catastrophe caused by the Nazi system; instead they attempted to shift the entire blame for the German policies of war and ruination onto Hitler, Himmler and Goebbels, all of whom had committed suicide. The majority of the population therefore believed that their severe punishment by the Allied court was appropriate. On the other hand, all too many Germans considered themselves as absolved from blame as a result of these trials. Such people hastened to point the finger at the former leading Nazis who had been brought before the courts, by whom they believed they had been deceived and misled, conveniently regarding themselves merely as harmless fellow-travellers. Thus the question of complicity amongst a wider swathe of the population for what it had been possible to do in the name of Germany between 1933 and 1945 rapidly receded from public gaze.

THE LATER TRIALS

The unanimity of the four victorious powers that was shown in the punishment of leading Nazis soon dissipated after the judgement at Nürnberg. In all four occupation zones there were a large number of subsequent trials against active Nazis; however these were conducted under the individual auspices of the zone concerned. Of particular importance were twelve subsequent Nürnberg trials against a further 184 hand-picked high functionaries of the Nazi regime held before US military courts. Those charged included generals, leaders of industry, jurists, high officials, commanders of SS squads, doctors, and those responsible for concentration camps. Four-fifths of the accused were convicted and half of the 24 death sentences were carried out. Apart from the punishment of the accused in accordance with individual levels of culpability, these trials were also concerned with clarifying for the benefit of the German public the extent of the criminality of the defeated regime. At an early stage, the US military courts concerned themselves with the SS guards of concentration camps such as Dachau.

The three western powers condemned over 5000 persons in military trials up to 1950, 806 of whom were given the death penalty. At least a third of these sentences were carried out. However, the outbreak of the Cold War between East and West soon caused the demands for punishment and expiation to fade into the background. The desire to draw a line under past events became widespread, also among the Western Allies. Most of the convicted Nazis were able to leave prison in the early 1950's, the last of them emerging in 1958. Soviet military tribunals convicted over 50,000 persons, of which 756 received the death penalty. One third of the convicted who were deported to Siberia as forced labour did not survive their terms. However, the Soviet tribunals did not only condemn as "fascists" actual or supposed Nazis, but also many opponents of Communism, including many democrats and young people, who were convicted of so-called "crimes" against the occupying power and the officials of the Soviet zone.

POLITICAL PURGES: DENAZIFICATION AND ITS CONSEQUENCES

Beside the conviction of war criminals, the denazification concept of the allies also implied a comprehensive political purge in occupied Germany. This began with the provisional internment of more than one hundred thousand incriminated Nazi functionaries in holding camps, and the dismissal of former members of the Nazi party from schools, the state administration and important positions in the economy. Finally, the professional and political past of millions of Germans was subjected to close scrutiny by means of detailed questionnaires.

THE WESTERN ZONES

From 1946 onwards, denazification courts under German control allocated the persons under examination to one of five categories: heavily incriminated, incriminated, slightly incriminated, fellow-traveller and not incriminated. On the basis of these categories, the appropriate punishments were handed down, ranging from imprisonment, through confiscation of property and fines, to temporary suspension of voting rights.

The expense incurred by the Western Allies, and above all the Americans, was massive, the results, however, somewhat variable. In the American occupation zone alone some 13 million people were obliged to fill in a questionnaire; 3.6 million of these theoretically required denazification, but only 1 per cent was actually punished. In Nordrhein-Westfalen, the most populous part of the British zone, only 90 persons were categorised as heavily incriminated or incriminated. Some critics have therefore condemned the western denazification policy as little more than a "production process for fellow-travellers" (*"Mitläuferfabrik"*—Lutz Niethammer). "Purge" and "rehabilitation" gradually became almost indistinguishable in a process that continued up to 1948. Many considered themselves unjustly treated, since the minor Nazis were the first to be brought to justice, and were treated with considerable severity, while the more important ones who gave the orders were generally dealt with later, and usually more mildly. Besides which, many of those who had formerly been convinced Nazis occupying high positions succeeded in concealing their past and in evading the arm of the law by accommodating themselves smoothly to the new dispensation—a form of unfinished business that was later to be a serious burden on the fledgling Bundesrepublik (Federal Republic of Germany, or West Germany).

THE EASTERN ZONE

In the Soviet zone, the process of denazification was carried out under the slogan of "anti-fascist democratic transformation". Structural intervention in society and the economy, such as the expropriation of landlords and the larger peasant holdings, and nationalisation of the major part of industry and the banks, were just as vital a part of the process as the purge of the government and administration. The latter affected about half a million former Nazis in offices of state. Most importantly, a large percentage of teachers, judges, public prosecutors and police officers were removed from their positions. In other areas, however, the former members of the Nazi party had less to fear: only every eighth party member was dismissed by the denazification commission presided over by the SED (*Sozialistische Einheitspartei Deutschlands*—Socialist Unity Party of Germany—*see Chronology*). In particular, the minor party members were treated leniently in order to integrate them as rapidly as possible into the new dispensation, which gave rise to the ironic remark: "Long live the SED, the big friend of the little Nazis" (Wolfgang Leonhard). Anyone who openly identified himself with the now dominant KPD/SED [the Communists] could make a career for himself, despite having a Nazi past. Numerous heavily incriminated Nazi functionaries, however, fled to the West. In February 1948 the Soviet military regime declared the denazification to be complete. Despite this, trials against actual or supposed Nazi continued to be held.

Although the denazification in the Western zones can hardly be described as a success story, the fact that several million former members of the Nazis party and its subsidiary organisations found themselves confronted with their individual political pasts did indeed result in a personal rejection of Nazism for many, and in the continuation of a change of direction that many had already embraced. In the Eastern zone, the denazification initiatives of the occupying power was overshadowed by the often arbitrary arrests of people

who earlier had not been Nazi activists at all, but who now opposed the policies of the SED and protested against the new lawlessness which characterised the seizure of power by the Communists.

WHAT WERE THE AIMS OF THE
OCCUPYING POWERS?

The common interest of the four victorious powers in a political cleansing
process did not prevent each from acting at its own discretion. This clearly
demonstrated how different were their concepts and priorities in respect of
Germany, and naturally these different concepts influenced their respective
occupation policies.

By means of denazification through questionnaires and hearings, the
Americans wanted to filter out the guilty from the rest of the Germans, clas-
sify their levels of guilt, punish them and generally "re-orientate the German
people" towards democracy. The British, junior partners to the powerful
USA, had a similar approach, but dealt with the problem more pragmatically; soon after the war had ended (and earlier than the US government in Washington), they began to concern themselves with the stabilisation of Western Europe, including the Western occupation zones, in the face of Stalin's
apparent attempts to extend the Soviet hegemony. For the French, the dismemberment of the German state and the control and exploitation of its economic potential had priority. The Soviets sought reparations for the devas-
tation of their country by the Germans to pay for its regeneration, the
establishment of a secure western border, as much influence as possible over
Germany as a whole, and in the medium term a restructuring of politics and
society, at least in their own zone of occupation; insofar as it could be
achieved, they wanted a Socialist Germany, as stated by Stalin at the beginning of 1945, although his remark was only later made public: "Whichever
power occupies a particular area will impose its own social system on it. Each
of us will introduce our own system over the greatest possible area its troops
can occupy. It could not be otherwise."

DEMOCRATISATION OF POLITICAL LIFE AND THE
ESTABLISHMENT OF POLITICAL PARTIES

One of the most important aims of the Allies was the creation of democratic structures in Germany. This was an aim shared with those Germans who
had survived the Nazi regime, and had been driven by it into illegality, into

opposition, into inner or outer emigration or into concentration camps. Based on their Social Democratic, Christian, conservative, Communist or liberal convictions, they were keen to make a contribution to the rebuilding of democratic structures in Germany, insofar as the occupying powers permitted. For this purpose however, there was a fundamental need to revive the political parties. The first politicians to engage with this problem looked to the traditions of the Weimar Republic, especially the Social Democrats and the Communists. There were, however, also new parties founded, that differed markedly from their Weimar predecessors, for example the CDU, the CSU and the FDP (*see Chronology*).

The Soviet occupation command allowed the Germans once more to form political parties in their zone earlier than did the Western Allies. An order concerning this was issued as early as the 10th of June 1945, whereas the Americans and the British waited until August–September of the same year and the French even until December. In every case, the occupying powers subjected the re-establishment of parties and their functionaries to strict control. The Western Allies, especially the Americans, were determined to ensure that the parties permitted by them were built from the base upwards, or in other words that they should genuinely represent the views of their members and not be controlled from the centre. The Soviets were not concerned with this principle; instead they encouraged centralised organisations, whose claims indeed extended to the whole of Germany. The very first party to be allowed was the KPD, which, in its first proclamation, presented itself as a democratic movement without specifically Socialist or Communist aims. A few days later the Central Committee of the SPD met in Berlin under the chairmanship of the former Reichstag deputy, Otto Grotewohl. It proposed radical nationalisation and proclaimed the need for the union of the two "antifascist" workers' parties. In his capacity as the spokesman for the newly reformed SPD [Social Democratic Party] in Western Germany, the former Reichstag deputy, Kurt Schumacher, rejected the leadership claims of the Berlin SPD; in particular, he resolutely stood out against the demand for a union with the Communists. In October 1945, the two-party leaderships agreed to a divided competence in the Eastern and Western zones.

In Berlin, Cologne, Frankfurt am Main (CDU) and in Bavaria (CSU), a political grouping took shape that was in essence a supra-confessional, Christian and bourgeois umbrella party. Moderate Catholics, Christian trades unionists and national-conservative Protestants joined together to form a people's party on the basis of shared Christian and humanitarian convictions. The Bavarian Christian–Social Union (CSU), which was more conservative and federalist than its sister organisation, remained a separate party. "Christian Social" ideas (Jakob Kaiser) formed the basis of the Union's programme in the early years. From 1948 onwards, however, they were overlaid with the concept of a social market economy resting on private enterprise. The dominant personality of the CDU from 1946 onwards was Konrad Adenauer, a prominent former centrist politician who had been the Mayor of Cologne from 1917 to 1933.

The founders of the liberal party in Berlin (Wilhelm Külz), Württemberg (Theodor Heuss) and Baden (Reinhold Maier) were at pains to overcome the old divisions between rightist and leftist liberal organisations in the Weimar Republic. Even so, the fissure between national liberal and leftist liberal ideas endured in the new party. Their common ground lay in their rejection of clerical influence in the state and in their support for private enterprise. In 1948 the various liberal parties in the Western zone came together to form the Party of Free Democrats (FDP) under the leadership of Theodor Heuss.

In the Soviet occupation zone, the Christian Democrats and the Liberals soon lost their independence. As part of the "anti-fascist" block, they were sucked into the Communist orbit, as also was the leadership of the eastern SDP by 1946. The latter (together with the KPD) was forcibly amalgamated with the SED in April 1946.

THE EMERGING DIVISION OF GERMANY

At the Potsdam conference of July–August 1945, the leaders of the USA, Great Britain and the Soviet Union could only agree on a pro forma compromise regarding the way in which Germany should be treated (demilitarisation, denazification, democratisation and decentralisation). No possibility of agreement existed between the enormous demands for reparations on the part of the Soviet Union and the insistence of the Western powers on the maintenance of the economic viability of Germany. Stalin's ruthless suppression of all non-Communist forces in East and South-East Europe, and in particular his sovietisation of Poland, was a further divisive factor affecting the relations between the former wartime partners.

An American compromise proposal served to cover over the splits in the alliance. Its basis was that, as far as reparations were concerned, Germany should be divided into two regions, a western and an eastern one, from which the Soviet Union on one side and the Western powers on the other should exact such reparations as they considered appropriate. In practice this meant that the Soviet occupation zone was given over exclusively to economic exploitation by the Soviet Union and the Western zone could benefit from the milder policy on reparations, as well as the general economic policies, favoured by the British and the Americans. However, this arrangement contradicted the existing agreement, whereby Germany was supposed to be treated as a single economic unit. The later political division of the country was thus foreshadowed in the decision to accept the American compromise. The two western powers could, by this means, at least thwart Stalin's aspiration to seize the Ruhr area. On the other hand, such a concession had to be paid for with the principle already agreed by Churchill, Roosevelt and Stalin during the war, whereby the easternmost region of Germany was to all intents and purposes amputated to the benefit of the Poles, and Poland's borders were moved westwards to the Oder and Lausitzer Neisse. It also meant the tacit acceptance of the expulsion of millions of people from Poland, Czechoslovakia and Hungary, often in barbaric circumstances, even if theoretically the "resettlement" was to be carried out in a "humane and orderly manner", as stipulated in the three-power agreement.

Apart from this compromise, it soon became clear that no agreement was possible across a whole range of important questions regarding the occupation and its aims (for example, the extent of the reparations, the permissible level of German industry, control of the Ruhr region etc.). As a result, the Allies, hardly having resiled from the dismemberment plans of the war years, nevertheless found themselves unexpectedly set on the path of a division of Germany.

THE EAST–WEST CONFLICT

On top of all this came conflicts in other parts of Europe and the world. In Eastern Central Europe, Stalin exploited his dominant military position to erect Communist satellite states, a process which was taken in the West as evidence of a fundamentally expansionist policy on the part of Moscow. In Iran, Turkey and Greece there were clashes between Anglo-American and Soviet interests.

Mistrust and division increasingly marked the relations between the former allies in the East and West, culminating in 1947 in the so-called Cold War. Its main field of action was to be occupied Germany, the division of which into western and eastern spheres of influence now seemed inevitable. The Allied Control Commission was rendered impotent, in the first instance by the obstructive policy of the French regarding the creation of a centralised German bureaucracy; but even more so because Stalin never missed an opportunity to force through his specific political aims for Germany. Without securing the agreement of the Western powers, he imposed a radical transformation of politics and society in the Eastern zone on the Soviet model, and consolidated the Communist hold on absolute power with terror, bribery and promises that were never intended to be kept. Great Britain and the USA reacted by amalgamating their two zones. They had already initiated democratic reconstruction in their spheres of influence, beginning at a local level with the recognition of political parties and the re-establishment of the Provinces (*Länder*).

In place of a joint control over the whole of Germany, the four occupation zones adapted to the policies of their guarantor powers. The Germans in the east were forced to set up a new socialist society from scratch on the Soviet model. Most of them did not want this, but were soon obliged to recognise that the promised democratic renewal in their zone had turned out to be a dictatorship imposed by the Soviets. On the other hand, the Germans in the Western zone somewhat unexpectedly got the chance to participate once more in the community of democratic states with America at its head, which promised both security and economic assistance. In the Western zones, under the watchful eye of the victorious Western powers, a grassroots democracy began to develop, with political parties, trades unions and democratically elected parliaments. For the convinced democrats amongst the Germans, this represented salvation from the years of oppression under the Nazis; and for the disillusioned fellow-travellers of the defeated regime, it represented a chance to rethink and reorientate.

CHRONOLOGY

1944

12 September 1944   London Protocol issued by the European Advisory Commission (EAC) set up by the USA, Great Britain and the Soviet Union to oversee the division of Germany and Berlin into occupation zones, or "sectors", following the anticipated victory of the anti-Hitler coalition.

25 September 1944   As a last ditch effort to stave off impending defeat, all males between the ages of 16 and 60 who are capable of bearing arms are called up for the "*Deutschen Volkssturm*" ("The Final Assault of the German People"), an operation placed under the command of Himmler.

16 October 1944   Soviet troops overrun East Prussia.

21 October 1944   The US army takes its first city (Aachen) on German soil.

1945

30 January 1945   The Red Army reaches the Oder.

4–11 February 1945	Conference at Yalta (in the Crimea): Roosevelt, Stalin and Churchill agree on the division of Germany into four occupation zones, and on the complete disarmament and demilitarisation of the country; also on the imposition of reparations, although there is no agreement on Stalin's demand for a total of 20 billion dollars of the latter, half of which should go to the Soviet Union.
7 March 1945	Collapse of the German west front; the Americans cross the Rhine at Remagen.
19 March 1945	As German troops retreat, Hitler orders that all industrial and supply facilities that might be of use to the enemy should be destroyed; however, through the intervention of the armaments minister, Albert Speer, at the beginning of April, this "Nero-like" order is not carried out. Nevertheless the Nazi leadership insists to the last on fanatical resistance.
12 April 1945	US President Roosevelt dies and is succeeded by Harry S. Truman.
19 April 1945	The SPD is refounded in Hanover on the initiative of the former Reichstag deputy, Kurt Schumacher, who had been held in a concentration camp for ten years.
25 April 1945	American and Soviet troops meet at Torgau on the Elbe.
30 April 1945	Hitler commits suicide in the *Führerbunker* in Berlin. His successor as President of the German Reich and Supreme Commander of the German army is Admiral of the Fleet Karl Dönitz. Soviet soldiers hoist the red flag on the Reichstag in Berlin. Exiled German Communists are flown to Berlin from Moscow to organise the regeneration of the German state along the lines approved by the Soviet occupation authorities. The "Ulbricht group" is responsible for Berlin. Ulbricht ordains that the process "must appear to be democratic, but we must have everything under our direct control".
2 May 1945	Capitulation of Berlin, the capital of the German Reich.
4 May 1945	The American commander in Cologne restores to office Konrad Adenauer, formerly Mayor of the city, but dismissed by the Nazis in 1933. At the beginning of October he is again relieved of his post, this time by the British military authorities.
7–9 May 1945	Unconditional surrender of the German army in the US military headquarters at Reims and in the Soviet headquarters in Berlin-Karlshorst. The suspension of all hostilities is set for the 8th of May.

| 12 May 1945 | The British Prime Minister, Winston Churchill, warns the US President, Harry Truman, of Stalin's ambitions in Europe: "Along the Russian front an iron curtain has fallen." |

14 May 1945   Directive JCS 1067 of the US General Staff, approved by Truman, comes into force; it establishes the US military government in Germany under General Eisenhower and his deputy, General Lucius D. Clay. Initially severe, this Directive remains in force until the middle of 1947, although in practice its provisions are soon applied with lenience.

23 May 1945   The Dönitz government falls and its members are arrested in Flensburg. There is now no longer a German central administration.
The former "Reichsführer SS", Heinrich Himmler, commits suicide.

28 May 1945   The US occupying forces set up a provisional government in Bavaria under Prime Minister Fritz Schäffer (the former leader of the Bavarian Volkspartei). On the 20th of September he is dismissed and replaced by Wilhelm Hoegner (SPD).

5 June 1945   The Berlin Declaration announces the defeat of Germany and the assumption of governmental functions by the four powers (USA, Soviet Union, Great Britain and France). "Germany will comply with any and all demands that now or later are made on her." Germany's 1937 borders are restored and the country divided into four occupation zones. There is joint occupation and administration of Greater Berlin. The four Supreme Commanders of the occupation zones constitute the joint Allied Control Council, which may only settle questions concerning "Germany as a whole" on the basis of unanimous agreement.

9 June 1945   The Soviet Military Administration of Germany (SMAD) is established in Berlin-Karlshorst.

10 June 1945   Earlier than the Western powers, the SMAD allows the formation of political parties and trades unions in the Soviet occupation zone (SBZ).

11 June 1945   Proclamation of the formation of the KPD following talks in Moscow between Ulbricht, Pieck, Ackermann and Stalin at the beginning of June: "We are of the opinion that to compel Germany to follow the Soviet path would be wrong."
In June and July follows the formation of the SPD, CDU, LDPD and the Union of Free German Trades Unions (FDGB) in the Soviet occupation zone.

26 June 1945	51 states sign the UN Charter in San Francisco.
1–4 July 1945	British and American troops leave those parts of Saxony, Thüringia and Mecklenburg that they had occupied and hand the area over to the Soviets. Western troops take up position in their occupation sector of Berlin.
9 July 1945	On the orders of the SMAD, five provinces are created in the SBZ: Brandenburg, Mecklenburg-Vorpommern, Thüringia, Saxony and Saxony-Anhalt.
14 July 1945	The permitted parties in the SBZ join together as "antifascist democratic parties", or "block parties", which are soon under the dominance of the KPD.
17 July– 2 August 1945	The "Big Three" (Truman for the USA, Stalin for the Soviet Union, and Churchill—from the 28th of July, Clement Attlee—for Great Britain) agree on the political aims of the occupation. France joins the agreement at the beginning of August. They are as follows: 1. Demilitarisation, denazification, democratisation and decentralisation is to be carried out in Germany, which should however be treated as "a single economic unit". 2. Claims to reparations are largely to be satisfied in the respective occupation zones by the removal of industrial assets and from existing production. In addition, the Soviets are to receive deliveries from the Western zone in exchange for agricultural products. Despite Soviet protests, no total for reparations is laid down, although the Soviet claim for the latter is pitched at 10 billion dollars. 3. The areas to the east of the Oder and the Görlitzer Neisse are placed partly under Soviet administration (Königsberg) and partly under Polish governance, pending a final peace treaty. 4. The "resettlement" of Germans from Poland, Czechoslovakia and Hungary is to be carried out in a "humane and orderly manner". 5. The Foreign Ministers of the victorious powers are charged with the task of working out a peace treaty with Germany and its former allies, and of clarifying questions of reparations and the details of measures to be taken during the occupation.
27 July 1945	Establishment of 11 German central administrations for the whole SBZ, acting in consort with the SMAD.
30 July 1945	First session of the Allied Control Council in Berlin.
6 August 1945	The American air force drops the first atom bomb on Hiroshima, and three days later on Nagasaki. Japan capitulates on the 2nd of September.

8 August 1945	The Allies agree on the punishment of major war criminals and on the setting up of an international military tribunal in Nürnberg.
27 August 1945	The establishment of democratic parties is permitted on a local basis in the US zone, in September in the British zone, and in December in the French zone.
3 September 1945	Land reform in Saxony. The other provinces of the SBZ follow suit; resistance comes from the CDU and the LDPD.
10 September– 2 October 1945	First conference of the four Foreign Ministers of the victorious powers in London. France demands the amputation of the Rhine-Ruhr region from Germany, the Soviet Union demands a central government for the whole of Germany and four-power control over the Ruhr region. The USA proposes a treaty incorporating the demilitarisation of Germany for a period of 25 years (the Byrnes Plan).
19 September 1945	Establishment of the provinces of Bavaria (without the Palatinate), Württemberg-Baden and Hesse in the US zone (Bremen is added later).
5–7 October 1945	Conference in Wennigsen near Hanover. Kurt Schumacher is nominated as spokesman for the SPD in the Western zone.
10 October 1945	Foundation in Würzburg of the Christian Social Union (CSU) by Adam Stegerwald.
19 October 1945	In Stuttgart the Lutheran Church issues a statement recognising its complicity with the Nazi regime.
20 November 1945	Commencement of the trials of 22 war criminals and members of six Nazi organisations (including the Gestapo and the SS) before the international military tribunals in Nürnberg (Robert Ley has already committed suicide and the industrialist Alfred Krupp is considered unfit to plead through illness).
20 December 1945	Law Number 10 on the punishment of war crimes is issued by the Control Council.

1946

20 January 1946	The first free elections in Germany since 1933 are held at local government level in the US zone. Local elections take place in the other occupation zones in September.
22 January 1946	Konrad Adenauer is appointed provisional Chairman of the CDU in the British zone and is confirmed in this position on the 1st of March.

9–12 February 1946	Founding of the Association of Free German Trades Unions (FDGB) in the SBZ.

5 March 1946 — The US zone passes a law entrenching the liberation of Germany from National Socialism and militarism. Every German over 18 years of age must fill out a questionnaire comprising 131 questions. In Fulton, USA, Winston Churchill speaks of an "iron curtain" in Europe.

7 March 1946 — Founding of the Free German Youth movement (FDJ) in Berlin. Its chairman is Erich Honecker (KPD).

26 March 1946 — The Allied Control Commission decides on a limitation of production for the German economy, fixed at 50 to 55% of the production in 1938.

21–22 April 1946 — In the SBZ, the union of the KPD and SPD is forced through, creating the Socialist Unity Party of Germany (SED) under the leadership of Wilhelm Pieck (KPD) and Otto Grotewohl (SPD).

25 April–12 July 1946 — No agreement over Germany is reached between the four Foreign Ministers, meeting in Paris. The Soviet Foreign Minister, Molotov, rejects the integration of the four zones, as also the proposal of the US Foreign Minister, Byrnes, that Germany should remain disarmed and be occupied for 40 years. Instead Molotov demands four-power control over the Ruhr region and 10 billion dollars of reparations for the Soviet Union.

25 May 1946 — The Deputy US Military Governor, Lucius D. Clay, orders a halt to the reparations deliveries into the SBZ, since the SBZ has failed to fulfil its side of the agreement.

30 June 1946 — A plebiscite in Saxony approves, with more than 77% in favour, the confiscation of the assets of major industries from "war criminals and Nazi activists".
The Control Council, on the initiative of the Soviets, introduces an interzone passport for journeys between the Eastern and Western zones.

23 August 1946 — Dissolution of the Prussian provinces in the British zone and foundation (on the 1st of November) of the new provinces of Nordrhein-Westfalen, Schleswig-Holstein and Niedersachsen.

30 August 1946 — Founding of the province of Rheinland-Pfalz in the French zone.

6 September 1946 — US Foreign Minister, James F. Byrnes, in a keynote speech held in Stuttgart, signals a change in American policy towards Ger-

many: "The American people wish to assist the people of Germany to find their way back to an honourable place among the free and peaceful nations of the world."

1 October 1946   Judgements of major war criminals are handed down at the Nürnberg trials. There are twelve death sentences, seven prison sentences and three acquittals.

15 October 1946   Premiere of the first post-war German film in Berlin. The film, made by Wolfgang Staudte, bears the title *The Murderers Are Among Us* (*Die Mörder sind unter uns*).

20 October 1946   Elections for the Provincial Parliaments in the SBZ. The SED emerges as the strongest party, but nowhere achieves an absolute majority, despite energetic assistance from the Soviet occupying power during the election campaign.

1 December 1946   Referendum on constitutions in Bavaria and Hesse, the first elections to the Provincial Parliament in Württemberg-Baden having already been held on the 24th of November.

2 December 1946   The British and the Americans come to an agreement on the economic integration of their two zones.

22 December 1946   The Saar region is incorporated into the French customs and economic zone.

2. Germany Is Set on a New Course: The Founding of Two States, 1947–1949

Earlier than the US government, the British saw through Stalin's double strategy in Germany. On the one hand the Soviet representatives in the Allied Control Commission and at the conferences of Foreign Ministers between 1945 and 1947 lost no opportunity of pressing for the reunification of Germany, since by these means they hoped to obtain influence, political leverage and economic advantages in the whole of Germany (and specifically in the Ruhr); on the other hand the Soviet occupying command simultaneously carried through profound social change in the area under its control, amounting almost to a revolution, while also demanding the integration of all the occupied zones.

REVOLUTION FROM ABOVE IN THE SOVIET OCCUPIED ZONE

Using the purge of "fascism" as cover, the Soviets carried out the expropriation of big landowners and the larger peasant holdings, nationalised industries and banks. They placed reliable Communist functionaries in the crucial administrative posts and built up a centrally controlled police apparatus, whose employees owed allegiance only to the new masters. As already mentioned, the Communists regarded denazification as a means for bringing the state entirely under their control. Comprehensive purges of the bureaucracy affected thus not only former Nazis, but soon also those who opposed the hegemony claimed by the Communists. According to figures released by the Soviet Ministry of the Interior in 1990, between 1945 and 1950, 122,671 people were held in special camps, some of which had previously been used as concentration camps by the Nazis. Among these, besides active and fellow-travelling Nazis, were to be found many opponents of Communism, including many young people. Again according to Soviet figures, 42,889 prisoners died of hunger or illness. Western authors assume a far higher figure.

The forced union of the SPD (Social Democrats) with the KPD (Communists) in April of 1946, creating thereby the "Party of Socialist Unity" (SED), widened the division of Germany. This was purely a manoeuvre by the Soviets and the German Communists to weaken the strong influence of the Social Democrats in their zone. Using a mixture of threats and promises, the chief functionary of the Communists, Otto Grotewohl, managed to bring about this fusion, notwithstanding that the majority of the SPD in the Soviet zone were against it. Percipiently, but vainly, the head of the West German SPD in Hanover, Kurt Schumacher, warned the Eastern party leadership against this tactic, whereby he anticipated that his party would simply be used as a "blood transfusion" for one whose real aim was the establishment of Communist hegemony in Germany. Soon the professional Communist revolutionaries of the SED controlled all the levers of power. Many Social Democrats were persecuted and others had to flee.

STEP-CHANGE IN THE POLICY OF THE USA TOWARDS GERMANY

In London, the government was well informed regarding developments in the Eastern Zone. The most influential British politicians no longer had any doubt that a separate Communist state was in the process of being formed in the East, from where pressure could be exerted on the rest of Germany. The British therefore felt that "something had to be done" against the "Russian menace". The US government still hesitated to throw overboard the Potsdam accord, although the British ambassador in Moscow was warning against the "militant, aggressive and expansionist" foreign policy being pursued by Stalin. The economic decline of all Western Europe appeared very likely unstoppable, should it become impossible both to stimulate rapidly the production of goods, and to ensure the food supply at Europe's heart (namely in Germany). The Ruhr, as the most important centre of energy supply and industrial production in Europe, needed to be placed at the disposal of its western neighbours, while trade and commerce needed to be kick-started. An increasing number of Western politicians were by now convinced that Stalin aimed to profit from the growing chaos in the western part of the continent.

The situation was indeed dramatic. In Great Britain, for example, even bread had to be rationed. A final attempt by the USA to avoid the imminent economic collapse in collaboration with, and not in opposition to, the Soviet Union foundered in the early summer of 1946. The suggestion of the US Secretary of State, Byrnes, that Soviet concerns about security in Germany should be satisfied by means of a neutralisation and demilitarisation of the occupied country, carried out under the strict supervision of the four powers and guaranteed for several decades, fell on deaf ears and was decisively rejected by Molotov. The British warnings, as well as those of the most important Germany expert on the spot, the Deputy Military Governor, General Clay, that co-operation with the Soviets was now no longer possible, now at last began to have an effect in Washington. A step-change in American policy towards Germany, one with far-reaching consequences, became apparent. At Stuttgart at the beginning of September 1946, Byrnes announced the imminent integration of the British and American zones to create a unified economic area, one which soon emerged as the core of a West German state.

In West Germany this move was greeted with considerable relief. For the first time the American world power had given the Germans a perspective on the future, indicated a route out of the present misery, and moreover (extremely important at the time) had shown itself willing (unlike after the First World War) to leave its troops in Germany and Europe for as long as was necessary. The greatest fear up till then was that the Americans would leave, but the Soviets would remain.

A UNIFIED ECONOMIC AREA

The founding of a "unified economic area" at the beginning of 1947 was an important preliminary decision for the future of Germany. It created an organisational framework stretching across zones, a German governmental and administrative structure on a federal basis with a parliamentary body (the economic council) in which the relative support for the diverse political forces represented in the eight *Landtage* (regional parliaments) of the British–American zone was reflected. The CDU/CSU (Christian Democratic and Christian Social Unions) and the SPD (Social Democratic Party) disposed over an equal number of deputies. The FDP (Free Democrats) held the balance. The Communists, the Centre Party (*Zentrum*), the German Party (*Deutsche Partei*) and the Association for Economic Renewal (*Wirtschaftliche Aufbauvereinigung*) played no significant role.

In outline, this already represents the later parliamentary configuration of the Bundesrepublik. For the time being, however, all laws and measures taken by the Economic Council were subject to British–American control. Nevertheless, what was more important, at least in the Western zone, was that German aspirations to self-determination in the context of a state framework were in accord with the aims of the Western Allies; these aspirations and aims included an end to starvation and need, normalisation of economic conditions, protection from Communist and Soviet threats and integration into the Western camp. That the Eastern zone had to be abandoned to the tender mercies of the Russian hegemony was accepted as a fact of life, since it was evident that nothing could be done to alter the situation.

The Policy of Containment

That the USA was now determined to prevent the spread of Communism, both in Europe and in the rest of the world, was underlined by President Truman's speech to the Congress in March 1947. He declared that the containment of the influence of Soviet Communism was now the central pillar of American policy on security. Its economic component was the European economic renewal policy, the so-called Marshall Plan, announced by the US Secretary of State, General George Catlett Marshall, in June 1947.

The Marshall Plan: Its Aims and Final Results

In order to avoid an imminent economic impoverishment of Europe, which the Truman government was convinced could only benefit the Communists and allow the Soviet Union to achieve hegemony on the continent, the USA offered all the countries of Europe generous financial help, as well as deliveries of raw materials to assist the rebuilding of the economy. However, only the Western countries took up this offer, as indeed Washington had anticipated.

Together with considerations of security in the context of the new policy of containment, the USA pursued a further aim in its application of the Marshall Plan. Because of the way the German and European economies were interwoven, the threatened collapse of the economy of Western Europe could only be prevented if West Germany was permitted to develop her industrial potential to the benefit of herself and Western Europe, but in a way that "would not make the Germans masters of Europe" (John F. Dulles). At the same time, above all France would never have accepted that aid should be given to Germany alone to rebuild her economy. By agreeing to the Marshall Plan, the European allies of the USA also accepted de facto the long planned political rehabilitation of the Western zone of Germany. Through the latter's integration into a common Western European–Atlantic economic area, a continuing control of the Germans was also effected—this being a requirement on which all the countries in Europe were agreed.

Although months were to pass before the American Congress finally approved the Marshall Plan, it was immediately taken up with enthusiasm by its potential beneficiaries, especially Germany. The greatest power in the world had stretched out its hand to the vanquished Germans! And Germany subsequently did indeed receive ten per cent of the sums (amounting to 14 billion dollars) that were transferred across the Atlantic up to 1952: England

and France were the main beneficiaries. However, of equal importance was the American concept that lay behind this material assistance, namely that of free world trade. This dovetailed with the particular German interest in having free access to markets and in the reactivation of its foreign trade: the crucial importance of the latter was that thereby the dollars could be earned that were necessary for the reconstruction of the country. The Marshall Plan developed into an aid programme with long-term benefits for West Germany, which may be summarised as follows:

1. It supplied the momentum for the creation of a West German state with an economic and social structure based on American precepts.
2. It accelerated the already increasing industrial production and thereby contributed significantly to an economic recovery.
3. It provided the Germans with a psychological orientation towards the Western democracies.

In West Germany, the mood of recovery grew rapidly, and was further strengthened by the economic and currency reforms of the summer of 1948. This three-fold economic course-setting constituted the first moves towards the foundation of a new state, leading finally in 1949 to the creation of the Federal Republic of Germany (*Bundesrepublik Deutschland*).

THE END OF RATIONING IN SIGHT

The rationing system for the British–American Zone (administered from Frankfurt am Main) was a form of shortage management. It led to constant conflicts with the different provinces, for example over the distribution of potatoes, coal and raw materials; it also encouraged the black market and put a brake on economic dynamism. Often the system functioned only on paper. The supply of food, fuel and clothing for the population did not immediately improve thereby, and this only began to change in the course of 1948.

In the Frankfurt Economic Council a new orientation towards the market economy was achieved in the face of strong resistance from the Social Democrat deputies. The main protagonist for the new approach was the American-supported new Economic Director, Ludwig Erhard, who was elected by the CDU/CSU and the FDP, but was at that time still an independent. In April 1948 he promulgated a radical change of course in economic policy. In the context of a general shortage of obtainable goods, whereby the average German attempted to make ends meet with his ration cards and by journeys to stock up directly at farmers, Erhard's words sounded pretty revolutionary: he announced that the whole system of economic management was to be deregulated, with the aim of freeing people from the command economy and giving free rein to market forces.

CURRENCY REFORM

The pre-condition for the new economic policy announced by Erhard and the inclusion of the Western zone in the Marshall Plan was, however, a radical reform of the currency. Some 380 billion nearly worthless Reichsmark were still in circulation, and there was no corresponding supply of goods. This was the consequence and late-arriving bill for Hitler's war, which had largely been financed by printing money, leaving a situation that demanded radical solutions. In place of "cigarettes as currency", real money was once again to be made available. That this nevertheless would mean that millions of German savers would lose their entire cash deposits was clear to all the experts.

American financial experts had already produced a plan for currency reform in 1946, the so-called "Plan for the Liquidation of War Financing and the Financial Rehabilitation of Germany", which the Soviets however rejected. Retaining financial control in their sector was more important to the Moscow leadership than having a say in the currency proposals for Germany as a whole. Further negotiations in the Allied Control Council collapsed definitively in the autumn of 1947. The US government now showed that it was determined to pursue currency reform without the participation of the Soviet Union. In extreme secrecy, the Moscow government ordered new currency to be printed for the Soviet zone as early as the beginning of December 1947. At this time also, and no less secretly, the new German banknotes for the Western zone, the Deutschmarks, were printed in Washington and New York. The Soviets wanted to wait until the Americans publicly announced a currency reform for the Western zone; however, an internal decision for a corresponding move in the East was taken early on for the Soviet zone, the currency to be distributed in the whole of Berlin.

In April 1948 the new banknotes came from America to Bremerhaven in 23,000 tightly packed chests, and were then transported to Frankfurt am Main, where they were stored in the cellar of a former building of the Reichsbank and shortly before their introduction were transported under military escort to the head branches of eleven West German provincial banks.

The currency reform was an initiative of the Americans, but the British and the French also gave their consent. A small group of German experts attended to the technical and logistical details and were able to exercise some influence over one or other of the conditions. Basically, however, the Americans carried through their concept for an effective currency reform: the debts of the German Reich were abolished, as indeed was 80 per cent of the wealth of every single West German.

This radical step was forced on the Germans by the victorious American power—to the great benefit of the former as it later turned out. The day fixed for the currency reform was the 20th of June 1948, a Sunday. On that day the Reichsmark became non-legal tender. Every single adult in the Western zone received 40 Deutschmark (and in August, a further 20 DM). Savers were almost completely expropriated, while the holders of property were spared; however, the latter were obliged later to make a compensating contribution of specific sums under a burden-sharing scheme. The currency reform was also carried out in the French zone. France was financially dependent on America and shared the fear of the Soviet Union that was now spreading across the whole of Western Europe. For this reason, France saw no alternative but to follow the American lead in respect of the founding of a West German state.

ECONOMIC REFORM

Simultaneously to the currency reform, the economic reform announced by Erhard some months before was now put in place. Together with the establishment of a new currency, it laid the foundation for the economic success of the later Bundesrepublik.

Without consulting Clay, the US military governor (and against the votes of the Social Democrats in the Frankfurt Economic Council), Ludwig Erhard carried through a far-reaching reform that largely ended rationing and lifted price controls on most commodities. The basic exceptions were items like rents and food staples. This indeed was an epoch-making achievement: the planned economy, introduced by the Nazis, discredited by the Communists in the Eastern zone and practised in the Western zone in the guise of administration of scarcity, was simply abolished. The end of official controls was at the same time the beginning of the social free market, which of course led at first to considerable price increases for many products and a sharply rising level of unemployment. Yet these proved to be transitional phenomena. The crucial point was that millions of frustrated German consumers could find, almost overnight, all those products in the shop windows which they had for years only dreamed of. The black market disappeared overnight. Hoarded and newly produced goods sought their buyers and the market mechanism of supply and demand soon began to demonstrate its effectiveness.

THE BERLIN BLOCKADE

The Soviet leadership was by no means taken by surprise by the currency reform in West Germany. For months, the leaders in Moscow had been planning to make it an issue for testing the resolve of the Americans, and to do so in Berlin, the most sensitive point of contact between East and West. The city, with its division into four sectors, lay like an island in the Soviet occupation zone, entirely surrounded by Soviet troops. The moment seemed opportune to bring the whole of Berlin into the Soviet sphere, since the Americans had signalled with their currency reform their determination to carry through the founding of a West German state. As early as April 1948, the Soviet command intensified its control over the movement of persons and goods to and from Berlin.

On the 24th of June 1948, the Berlin crisis finally escalated into a dangerous confrontation between East and West. Meanwhile, the Soviet zone was also provided with a new currency ("East Deutschmarks"—DM-Ost) on the 23rd of June 1948, which the Soviets ordered should be the legal tender also for the whole of Berlin. The Western Allies declared this order to be "null and void" and immediately introduced in their three sectors the new D-Mark West, in exchange for the Ostmarks brought into circulation by the Soviets, which were accepted for a period of several months. Immediately after this, the lights went out in West Berlin and the Soviets imposed a complete blockade on the western part of the city. All railway access, as well as access by road or water, were blocked, while the supply of electricity and food from the eastern part of the city and the Soviet zone was discontinued. Two million West Berliners and eight thousand allied soldiers were caught in a trap.

The aim of Moscow was to compel the Western powers to withdraw their troops stationed in Berlin so that the Soviets could occupy their areas. The American project of a West German state would thereby collapse, or so it was thought.

However, to the manifest surprise of the Soviet leadership, the British and the Americans refused to knuckle under, but reacted with an air bridge, the largest and most sustained airlift that the world had ever seen up to that time.

For almost a year American and British pilots transported everything that over two million people in Berlin needed for living and for work: milk powder, coal, dried potatoes and petrol, knitting needles and paper, medicines and clothing—and much more. Every two to three minutes a plane (known as a "raisin bomber") would land at one of the three airports of West Berlin. The trick was to hold the besieged "fortress" of West Berlin without the use of force, since the Soviets also respected the agreements made in 1945 concerning the use of an air corridor to and from Berlin.

However, the Western powers were unable to prevent the division of the city. Under pressure from the Soviets, the democratically elected Berlin city council fled in the autumn of 1948 to the western sector of the city and from there, under the leadership of the Social Democrat, Ernst Reuter, demonstrated the West Berliners' will to resist. Only a very few of the latter responded to the Soviet enticements to go over to the eastern sector of the city and register in the Soviet zone, where they were promised that fresh vegetables, milk and potatoes would be available.

On the 12th of May 1949, the Soviets gave in. They had not managed to achieve their aim, but on the other hand they had certainly ensured that those Germans who were able to do so, irrevocably and with feelings of relief and gratitude, opted for the Western camp. The foundation of the West German state was not prevented, but rather brought forward. America, the victorious power, was now also the protecting power guaranteeing West Germany.

THE FOUNDATION
OF A STATE IN THE WEST

While the Americans and the British were supplying the Berliners from the air and many people feared that there would be a new war, in West Germany a new state was taking shape. From the spring of 1948, the three western occupying powers, together with Belgium, Holland and Luxembourg, held consultations regarding the details of the planned foundation of the Federal Republic. France also gave her consent, after having secured guarantees for its security in regard to a West Germany that had the potential to become extremely powerful, politically and economically. On the 1st of July 1948, the three military governors of Great Britain, France and the USA summoned the eleven West German regional Prime Ministers to the US High Command in Frankfurt am Main and commissioned them to begin consultations regarding the constitutional form of a prospective West German state. For this purpose, they were to call into being a constitutional assembly. The Western Allies demanded that the new state should be democratic and federal (thus with extensive autonomy for the *Länder*), and must safeguard the human rights of its citizens. A statute of occupation designed to regulate relations between the future government and the Western Allies was also promulgated.

The order concerning the founding of a state was seen by the West German politicians as a chance to regain from the victorious powers a measure of political autonomy. They too wanted a free democracy, one, however, in a form that could not be seen as acceptance of a final division of Germany. For this reason the new constitution was to apply only provisionally, until the day that Germany was reunited. This idea was to be articulated through the concept of a "Basic Law" (*Grundgesetz*). The West German state now being created was to be the core of a future free and united Germany; it was, however, to be capable of political action and thus more than simply a makeshift construct born of necessity.

Following an invitation from the Bavarians to Herrenchiemsee, a convention of carefully selected experts prepared a strongly federalist legal model that was ready in August of 1948. This was laid before a parliamentary council consisting of 65 representatives of the provincial parliaments. From the 1st of September 1948, the latter began to work out the Basic Law in Bonn. The two largest political factions, CDU/CSU and SPD, were strongly represented with 27 delegates each; at the same time, the FDP, despite only mustering five delegates, had a significance out of proportion to its numbers.

All were concerned to learn the lessons of history, to avoid repeating the mistakes of the Weimar Republic and to draw the relevant conclusions from the experience of the inhuman Nazi dictatorship. Justice was to have precedence over politics, the state must exist to serve the people, human dignity was to be paramount and the total control of the state was to be replaced by the autonomous and inviolable status of the free individual: these were the constitutional guidelines upon which agreement was speedily reached.

It was important that the Basic Law should be established by mutual agreement. Nevertheless, within the parameters of basic principles, party politics also played a role in the consultations of the delegates. The occupying powers also influenced the course of the consultations considerably. As a result, during the nine months of discussion there were repeated and heated controversies between the political forces represented on both the German and the Allied side, particularly in regard to the question of the division of power between the Federal Government and the *Länder* (for example, concerning respective tax-raising powers and the role of the provincial chambers).

On the 8th of May 1949, exactly four years after Germany's unconditional surrender, a large majority was able to reach agreement over the Basic Law, which was approved by the Allied military governors and all the West German provincial assemblies with the exception of Bavaria. The Bavarian parliament, with its CSU majority, rejected the constitution on the grounds that its vision of government was too centralised, but at the same time it accepted the decision of the other federal states to make the validity of the Basic Law binding in the whole of West Germany. On the 23rd of May 1949, the Basic Law came into force. This was the hour of West Germany's birth.

At the election of the first German Parliament in August 1949, the Union parties (CDU/CSU) were victorious with 31% of the vote, over the SPD with

29.2%. The narrow margin of victory for the Union was interpreted in the Federal Republic as approval of the policies favoured by Adenauer, and above all by Erhard, which sought to orientate the country towards a market economy. Together with the FDP and the Deutsche Partei (DP), the Union formed a government under Chancellor Adenauer, who was elected by a majority of just one vote at the Bundestag (Federal Parliament) in Bonn in September. The first Federal President was the candidate of the FDP, Theodor Heuss. The role of the Leader of the Opposition in the Bundestag was assumed by the chairman of the Social Democrats, Kurt Schumacher. In this way a state emerged within the Western occupied zones, but one which of course still operated under the watchful eye of the Western Allies.

THE FOUNDATION OF A
STATE IN THE EAST

The answer of the Soviet Union to the founding of the Federal Republic had been prepared long in advance, yet Stalin deliberately kept the status of the Soviet occupied sector in doubt until the end of 1948. Probably he still hoped to exert influence on Germany as a whole; the main aim of his strategy was that the Western powers should clearly be seen as responsible for the division of Germany. On the other hand, the leadership of the SED around Wilhelm Pieck, Walter Ulbricht and Otto Grotewohl was working towards a rapid consolidation of its position, correctly assuming that the Communist version of "a new democratic order" could only be realised in the East under the protection of the Soviet army.

Without the presence of Soviet power there would have been no formation of the *Deutsche Demokratische Republik—DDR* (German Democratic Republic—GDR). The East German Communists, who had committed themselves to "a specifically German path to Socialism" under the aegis of the SED, would have had no chance to form a government through free elections. Privately, the Soviets assumed that the East-CDU would get 50% of the vote in a free election held in the Soviet occupied zone. For that reason alone, it was important to ensure that no such free election was held.

The claims to leadership of the country made by the SED in the Soviet zone were opposed at the outset by the Christian Democrats (CDU) and Liberals (LDP), and not without success. At the Council and Provincial elections of 1946, the SED only just came out on top (with 57% and 47% of the vote) after the Soviet military administration intervened in the campaign massively in its favour and arrested large numbers of the supporters of the bourgeois parties. In Berlin as a whole, the SED was heavily defeated, achieving there only just 20% of the vote. The SED was also damaged by resistance from the supporters of the SPD working illegally.

In order to limit the influence of the two bourgeois parties, the SED and the Soviet occupying power jointly promulgated a "German People's Congress for Unity and a Just Peace" towards the end of 1948. This and the subsequent People's Congresses were cosmetised parliaments manipulated by the Soviets to give the impression of popular support for their German policy, which consisted of agitation abroad for the maintenance of the unity of Germany.

The SED, with the help of the Soviets, dominated also the trades unions, the Youth Organisation (FDJ) and all the recently re-established state institutions, such as the police. With the founding of a "German Commission for the Economy" on Soviet orders in the summer of 1947, the first stage in the formation of the later GDR government was achieved. This centralising economic authority, endowed with dictatorial powers, was firmly in the hand of the SED. Within the SED itself, the Communist functionaries increasingly determined the party's policies, and from 1948 formed a small dictatorial clique of professional revolutionaries in the Stalinist mode.

At the end of 1948, the SED leaders received approval from Stalin for the founding of a state in the Soviet zone, and set to work on the preparations for the same, clothing their deliberations in the mantle of unification propaganda. The People's Congress movement again served in May 1949 to conceal the actual aims of the SED, namely to exercise permanent power in East Germany without risking free elections, but putting forward a manipulated unified list of candidates for representative functions. Stalin agreed to the urgent request of the SED to postpone the Parliamentary elections by a year—so that the pre-planned SED victory should at least appear plausibly democratic. By then the German Communists believed they would have the bourgeois parties under control, as indeed proved to be the case by 1950. From the People's Congress and its representative body, the People's Council, the Provisional People's Assembly of the German Democratic Republic (*Provisorische Volkskammer der Deutschen Demokratischen Republik*) emerged finally on the 7th of October 1949. The SED never received democratic confirmation through a free vote. A few days after the founding of the GDR, Pieck was elected to the post of president and Grotewohl to that of the head of the government. The strong man, who actually held the reins of power, was of course Walter Ulbricht, the First Secretary of the SED. The division of Germany into two states was thereby complete.

CHRONOLOGY

1947

1 January 1947	Merging of the American and British zones into a "United Economic Area" (British–American zone—*Bizone*).
25 February 1947	The Allied Control Council dissolves the State of Prussia, which "has always been the standard bearer of militarism and reaction in Germany".
10 March– 24 April 1947	The conference of Foreign Ministers in Moscow breaks up over unresolvable differences concerning Germany.
12 March 1947	US President Truman appears before Congress to declare the determination of his government to support the free peoples of the world against the threat of Communism (the Truman Doctrine).
22–25 April 1947	Founding of the German Trades Union Confederation (*Deutscher Gewerkschaftsbund*—DGB) in the British zone. Its first President is Hans Böckler.
29 May 1947	British–American agreement over the institution of an "Economic Council" (Economic Parliament) for the *Bizone* with its headquarters in Frankfurt am Main, to preside until "governmental and administrative structures for the whole of Germany have been put in place".
5 June 1947	US Secretary of State, George C. Marshall, announces a programme of reconstruction and economic assistance for the countries of Europe, including Germany (the Marshall Plan).
6–8 June 1947	A conference of all the local government leaders of Germany is held to consult on the economic emergency. The conference collapses before it even begins because the head of the Soviet zone walks out, on the grounds that the agenda cannot be agreed. The SED had demanded that the latter should negotiate a central government for the whole of Germany.
11 June 1947	Establishment of the German Economic Commission in the Soviet zone by the Soviet occupying power, with the aim of centralising the East German economy.
25 June 1947	The Economic Council of the *Bizone* is established in Frankfurt am Main.

12 July– 22 September 1947	The Marshall Plan Conference takes place in Paris with 14 European nations involved, but in the absence of the Soviet Union, which also prevents Poland and Czechoslovakia from participating.
16 September 1947	Young writers found the "*Gruppe 47*".
25 November– 15 December 1947	The London Conference of Foreign Ministers ends in failure. It is unable to achieve a joint policy on Germany to which all the four victorious powers can subscribe.
6–7 December 1947	The first "German People's Congress for Unity and Peace" is held in Berlin under the leadership of the SED.

1948

9 February 1948	New constellation of the United Economic Area; doubling of the number of delegates in the Economic Council to 104; introduction of a provincial assembly as a second chamber with the right of veto and the right to initiate laws; an administrative council is set up with administrative directors (for the economy etc.) and a director-general at the top. The basic features of this body foreshadow the internal structure of the later Federal Republic (Bundesrepublik).
23 February– 6 March 1948	The USA and Great Britain arrange a conference in London, which includes France and the Benelux countries, to discuss the question of Germany.
25 February 1948	The Communists seize power in Czechoslovakia.
1 March 1948	Founding of the *Bank deutscher Länder* (later the Bundesbank—Federal Bank, Germany's Central Bank) in Frankfurt am Main, at the instigation of the military governors of the three Western zones.
2 March 1948	The Frankfurt Economic Council elects Ludwig Erhard to the post of Economic Director.
17 March 1948	Great Britain, France and the Benelux countries conclude a treaty in Brussels, whereby they form the Western European Union with the aim of collective defence.
20 March 1948	End of the four-power administration of Germany: the Soviet representatives on the Allied Control Commission leave this body in protest at the London Six Power Conference.

16 April 1948   Foundation of the European Organisation for Economic Co-ope-
                       ration (OEEC) dedicated to co-ordination of the assistance pro-
                       vided under the Marshall Plan for the economic regeneration of
                       Western Europe. There are 16 member states, while West Ger-
                       many is represented by the Military Governors.

20 April–2 June 1948   Continuation of the London Six Power Conference. The end re-
                       sult is that it is agreed that the three Western zones, still under
                       the aegis of the three western powers, should acquire "govern-
                       mental responsibilities". The West German heads of provincial
                       governments are to draw up a constitution on the federalist mo-
                       del (the London Recommendations—*Londoner Empfehlungen*).

20 April–8 June 1948   At Rothwesten near Kassel German currency experts are asked
                       by the Allies to prepare the technical basis for a currency reform.

21 April 1948   Ludwig Erhard presents his programme for the reorientation of
                       the *Bizone* to the market economy.

18 June 1948   The decision is made to bring in the market economy: the major-
                       ity of the CDU/CSU and FDP pass the "Law of Guiding Prin-
                       ciples" (*Leitsätzegesetz*) presented by Erhard to the Economic
                       Council, which provided for the abolition of the command econ-
                       omy and the deregulation of most prices. The law comes into
                       force on the 24th of June.

20 June 1948   Currency reform in the three Western zones and introduction of
                       the D-Mark by the Western Allies.

23 June 1948   Currency reform in the Soviet zone: the new Ostmark is sup-
                       posed to be valid currency in the whole of Berlin, but is rejected
                       by the Western commanders, who introduce the new West Ger-
                       man Deutschmark into the Western sector.

24 June 1948   The blockade of Berlin by the Soviet Union begins. By means of
                       an "air-bridge" that was initiated two days later, the American
                       and British air forces ensure the provision of supplies to the West
                       Berlin population.

1 July 1948   The military governors of the Western zones give the eleven Prime
                       Ministers of the West German *Länder* a formal commission
                       through the three "Frankfurt Documents" to work out a cons-
                       titution for a new state in the context of a statute of occupation.
                       Willy Brandt takes up German citizenship again after 15 years'
                       exile in Norway and Sweden.

8–10 July 1948   A conference is held in the Hotel Rittersturz in Koblenz attend-
                      ed by the Prime Ministers of the *Länder* to discuss the Frankfurt
                      Documents: the three occupation zones are to be united as a Pro-
                      visorium under a Basic Law. In the following weeks the Allied
                      governors make it clear to the German politicians that the Lon-
                      don Recommendations concerning the foundation of a new state
                      are regarded by them as binding, but nevertheless indicate that
                      they are prepared to accept the idea of a Provisorium: the future
                      constitution is thus to be called the "Basic Law" and the assembly
                      that formulates the constitution is to be called the "Parlia-
                      mentary Council".

26 July 1948   After several conferences, the Prime Ministers reach agreement
                      with the military governors in Frankfurt am Main over the foun-
                      dation of a West German state.

10–23 August 1948   On the initiative of the Bavarian head of government, Hans
                      Ehard, an expert commission (the *"herrenchiemseer Konvent")*
                      puts forward a Basic Law for the Parliamentary Council in Bonn.
                      Many of its fundamental points are later incorporated into the
                      Constitution itself.

18 August 1948   The borders between the three Western zones are opened and
                      restrictions on travel, together with passport controls, are abol-
                      ished.

1 September 1948   The Parliamentary Council begins its work in Bonn; it consists of
                      65 representatives elected by the Provincial Diets and five repre-
                      sentatives from Berlin without voting rights. Konrad Adenauer
                      (CDU) is the President, while the Chairman of the main com-
                      mittee is Carlo Schmid (SPD).

6 September 1948   Following demonstrations inspired by the Communists, the Ber-
                      lin City Assembly moves its seat to West Berlin. In this way the
                      administrative separation of Berlin is sealed. From the end of
                      November, Friedrich Ebert of the SED holds the post of Mayor
                      in East Berlin, although he has not been elected; after elections
                      in the three western sectors, Ernst Reuter (SPD) becomes the
                      Mayor of West Berlin at the beginning of December.

22 September 1948   Founding of the Freie Universität Berlin (Free University Berlin).

12 November 1948   General strike of the trades unions in the *Bizone* in protest
                      against Ludwig Erhard's economic policy.

28 December 1948	The decision is made by the Western powers and the Benelux countries to place the West German coal and steel industry of the Ruhr under international control (*Ruhrstatut*); West Germany is at this time represented by the military governors.

1949

January 1949	The SED characterizes itself as a "new type of party" and the "Marxist-Leninist party of struggle". In every respect Stalin's Soviet Union is its model.
4 April 1949	Signing of the NATO treaty in Washington.
10 April 1949	The Statute of Occupation is published and comes into force on the 21st of September.
8 May 1949	With 53 votes for, and 12 against, the Parliamentary Council passes the Basic Law.
12 May 1949	End of the Berlin blockade. The three military governors approve the Basic Law, which is then ratified by the Provincial Diets between the 18th and the 21st of May.
15 May 1949	The population of the Soviet zone elects from a composite list the Third German People's Congress, which passes a constitution at the end of May, the latter partly oriented towards the constitution of the Weimar Republic. The SED dominates the "Parliament of the German People's Council", a fake democratic body that emerged from the "People's Congress". By means of electoral manipulation, the SED achieves 66% of the composite list vote.
20 May 1949	The Bavarian Diet rejects the Basic Law by 101 votes to 63, but nevertheless accepts it legal validity in Bavaria.
23 May 1949	Proclamation of the Basic Law for the Federal Republic of Germany in the final sitting of the Parliamentary Council in Bonn. It comes into force at the end of the day.
15 July 1949	The CDU published the Düsseldorf "Announcement of Guiding Principles" (*Leitsätze*): The market economy is to be the basis of the party's electoral programme.
23 July 1949	Thomas Mann's first visit to Germany after sixteen years of exile.
14 August 1949	Election to the first German Parliament. CDU/CSU (the "Union") wins 31% of the vote; SPD: 29.2%; FDP: 11.9%; KPD: 5.7%.

7 September 1949	The Bundestag (Federal Parliament—the Lower House) and Bundesrat (Federal Council—the Upper House) meet in session for the first time.
8 September 1949	In joint session, the assemblies elect the FDP candidate, Theodor Heuss, to be the first Federal President.
15 September 1949	Konrad Adenauer (CDU) is elected Federal Chancellor by a majority of just one vote.
18–23 September 1949	First Frankfurt Book Fair.
7 October 1949	Founding of the German Democratic Republic (GDR) in East Berlin. Otto Grotewohl (SED) becomes Prime Minister, Wilhelm Pieck (SED) becomes President of the GDR. Stalin calls the founding of the GDR a "turning point in the history of Europe".
8 October 1949	Agreement is reached over trade within Germany (intra-zonal agreement), which was to remain in force until the end of the GDR (1990).
12 October 1949	Founding of the German Trades Union Congress (DGB) in Munich. Hans Böckler becomes its first President.
21 October 1949	Federal Chancellor Adenauer announces that the Federal Republic of Germany is alone entitled to speak for the German people ("claim to exclusive representation").
22 November 1949	The three High Commissioners and Chancellor Adenauer sign the Petersberg agreement: the Federal Republic joins the Ruhr authority and the European Council. Consular representation is initiated with the Western states.
2 December 1949	Foundation of the Standing Conference of the Minister of Culture, Education and Church Affairs in Bonn.

3. The Federal Republic Orientates to the West: Western Integration and the "Economic Miracle" in the Adenauer Era, 1949–1963

CONDITIONAL FREEDOM

From September 1949, the Federal Republic enjoyed a democratically elect-ed government, but was nevertheless under foreign control as a protectorate of the Western Allies. The new freedom, guaranteed by France, the USA and Great Britain, was thus conditional, and was moreover accompanied by the mistrust of the peoples of these, the victorious countries, who expected their governments to continue to keep the Germans on a short leash. Thus the effective constitution in the land was the Statute of Occupation, agreed in April 1949 between the three victorious powers, and effective from the fol-lowing September.

THE HIGH COMMISSIONERS

This regulatory situation was in no way altered by the fact that, in place of military governors, there were now High Commissioners. It was under this new title that the former British military governor, General Lord Brian Ro-bertson, now operated in a civil capacity. France was represented by a career diplomat, André François-Poncet, who had been the ambassador to Berlin in the 1930's. He was well-versed in German civilisation and culture, but made no secret of his mistrust of the Germans and lost no opportunity of letting his German interlocutors know who was boss. The US government sent John McCloy, one of the formative experts of the American war and post-war years, who was also a man who knew Germany extremely well, and was not without sympathy for the country that he both watched over, and at the same time sought to bind into democracy and the western community. Since he represented the strongest power in the High Commission, his word carried most weight. In cases of doubt, the strengthening of Western Europe and the inclusion of the Federal Republic in its sphere was more important to him than the exercise of petty controls. After a short while, he got on well with Konrad Adenauer, the new head of the Bonn government, so that even dur-ing the period of occupation, German–American relations prospered. In the following years, McCloy became the architect of the close co-operation between America and West Germany.

CONTROL EXERCISED THROUGH THE
STATUTE OF OCCUPATION

At the beginning, everything operated on a very formal basis. The High Commissioners resided on the Petersberg, high over the Rhine, overlooking the provisional federal capital. Its control apparatus was large and expensive. At the beginning of the fifties, it still employed more than 10,000 Allied officials and several hundred officers. The Allied occupation force consisted of 100,000 men. In addition, there were the families of these and their German service infrastructure. A good one third of the federal budget was devoted to covering the costs of all this.

No law could be passed by the Federal Parliament without the approval of the High Commission. Further, the Commission still determined all matters concerning trade and foreign policy. The fact that they were entitled to remove all competences from the Federal Government and the Parliament "on grounds of security or in order to preserve the democratic form of government in Germany" could be seen as a standing threat and was naturally resented by the German politicians. When and to what extent the Western Allies might be prepared to forego their rights of occupation, above all in foreign policy matters, remained open, although it was promised that this would be looked at in 18 months time.

SOVEREIGNTY AND WESTERN ORIENTATION
AS POLITICAL AIMS

It was fairly obvious that the seventy-three years old Chancellor, Konrad Adenauer (CDU), who owed his position to a single vote majority, would work to find ways of bringing about independence for the young state, as indeed he made clear in his first governmental declaration. "The only route to freedom is to collaborate with the High Commission, so that we may try to regain our freedoms and competences step by step." Adenauer's main political aims, which from the first day of his government he stubbornly pursued against all resistance, was the removal of all limitations imposed by the occupation, and the transformation of the Federal Republic from a political object defined by the politics of the Western powers into a full partner with equal rights, a process that would thereby bind West Germany firmly to the western world.

Probably any Chancellor would have made the regaining of sovereignty and western orientation his highest priority. However, by contrast to his greatest political rival in the opposition SPD, its leader Kurt Schumacher,

Adenauer showed understanding for the Allied insistence on an effective control of the German economic potential in the Rhine and Ruhr areas. The conditions they imposed allowed only slow progress to be made by Adenauer in convincing them of the justness of German interests, and the Germans had therefore to accept considerable delays and disadvantages. Schumacher, on the other hand, self-confidently demanded that Germany be treated as an equal to the powers, a position that was illusory at that point in time.

In order to win trust, Adenauer showed willingness to compromise, above all in respect of French demands and interests in the coal and steel sector of the Ruhr and in Saarland. At the same time, he adroitly included in the deals he made clauses that were favourable to Germany, above all the immediate cessation of the demolition of industrial plants. He was not in fact "the Federal Chancellor of the Allies" as Schumacher once criticised him in Parliament, but rather a shrewd pragmatist, who never forgot that the Germans were dependent on the good will and the individual interests of the Western Allies. He had no time for nationalistic slogans or feelings, some of which were shared even within the ruling coalition of CDU/CSU, FDP and DP. It was the security of the people of West Germany that he considered paramount. At the same time he felt that it would be possible to achieve a community of interest between the Western victors and the defeated nation by binding the Federal Republic into the western sphere of influence.

THE FIRST FEDERAL CHANCELLOR: A POLITICIAN WHO UNDERSTOOD POWER

Konrad Adenauer, born in Cologne in 1876, was for many in the chaotic post-war period a beacon of orientation who personified the "good old days" of the Empire. He looked back on a successful political career as Mayor of Cologne from 1917 up to his removal by the Nazis in 1933. He was one of the most important Centrist politicians of the Weimar period, yet, as a local government figure, was not identified with their failure. He survived the Nazi period as a private individual in his house in Rhöndorf, although in the last few months of the war he was imprisoned by the Gestapo, together with his wife. Immediately the war ended, the Americans reinstated him as Mayor of Cologne; five months later, the British (now the authority in the area) dismissed him, officially for incompetence, in reality because he sympathised with the French idea of the creation of a Rhineland state, and because of his anti-Socialist views. The idea was that he should be forced out of politics once and for all. However, his exclusion was lifted a little later and within two years he made a "lightning progression" (Rudolf Morsey) through assorted offices of the Rhineland CDU. As President of the Parliamentary Council, he became in 1948–49 "Speaker for the incipient Federal Republic in dealing with the Western powers" (Theodor Heuss). A talent for organisation, voter appeal, personal contacts and a keen appreciation of how to use power helped him finally to capture the testing office of Chancellor of the Federal Republic of Germany.

The patriarch from Rhöndorf near Bonn was indeed a happy discovery for the Germans at a time when they were faced with suspicion all over the world. The victorious Western powers, in particular the USA, saw in him a guarantee for the definitive abandonment by Germany of all illusions of overmighty power. The Federal Republic was viewed as the core state to which, at some time unknown, the Soviet zone, now the GDR, would also belong.

THE IMPLICATIONS OF THE FEDERAL REPUBLIC'S COMMITMENT TO THE WEST

Adenauer's principal policy objective was the binding of the Federal Republic to the Western powers by treaty. The political, economic, and finally also the military location of the Federal Republic in the Western camp, and in a united Europe, became thereby the hallmark of the Adenauer era.

Adenauer was convinced that the Germans, whose political maturity he mistrusted, could only be protected from themselves through a close alliance with the West. The historical and fatal German tradition, represented by a striving to consolidate their position between East and West, was to be relinquished once and for all. Alliance with the West meant also protection for the young democracy from the threat posed by the Communist Soviet Union. At the same time, it was a guarantee that the joint victors in 1945 should never again be in a position to decide the fate of the nation over the heads of the Germans. The nightmare of Potsdam was constantly in his thoughts.

NO ACCOMMODATION WITH THE SOVIET UNION

Finally Adenauer saw in a western alliance a realistic chance of reuniting "in peace and freedom" the larger part of Germany that had escaped the Russian grasp with its counterpart, an aim he never tired of stressing to his critics in Parliament and among the public. He rejected decisively agreements with the totalitarian Soviet Union, such as the neutralisation of the whole of Germany, which was repeatedly offered by Moscow. He did so because he saw in such arrangements the beginning of the end of democratic renewal in Germany. Adenauer saw that the only chance even to negotiate with Moscow on the German question lay in establishing a position of strength that could only stem from a close alliance with the West, particularly the United States. His opponents, including those in his own party, saw this as paradoxical. Yet Adenauer, as his later electoral success demonstrated, had touched a nerve in the people of West Germany with his *Realpolitik*, which accurately reflected their hopes and fears. Most Germans, in view of the recent catastrophe, including that in the Soviet zone, had a simple desire for economic and political security, and only the West under the leadership of the new world power of America provided such security. Adenauer's assumption, that the West could only persuade Moscow to forego its German booty if it acted from a position of strength, was certainly controversial; yet it dovetailed exactly with the policy of the United States under Presidents Truman (1945–1952) and Eisenhower (1953–1960) (or at least during Eisenhower's first period of office). The reunification of Germany, which was a policy to which the American leadership was fully committed, was therefore also for Washington a long-term aim, in the context of a reordering of Europe; it was not, however, an immediate aim that could be realised against the will of the Soviet nuclear power.

WESTERN ORIENTATION

Following the entry of the Federal Republic into the Organisation for European Economic Co-operation (OEEC), which co-ordinated the Marshall Plan, and into the European Council at Strasburg (1950), which for the first time afforded German politicians an international forum for the exchange of political ideas, the creation of the European Coal and Steel Community (1951) became the foundation for the economic integration of Western Europe and at the same time opened the way to the successful overcoming of German–French animosity. Above all, the rearmament of West Germany placed the seal on the successful integration of the Federal Republic with the West.

REARMAMENT AND ENTRY INTO NATO

Adenauer's first period of office (1949–53) was overshadowed by the Korean War (1950–53). The war made the East–West divide more acute and accelerated the decision-making process of the Americans and the West

Europeans, so that an effective defensive military alliance directed against the Soviet Union, one that included West Germany, was quickly achieved. Following the North Korean attack on South Korea in the summer of 1950, concern became widespread in West Germany that there might be an attack against it by the East German security forces. But also other Western European countries felt threatened by Soviet power. Consequently they abandoned their reservations regarding the rearmament of the Federal Republic that America was demanding, and that Adenauer subsequently managed to push through despite strong domestic opposition, especially from the SPD and the trades unions.

This success was also something that the Soviet dictator, Stalin, was unable to prevent. As a last ditch throw, he suggested in March 1952 to the Western powers, and specifically to West Germany, that a reunification might be possible, as long as the western part of Germany remained neutral. This offer was designed to stymie the burgeoning western alliance. We now know that this was primarily a propaganda ploy. At no time was the Soviet Union really prepared to sacrifice the East Berlin regime to the reality of a neutral non-Communist united Germany. In Moscow, nevertheless, it was seriously believed that this offer might mobilise the "masses" against the Adenauer government and might bring about its fall. Thereafter, it was thought, the cards would have to be reshuffled. In fact, the Western powers displayed exactly the same indifference to this "offer" as did Adenauer and the overwhelming majority of the population.

As a quid pro quo for the West German defence contribution, the Western powers declared their willingness in 1952 to end the occupation regime in Germany (*Deutschland-Vertrag*). Nevertheless the majority of the population were against rearmament at this point in time. The feeling that if this was done, it was being done "without [the individual's] consent" was widespread. When the planned European Defence Community (EDC), which was to include the Federal Republic, came to nothing in 1954 because of French resistance, the Federal Republic was incorporated into NATO on the initiative of Great Britain and the USA (1955) and at the same time the occupation of West Germany was declared to be at an end.

The peculiarity of the German membership of NATO lay in the fact that, in contrast to other members, the Germans were obliged even in peacetime to place all their military forces under the supervision of the Alliance. In addition, an upper limit of 500,000 men under arms was laid down; and finally the Federal Republic agreed to forego the production of ABC [atomic, biological and chemical] weapons, and also to forego their deployment. With these stipulations, the concerns of France, the most reluctant NATO member, were addressed and evidently met.

THE QUESTION OF THE SAARLAND

In the question of the Saarland, which bedevilled Franco-German relations for many years, a compromise was worked out. The Saar area was to be politically "Europeanised" (*Saarstatut*), with strong economic ties to France, as long as the Saarland population approved this in a referendum. Against the expectations of the government in Paris, a significant majority voted, however, for the reincorporation of the Saarland into the Federal Republic (1957), a result that the French thereupon accepted.

THE FEDERAL REPUBLIC REGAINS SOVEREIGNTY

With this solution, the Federal Republic with unexpected rapidity became a largely sovereign state. Only in the question of Berlin, and in that of the potential reunification of Germany, did the western victorious powers retain their original victors' rights ("Four Power Status") until 1968. At the same time, they declared themselves willing to accept a reunification of Germany based on democratic principles—an important concession first made in 1955, which was finally honoured in 1990.

By means of a shrewd policy of real performance (Petersberg Agreement 1949: Entry into the Ruhr authority to prevent the further dismantling of industrial plants), confidence-building (entry into the European Council, 1950, and inclusion in the Schuman-Plan, 1950–51), as well as by offering to place the economic and industrial potential of West Germany in the service of European–Atlantic partnership led by the USA, Adenauer achieved the following:

1. Reduction of the mistrust of Germany in the Western world.
2. A guarantee of the security of the Federal Republic underwritten by the USA.
3. The binding of the young Bonn democracy definitively into the western community of states, to which, as Adenauer stressed, the Germans naturally belonged by reason of their "origin and convictions".

The Shadow of the Past: Between Repression and a Reckoning with the Past

Less glorious than the successful binding of West Germany into the community and values of the western democracies was the Adenauer era in terms of confrontation with the Germans' recent past. As the time gap increased between the present and the self-inflicted catastrophe of 1945, ever fewer of the new federal citizens wished to engage with the causes and the extent of the crimes committed during the Nazi hegemony in Eastern and Western Europe, especially the crimes committed against the Jews. Officially nobody now defended National Socialism—a short-lived successor party of NSDAP, calling itself the Socialist Empire Party (SRP) was forbidden by the Constitutional Court in 1952. However, the opinion polls of the 1950's showed that the "brown" [i.e. Nazi] way of thinking was by no means absent from the minds of a significant minority.

Thus it is no surprise to find that the engagement with the Nazi past had become by now at best sporadic. However, the judicial balance of dealing with Nazi crimes was positive: apart from the military tribunals of the Allies already mentioned, which lasted from the late 1940's until around 1951, West German courts with special competence for Nazi crimes against Germans brought many Nazi criminals to trial. In this way, 5487 people were convicted, including those indicted for participation in attacks on Jews in the so-called *Reichskristallnacht* of 1938. Others were condemned for "euthanasia" murders against handicapped people. However, with these results in the bag, a large part of the population believed that all those responsible for Nazi horrors had finally been brought to justice. The enthusiasm of the people, and especially of politicians, to continue to pursue Nazi criminals evaporated very quickly.

In the following years, the judicial pursuit of criminals virtually came to a halt. Difficulties of state prosecutors in pursuing Nazis criminals beyond the borders of Germany, especially in Eastern Europe, played a part in this. However, what was really characteristic of this climate of forgetting was the official federal policy of integrating many former Nazis into the democratic state. The need of the hour seemed not to be exclusion and punishment, but reconciliation with all those who had not committed any major crimes. Virtually all the politicians, both on the government side and in the opposition, were in agreement with this policy, not least because they wished to tap the substantial reservoir of votes that ex-Nazis represented. Even combative democrats, like Kurt Schumacher, the leader of SPD, and the Berlin Mayor, Ernst Reuter (SPD) followed this line, although in public speeches they continued to highlight the crimes of Nazism and warned that they should not be treated lightly or as passing aberrations.

The exigencies of the day diverted the energy and attention of the vast majority of the new federal citizens towards reconstruction, and the threat that seemed to be burgeoning in the East. In the Bundestag there was a cross-party consensus in favour of drawing a line under the recent past. In this way it was thought that a stable society could be achieved, a belief held even more emphatically on the government side than in the SPD opposition. Nevertheless, the most significant legislative initiatives were accepted by an ever-growing majority: more immunity from prosecution, applications to the Western Allies for amnesties for the German war criminals in Landsberg and other measures, above all the re-employment of some 150,000 government officials who had been dismissed on account of their membership of the Nazi party and the recognition of their pension rights. Prominent churchmen also persistently lobbied for this. The legislators did not display a similar generosity towards some groups of Nazi victims, but took refuge behind complicated bureaucratic procedures required for the recognition of victim status.

The political price for this integration policy, which was nevertheless probably inevitable in view of the many millions of Nazi party members and sympathisers, was the recurrent uncovering of scandals regarding the Nazi past of individual members of the government, or of high officials such as Hans Globke, Adenauer's closest confidant and head of the Bundeskanzleramt, (office of the Federal Chancellery), who nevertheless retained his position to the end of his legal term, ignoring all criticism. These scandals fuelled the protests of the young generation in the 1960's, who harshly criticised the shortcomings of the "blind eye" policy towards former Nazis.

DRAWING A BALANCE OF NAZISM

The coming to terms with the Nazi past was a Janus-headed affair, so that failures and successes were not always easy to separate from each other. The so-called "epidemic of pardons" (Robert W. Kemptner) that characterised the early years of the Bundestag and benefited those implicated in the Nazi regime contrasted sharply with the passionate debates in Parliament during the 1960's and 1970's. These resulted in further pursuit of Nazi murderers; in particular, pressure from victims and their supporters ensured that the crime of murder, from 1979, was no longer subject to the statute of limitations. Right from the beginning, two phenomena ran parallel: uncompromising public condemnation of the Nazi regime and its crimes delivered by politicians, in the media, academe and education was coupled with what was in practice an indulgence of the "brown" past of many who were active in precisely these areas of activity. The "right to make a political error" (Eugen

Kogon) was claimed by the new democrats who were prepared to be reconciled with the new order, and this right was indeed granted them in a most generous way. However, the incorporation of such people, who had been part of the Nazi leadership and who now suddenly discovered their loyalty to the Bonn democracy, while it helped to stabilise the young Federal Republic, was morally dubious and above all completely unacceptable from the point of view of the Nazi victims. On the other hand no politically relevant potential of diehard reactionaries emerged from the former Nazis which could be said to endanger democracy.

Any overall judgement has to recognise the consequences of the half-hearted attempt to deal with the past that was characteristic of the fifties. Against this should be set the parallel laws for compensation, that were energetically pushed through, and designed to compensate Jewish and non-Jewish victims of the Nazi regime, producing a fund which is now calculated to be worth some 100 billion DM. Nevertheless, it has lasted until 2000 and beyond before the millions of Eastern Europeans used as forced labour as part of the Nazi war machine were considered for compensation. Over half a century after the end of the war, the German state and German industry (the latter not quite voluntarily) declared themselves ready to pay several thousand DM in compensation for the victims who were still alive, a total payment of about 10 billion DM.

LATE INVESTIGATIONS AND TRIALS

The systematic investigation and pursuit of Nazi criminals really began with the founding of the Central Office of Regional Judicial Administrations (*Zentrale Stelle der Landesjustizverwaltungen*) in Ludwigsburg in 1958, which was devoted to the uncovering of Nazi criminality. The result of this was that the public could witness several major trials against SS functionaries, such as those who had administered Auschwitz and other extermination camps, who went before the jury court in Frankfurt am Main (1963–65), or such prosecutions as the Majdanek trial held in Düsseldorf (1975–81). Suddenly the Third Reich did not seem to lie so far in the past as had appeared to be the case in the 1950's. By using judicial procedure, an attempt was now made to punish the worst crimes of the Nazi regime. It often required years of investigation to discover the culprits, to interview witnesses and to retrieve and evaluate documents. In one of the last large-scale Nazi trials in Stuttgart in 1992, a former SS camp commander was sentenced to life imprisonment for murder and complicity in murder. Between the 8th of May 1945 and 1999 a total of 6495 former Nazis were prosecuted and convicted by the West German courts, of which 750 were convicted after 1958. This is a small number in view of the 106,496 investigations, but a lot if one considers the actual difficulties involved, which were unparalleled given the complexity of the task. Nor should one forget that the servants of dictatorship and genocide now profited from the protection of their civil and legal rights as guaranteed by the rule of law, whereby an individual is only convicted in the event that his or her individual guilt can be proved beyond reasonable doubt. It was precisely this that was often lacking when witnesses could be shown to have faulty memories of events. Another highly unsatisfactory outcome was that, with a very few exceptions, no Nazi judges were brought to justice for abuse of their position, not even Freisler's bloodstained assistants of the People's Court (*Volksgerichtshof*) in Berlin. Likewise most of the "desk criminals" (*Schreibtischtäter*) of the main office of Reich security (*Reichssicherheitshauptamt*) in Berlin, the central organ of Nazi terror got off scot-free, with the exception of Adolf Eichmann, the former head of its Jewish Department, who was abducted by the Israeli secret service from Argentina in 1960 and condemned to death by a court in Jerusalem in 1962. It is only since the seventies, and even more in the eighties, that the memory of the massacre of European Jewry has become common knowledge to the majority of German citizens, not least because they themselves were not personally involved in this dark epoch of German history, which still casts such a long shadow. This generation had access to the results of historical research, as well as the opportunities provided by political education within and beyond the school system, and finally also to highly effective film representations of the Nazi past, for example the American TV series "Holocaust" (1979), which attracted over 16 million viewers in West Germany.

CONTROLLED PARTNERSHIP:
EUROPEAN INTEGRATION

Apart from the entry of the Federal Republic into the defensive alliance of the West, the Adenauer era also saw the laying of the foundation for the economic cooperation of a growing number of European states. As a result of "europeanisation", which brought the resolution of seemingly unresolvable conflicts and differences of interest (the Saarland question, the Ruhr coal problem, rearmament), the trick was achieved of bringing two aims that appeared incompatible into harmony, that is the urgent need of the Bonn politicians for the equal status and security of the Federal Republic to be recognized, and the demand of the peoples of Europe for security from a renascent Germany. "Integration" became the key concept of the epoch. The controlled partnership with Germany replaced one-sided control and imposed measures, which an economically weaker France had long advocated.

What had still seemed incredible at the beginning of the fifties became reality a decade later: a Franco–German reconciliation in the context of the unification of Europe. The starting gun for this was fired by the founding of the European Coal and Steel Community (Montan-Union) in 1951, which, with the participation of the Benelux countries and Italy, placed the production of the coal and steel of these countries under the aegis of a supranational West European organisation. With the Treaty of Rome in 1957, the pioneering European unifiers widened the scope of economic integration (European Economic Community, Euratom) with the aim of creating a single European market, the predecessor of the European Union.

The Franco–German reconciliation was able to flourish on the basis of this stable foundation. The Federal Republic had no difficulty in accepting the leading political role of France in Europe; France, for its part, no longer felt threatened by a Federal Republic that was to grow within a few years into a major economic power. With the signing in 1963 of a Franco–German treaty of friendship by Chancellor Adenauer and President de Gaulle, a line was drawn under the centuries-old enmity of the two countries.

ECONOMIC MIRACLE: PROSPERITY FOR ALL

At the beginning of the Adenauer era, the economic position was weak. The "social market" was brought into question by rising prices, a widening gap between average earnings and those of the rich and substantial unemployment. In the winter of 1951–52, around 12% of those available for work, almost two million people, were out of a job. In some cases there was also a shortage of bread, wheat and sugar.

In the second half of 1952 however, following the Korean War, demand for German goods increased sharply worldwide. Ludwig Erhard, the Minister for Economics, was able to forego dirigiste measures and to liberalise further the economic exchange of goods. With the upswing, largely the result of foreign trade and the return of Germany to world markets, a long boom set in, which in turn ushered in the German "economic miracle". Exports rose continuously and the construction industry flourished; the automobile industry forged ahead and shipbuilding reached pre-war levels, while the Federal Bank soon presided over reserves of 1.7 billion dollars. Unemployment halved and by 1955 reached 5.5% for the first time since the war—despite the sharp increase in jobseekers caused by those fleeing from the GDR. Soon there was full employment (in 1960 unemployment was

1.2%). From 1955, employees from abroad had to be sought. The last restrictions on the Deutschmark were lifted in 1958 and the Mark became a freely convertible currency.

"Prosperity for all" was Ludwig Erhard's message and optimism was the hallmark of the times. Everyone profited from the unusual economic upswing of those years, albeit in a very unequal fashion. The performance of the Federal German economy became the foundation for an exemplary social security net, which guaranteed social harmony, and this in turn contributed to economic productivity. Among many important measures, such as the introduction of generous pensions in 1957, perhaps the most significant was the "equalisation" of 1952, by means of which more than ten million exiles and refugees, as well as others disadvantaged by the war, were compensated. The payments made up to 1989 amounted to over 130 million DM.

STABILITY AND CONSENT

The economic miracle and the successful re-entry of the Federal Republic into the western community of nations helped Adenauer to landslide victories both in the elections of 1953 and above all in 1957 (with 45.2% and 50.2% of the vote respectively), which were seen as quasi-plebiscites in which the majority of the population approved the economic and foreign policy of the Federal Government. The CDU/CSU developed into a dominant people's party. For its part, the SPD only accommodated itself to the trend at the end of the 1950's, when it saw the need to become a modern centrist party open to all voter groups, while at the same time falling into line with Adenauer's western-oriented foreign policy, primarily on the urging of Herbert Wehner and Willy Brandt.

THE DIVISION OF GERMANY
BECOMES ENTRENCHED

In one area, of course, Adenauer remained unsuccessful, namely that of the reunification of Germany. The nuclear treaty between the two world powers had led to the entrenchment of the division of Europe and thus also of Germany. The politics of strength was thereby rendered ineffective. Adenauer evidently saw this himself, because he tried several times (albeit in great secrecy) to persuade Ulbricht to allow the people within his area of domination more freedom and more opportunities to make contact with West Germans. As a *quid pro quo*, the Bonn government signalled that it would be prepared in practice to accept the status quo in the GDR. The SED, however, was not interested in these approaches, no more than were their string-pullers in Moscow.

The Soviet power was faced several times with uprisings among its satellites (1953 in the GDR, 1956 in Poland and Hungary) which it put down ruthlessly, thereby asserting Communism's claim to absolute hegemony in these countries. A second Berlin crisis blew up in 1958, when the Soviet leader Khrushchev attempted to incorporate West Berlin into the GDR in order to stabilise the power of the SED. The crisis came to a head on the 13th of August 1961 with the building of the Berlin Wall, and only gradually receded after the ending of the Cuba crisis of October 1962.

The fact that Eisenhower, from the end of the fifties, and even more his successor as President, John F. Kennedy (1961–63), accepted the status quo in Europe and thereby the division of Germany, aroused dismay and mistrust in Adenauer. In addition, the frequently announced plans for withdrawal of part of the American troops from Europe caused the Chancellor profound anxiety. He had serious doubts as to whether the Americans would use their nuclear weapons to defend Western Europe, and in particular the Federal Republic, in the event of an attack by the Soviet Union. For this reason he sought alliance with France. The French President, Charles de Gaulle appeared to him the only one of the western heads of state and government who was to be trusted in the German question. The Franco–German Friendship Treaty of 1963 was the direct result of this view.

THE TWILIGHT OF THE CHANCELLOR

By the election of September 1961, Adenauer had passed the zenith of his power. The Union lost its absolute majority (45.3%) and the SPD, led by the incumbent Mayor of Berlin, Willy Brandt, achieved its best result since 1919 (36.2%). The FDP under Erich Mende, who advised against a fourth period of office for Adenauer during the campaign, and who proved extremely voter-friendly (12.8%), finally declared that he would support a renewed coalition with the CDU/CSU under Adenauer, on condition that the latter would retire from the post of Chancellor before his period of office was over.

The final period of office of Adenauer was overshadowed by internal party bickering concerning a suitable successor for the "old man of Rhöndorf", who was reluctant to relinquish power and did everything he could to prevent the economics minister, Ludwig Erhard, from succeeding him. Adenauer also lost much public respect as a result of the "Spiegel affair" in the autumn of 1962, when he and his Defence Minister, Franz Josef Strauss, professed to see "treachery" in an article about NATO in *Der Spiegel* magazine and ordered the arrest of several *Spiegel* editors and even the publisher. Many people saw this as an attack on press freedom and a government crisis ensued: Strauss, under pressure from the FDP, was obliged to resign, and the FDP also forced Adenauer to supply a firm date for his retirement from government. In October 1963, the 87-year-old founding Chancellor of the Republic resigned and made way for the "father of the economic miracle", Ludwig Erhard.

It was to be many years before the bitterness of the party political struggle of this time was allowed to settle, and the Adenauer era (but above all the man who gave it its name) began to receive the positive recognition it and he deserved. With his stubborn determination to anchor the Federal Republic in the Western European–Atlantic alliance, despite all obstacles, Adenauer had laid the foundations for a new and even revolutionary orientation in German history. His policy had not only political, but also no less important cultural and value-oriented components. Without the security that was guaranteed thereby, the Federal Republic would never have reached the status of a leading world economic power.

CHRONOLOGY

1950

8 January 1950   Founding of a right-wing alliance in Kiel for "Those Expelled and Deprived of their Rights" (BHE) to represent the refugees from the East; its Chairman is the former SS-Hauptsturmführer, Waldemar Kraft, who later also becomes Chairman of the political party that emerges from the alliance.

13 January 1950   The Soviet Union withdraws from the Security Council of the UNO (until 1st of August 1950).

8 February 1950   Two million unemployed are recorded in the Federal Republic, representing 13.3% of those seeking work.

7 March 1950   In an interview with an American newspaper, Adenauer suggests that there should be a political union between France and Germany.

8 March 1950   The Federal government declares West Berlin to be an area of economic emergency. It is to be assisted by the Marshall Plan and by transferring 22 federal agencies to West Berlin (including the Federal Administrative Court).

16 March 1950   In a speech in the House of Commons, the leader of the British opposition party, Winston Churchill, becomes the first leading politician to support the idea of a German contribution to Western European defence.

28 March 1950   The Bundestag passes its first law to stimulate housebuilding: within six years 1.8 million homes are to be built with state financial support.

1 April 1950   An Office for Foreign Affairs is set up in the Bundeskanzleramt.

2 April 1950   In the current year's budget, 4.6 billion DM is allocated for the costs of the occupation forces (23.2% of the federal tax income).

3 April 1950   US President Truman approves the concept of a "policy of strength" in respect of the Soviet Union.

27 April 1950   The Bundestag passes a measure to assist former prisoners of war on their return home.

1 May 1950   End of rationing. The largest political rally since the war is held in West Berlin: 600,000 Berliners demonstrate against "unity in chains" and for "peace and freedom".

4 May 1950   Redistribution of 600,000 refugees located in Bavaria, Schleswig-Holstein and Lower Saxony to other Federal States.

9 May 1950   The French Foreign Minister, Robert Schuman, proposes the founding of a European Coal and Steel Community (Schuman Plan).

16 June 1950   The first Consulate of the Federal Republic is set up in London.

25 June 1950   The Korean War breaks out. The UNO Security Council, with the Soviet Union absent, condemns the attack of North Korea on South Korea.

17 July 1950   The Central Council of Jews in Germany is set up in Frankfurt am Main.

28 July 1950   The Bundestag passes a measure establishing an office for the protection of the constitution.

6 August 1950   The associations of expellees and refugees from East Germany formulate a "Charter of Expellees", which demands the right to a homeland, abstinence from acts of revenge and the creation of a united Europe.

7 August 1950	Entry of the Federal Republic into the Council of Europe, at first without voting rights. From 5th of May 1951, full member.
11 August 1950	Churchill's proposal for the creation of a European army, to include also West German contingents, receives majority approval in the European Council.
16 August 1950	The US High Commissioner, McCloy, initiates the issuing of pardons, which benefits some who had been condemned as German war criminals.
17 August 1950	Chancellor Adenauer hands the three High Commissioners a memorandum in which he declares the willingness of the Federal Republic to rearm in the context of a European army, and at the same time demands the removal of occupation controls. This suggestion had in fact been made to the High Commissioners privately in June and was now again presented in mid-August, but was not discussed in cabinet.
12–18 September 1950	The Foreign Ministers' Conference in New York of the three Western powers provides the Federal Republic with security guarantees.
19 September 1950	The federal government bans state officials from membership of 11 Communist and 2 extreme right organisations.
30 September 1950	For the first time there are fewer than 500,000 unemployed in the Federal Republic.
5–10 October 1950	Secret conference of German military experts (including the former Wehrmacht Generals Heusinger and Speidel) in the Himmerod monastery in the Eifel region. The discussion revolved around the necessary preconditions for a German contribution to defence. The discussion was summarised in the "Himmeroder Memorandum".
10 October 1950	Resignation of the Minister of the Interior, Gustav Heinemann (CDU) in protest against the rearmament policy of the Chancellor.
19 October 1950	The Bundestag passes a measure to assist war victims, which will involve an annual expenditure of 3.2 billion DM.
20 October 1950	The French Prime Minister, René Pleven, proposes a plan for a European army as a precondition for the participation of the Federal Republic in the defence of Europe. Adenauer welcomes the suggestion. The leader of the opposition, Kurt Schumacher,

rejects it. In the following period the topic of German rearmament dominates political debate in the Federal Republic and polarises the political camps.

4 November 1950	In Strasbourg the European Convention on the Protection of Human Rights and Basic Freedoms is signed.
26 November 1950	Chinese offensive against UN troops in North Korea.
30 November 1950	The Prime Minister of the GDR, Otto Grotewohl, proposes an "All-Germany Foundation Council", whereby both German states should have equal status in deciding how to compose a common German government.
16 December 1950	A national emergency is declared in the USA due to the Korean War.

1951

23 January 1951	The NATO Supreme Commander, Dwight D. Eisenhower, makes a public statement of contrition on behalf of German soldiers.
15 February 1951	The Pleven Plan Conference concerned with the creation of a European army begins in Paris.
6 March 1951	Revision of the Statute of Occupation. The Federal Republic acquires greater competence in foreign policy and recognises German debts abroad.
15 March 1951	Chancellor Adenauer takes over the newly created office of Foreign Minister.
10 April 1951	Law 131: Rehabilitation of most public officials who, after 1945, through flight, expulsion or denazification had lost their offices or been dismissed.
18 April 1951	Signing of the treaty setting up the European Coal and Steel Community in Paris by the Foreign Ministers of the Federal Republic, France, Italy and the Benelux States. With this, the process of European integration begins. The Bundestag ratifies the treaty on the 11th of January 1952 and it comes into force on the 25th of July 1952.
11 May 1951	Law on compensation for victims of illegal acts by the Nazis.
21 May 1951	Parity participation for decision-making in the Montan industry is introduced for the workforce.

9 July 1951   Official end of a state of war in Germany proclaimed by the three Western powers.

30 July 1951   The Bayreuth Festspiele are resumed under the direction of Wieland and Wolfgang Wagner.

7 September 1951   Founding of the Federal Constitutional Court in Karlsruhe.

15 September 1951   The People's Chamber of the GDR appeals for Germans to sit "at one table".

27 September 1951   The Federal government declares its willingness to pay compensation to Israel.

16 November 1951   The Federal government applies to the Constitutional Court to have the *Socialistische Reichspartei* (SRP) and the *Kommunistische Partei Deutschlands* (KPD) banned.

21 November 1951   The former Minister of the Interior, Gustav Heinemann (CDU), and the Chairman of the Centre Party, Helene Wessel, found the "Association for Mutual Assistance to Establish Peace in Europe" (*Notgemeinschaft für den Frieden in Europa*) in an attempt to prevent rearmament.

1952

8 February 1952   The Bundestag, without the support of the SPD, accepts in principle a German defence contribution in Europe.

10 March 1952   Stalin offers reunification under the precondition of German neutrality. The exchange of notes between the Western powers and Moscow, whose main point of disagreement is the provision of effective guarantees for free elections, ends in September without result.

16 March 1952   Adenauer's policy is vindicated: namely, that only from a position of strength can the West successfully negotiate with the Soviet Union.

22 April 1952   Kurt Schumacher, the opposition leader, demands immediate four-power negotiations to consider Stalin's reunification offer.

26 May 1952   The German Treaty is signed in Bonn. The state of occupation is lifted; the Western powers retain certain rights concerning a potentially unified Germany and with regard to Berlin. The GDR institutes a no-go area along its border.

27 May 1952   Signing of the European Defence Agreement in Paris.

24 June 1952	The *Bild* newspaper appears for the first time in an edition of 250,000 copies selling at 10 Pfennig.
10 July 1952	A law spreading the burden of hardship passes through the Bundestag; it is primarily concerned with regulating compensation due for damage sustained during and after the war.
19 July 1952	The Bundestag passes an Industrial Democracy Act.
20 July 1952	The Mayor of Berlin, Ernst Reuter, lays the foundation for a memorial to the events of 20 July 1944 in the inner courtyard of the Bendler apartment block.
2 August 1952	The Federal Republic joins the International Monetary Fund and the World Bank.
20 August 1952	Kurt Schumacher dies. Erich Ollenhauer succeeds him as leader of the party and of the parliamentary party (SPD).
10 September 1952	A compensation agreement is reached between the Federal Republic and Israel.
30 November 1952	Federal President Theodor Heuss inaugurates a memorial in the former concentration camp of Bergen-Belsen.
4 November 1952	Dwight D. Eisenhower is elected President of the USA.
26 December 1952	Four thousand households watch the *Tagesschau* (television news) for the first time.

1953

27 February 1953	Agreement is reached in London between the Federal Republic and 19 creditor states: West Germany takes on the pre- and post-war debts of Germany amounting to a total of 15 billion DM, which in the event will be annulled some years later.
5 March 1953	Death of Stalin.
19 May 1953	A law is passed for the rehabilitation of expellees and refugees.
17 June 1953	People's revolt in the GDR. In a law of 4th August 1953, the Bundestag declares that the 17th of June shall be the "Day of German Unity".
6 September 1953	Elections to the second German parliament are held, for the first time with the 5% hurdle in place. CDU/CSU: 45.2%; SPD: 28.8%; FDP: 9.5%; GB/BHE: 5.9%; DP: 3.2%. Konrad Adenauer is elected Federal Chancellor.

18 September 1953   Law regulating the compensation to be offered to Nazi victims.

1954

30 March 1954   Theodor Heuss is again elected Federal President.

4 July 1954   With a 3:2 win over Hungary, the Federal Republic wins the Football World Championship in Bern.

30 August 1954   The French National Assembly rejects the planned European defence alliance.

1 October 1954   The ARD TV channel begins broadcasting.

23 October 1954   Signing of the Paris Treaties. These encompass the ending of the occupation administration, security guarantees from the Western powers for the Federal Republic and Berlin, recognition of the autonomy of representation of the Federal Republic, and entry into NATO and to the Western European Union (WEU). There is a separate Franco–German agreement on the Saar region.

1955

15 January 1955   The Soviet Union offers to negotiate over the reunification of Germany, provided the Bundestag refuses to ratify the Paris Treaties.

29 January 1955   Rally in the Paulskirche in Frankfurt against rearmament, in which the SPD leader takes part.

5 May 1955   The Paris Treaties come into force. End of the occupation. The Federal Republic is a sovereign state, albeit with some restrictions.

9 May 1955   Entry of the Federal Republic into NATO.

14 May 1955   Founding of the Warsaw Pact.

17–23 July 1955   The Geneva Conference on Germany attended by the Four Powers ends without achieving any results.

24–27 July 1955   In the GDR Khruschchev and Bulganin proclaim the new Soviet doctrine of two German states: reunification was to be "a matter for the Germans", but would only be possible in the context of safeguarding the "socialist achievements" of the GDR.

8–14 September 1955 Adenauer makes a state visit to Moscow: diplomatic relations are established and around 10,000 German prisoners of war and interned civilians are released.

23 October 1955	The population of the Saarland rejects the "Europeanisation" of the Saar region in a referendum, with 67.7% voting against. The area is incorporated into the Federal Republic on the 1st of January 1957, with economic integration following in 1959.
9 December 1955	Foreign Minister Heinrich von Brentano announces that the establishing of diplomatic relations with the GDR by any third party will automatically be followed by the breaking of diplomatic relations with Bonn (Hallstein Doctrine).
20 December 1955	The first agreement concerning the recruitment of guest workers (*Gastarbeiter*) is signed between the Federal Republic and Italy.

1956

7 July 1956	The Bundestag approves with a majority of 270 over 166 votes (141 from the SPD) the introduction of national service, with a proviso for the right to refuse military service on grounds of conscience.
17 August 1956	The Constitutional Court bans the KPD (Communist Party).
16 October 1956	Franz Josef Strauss of the CSU becomes the Minister of Defence.
23 October 1956	Popular uprising in Hungary.

1957

23 February 1957	Pension reform ("dynamic pensions").
25 March 1957	Founding of the European Economic Community (EEC) and the European Atomic Energy Community (Euratom) in Rome by the Federal Republic, France, Italy and the Benelux States.
1 April 1957	Calling up of the first national servicemen in the Federal Republic.
3 July 1957	Anti-monopolies (anti-trust) legislation (cartel law).
4 July 1957	The Deutsche Bundesbank (German Federal Bank) replaces the Bank of the German Provinces established under the Allied occupation. It begins its activity on 1st August in Frankfurt am Main. By law it is independent of government.
15 September 1957	Third German general election. With 50.2% of the votes, the Union under the leadership of the 81-year-old Konrad Adenauer achieves an absolute majority. SPD: 31.8%, FDP: 7.7%. Adenauer is again elected Chancellor. A government is formed from the CDU, CSU and the Deutsche Partei (DP).

3 October 1957	Willy Brandt (SPD) is elected Mayor of (West) Berlin.
4 October 1957	Successful launch of the first satellite ("Sputnik 1") by the Soviet Union.

1958

19 April 1958	Mass demonstrations against the atom bomb in many cities of the Federal Republic.
1 July 1958	The law providing for equal rights of men and women (1957) comes into force.
27 November 1958	Khrushchev's Berlin ultimatum.
1 December 1958	Establishment of the Central Office for the Prosecution of Nazi Crimes of Violence in Ludwigsburg.

1959

11 May– 15 August 1959	Final conference on Germany of the four victorious powers of the Second World War in Geneva ends without achieving anything. The Federal Republic and the GDR are present as observers.
1 July 1959	Heinrich Lübke (CDU) is elected Federal President in Berlin.
15 November 1959	Godesberg Programme agreed by the SPD.

1960

30 June 1960	Keynote speech of the deputy chairman of the SPD, Herbert Wehner, in the Bundestag. The SPD now aligns itself with Adenauer's foreign policy of integration with the West, which is to be a precondition of any reunification of Germany.
8 July 1960	The IG Metall union and the Gesamtmetall employers' organisation agree on the step-by-step introduction of the 40 hour week.
8 November 1960	John F. Kennedy is elected President of the USA.

1961

6 June 1961	Founding of the *Zweiten Deutschen Fernsehen* (ZDF—second German TV channel).
25 July 1961	US President Kennedy stresses in a televised address the three "fundamental elements" of American policy towards Berlin, which is based on guaranteeing the freedom and viability of West Berlin.
13 August 1961	The Berlin Wall is built.

17 September 1961   Fourth Federal Parliamentary elections: the Union loses its abso-
                      lute majority, remaining however, with 45.3% of the vote, the
                      strongest party. SPD: 36.2%; FDP: 12.8%. Konrad Adenauer
                      (85) is again elected Chancellor on 7 November, but declares
                      himself willing to retire before the next election. A coalition gov-
                      ernment is formed of CDU/CSU and FDP.

27–28 October 1961   American and Soviet tanks confront each other at the Fried-
                      richstrasse border point in Berlin.

30 October 1961   An agreement is made regulating the recruiting of "guest work-
                      ers" (*Gastarbeiter*) from Turkey.

15 November 1961   The provincial judiciary in Salzgitter sets up an office to record
                      criminal killings carried out on the internal German border, and
                      to keep track of political convictions and arbitrary acts against
                      political prisoners in the GDR.

11 December 1961   Adolf Eichmann, the former SS-Obersturmbannführer and
                      "official in charge of the Jews" in the Berlin *Reichssicherheits-
                      hauptamt*, is condemned to death in Jerusalem and executed at
                      the end of May 1962.

1962

4–9 September 1962   State visit to the Federal Republic by President Charles de Gaulle,
                      during which he is enthusiastically received by the German
                      public.

14–28 October 1962   Cuban missile crisis.

7–9 November 1962   Debate in the Bundestag over the so-called *Spiegel* affair, which
                      leads to the withdrawal of the FDP ministers from government,
                      as well as the enforced resignation of the Defence Minister,
                      Franz Josef Strauss.

1963

22 January 1963   Signing of the German–French Friendship Treaty in Paris by
                      Adenauer and de Gaulle.

March 1963   Trade agreement with Poland and the establishment of a Ger-
                      man trade representative in Warsaw.

15 October 1963   Resignation of Adenauer as Federal Chancellor, who is succeed-
                      ed by Ludwig Erhard.

4. Hegemony Against the Will of the People: The German Democratic Republic, 1949–1961

The Dictatorship of the SED

With the founding of the German Democratic Republic (GDR, German acronym: DDR, standing for *Deutsche Demokratische Republik*), the openly totalitarian party dictatorship of the SED (*Sozialistische Einheitspartei—* Socialist Unity Party) began in the eastern part of Germany. The democratic opposition of the CDU and the LDP was suppressed. Those politicians brave enough to resist the Communist pressure were soon removed from office. Many were obliged to flee to the Federal Republic. The block parties were amalgamated and placed under the leadership of functionaries congenial to the SED. The unions, the youth organisation (*Freie Deutsche Jugend*), women's organisations and all other so-called mass organisations were turned into extensions of the SED.

The SED consolidated its power at the first elections for the *Volkskammer* (People's Assembly) in 1950 by means of relentless propaganda, pressure on the population, terror directed against political opponents, the introduction of a unified electoral list which prevented genuine choice between the parties, and finally by vote rigging. This election, and practically every subsequent sham election produced results of almost 100% support for the unified list of candidates, and were then trumpeted by the SED leadership as evidence of the permanent and overwhelming approval of the population for its policies. However, these faked results were hiding what the citizens of the GDR really wanted, which was demonstrated somewhat more plausibly by their attempts to "vote with their feet". 2.7 million of them fled the GDR between 1949 and 1961, passing over the still open border to the western part of Germany; among them were very many of the younger generation.

Stalin's Soviet Union as the Model for the GDR

Under the authoritative leadership of the long-standing Communist, Walter Ulbricht, the one-party model of the Soviets was adopted by the SED; until well into the fifties, the Stalinist system of the Soviet Union was assiduously replicated in every aspect of the state, economy and society. A command

economy and political dictatorship, Marxist Leninism as a kind of state reli-
gion, and the subordination of all opinion and information to the requirement of the SED were the hallmarks of this system. Its representatives never
tired of praising the GDR as the "better" Germany, in which everything was
done for the people, the workers were no longer exploited and the disastrous
Fascist past had finally been overcome.

THE PARTY IS ALWAYS RIGHT

The claim to absolute power of the SED, both in the state and in society, was
expressed in a key propaganda formulation: "The Party is always right."
Anyone daring to speak out against the policy of the rulers in East Berlin
risked losing his job or was hauled before the courts as a "class enemy",
often on fabricated charges. In the early fifties, there were some 50,000 political prisoners in the gaols. Political trials were also intended to intimidate the
population. Even schoolchildren who had distributed flyers with criticism of
Ulbricht, received long prison sentences (for example in Werdau in Saxony).

Real or supposed backsliders within the SED itself were equally not to be
tolerated. At the beginning of the fifties, and ever more frequently thereafter,
Ulbricht ordered purges of the Party, which adversely affected over 150,000
ordinary members, mostly former members of the SPD, but also leading functionaries. The latter often had to be made scapegoats for failures and malfea-
sance in the economic sector or in the supply of food. Nevertheless, the SED
never managed to dampen the increasing anger of the population, since living
standards failed to improve and most of the 18 million inhabitants of the
Eastern zone were aware of the better life available in the Federal Republic.

Realistically calculating that the resistance of the peasants, craftsmen, artisans, entrepreneurs and even industrial workers to the Communists' command economy could not be overcome with constant state propaganda, the
SED leadership around Walter Ulbricht, with the "friendly" support of the
Soviet Control Commission in Berlin-Karlshorst, used the secret service
and a corrupt judiciary in order to take out all the real or imagined opposition to the Party.

WALDHEIMER TRIALS

In the GDR, there was no genuine coming to terms with the German past.
The Communist leadership interpreted the founding of the "first worker and
peasant state" on German territory as a victory for anti-fascism. Ritualistic

proclamation of the heroic struggle of the Communists against the Nazis served to obscure uncomfortable questions regarding the involvement of East Germans in the defeated regime. After a purging of personnel and economic transformation during the period of occupation and later, show trials against real or imagined Nazis chiefly served to underpin the propaganda claim that the GDR (in contrast to the Federal Republic) was taking the prosecution of Nazis seriously. Thus, between April and June of 1950 the Waldheim trials were staged, all of them making a mockery of the principles on which the rule of law is founded. Under the direct command of the SED, tame judges convicted more than 3300 people to long imprisonment in rushed trials and without any legally acceptable evidence of individual guilt. Defence lawyers were not allowed and witnesses were not cross-examined. Of the numerous death penalties handed down, 24 were carried out. Most of those convicted were people who were persecuted in the post-war period simply because of their past membership of, or function in, the NSDAP. Only a few had participated in Nazi crimes. Many were arrested on account of groundless denunciations, others because of their opposition to the policies of the Soviet occupiers.

COMPULSORY SOCIALISM

As early as June 1951, the SED was proclaiming that "to learn from the Soviet Union means to learn how to be victorious". In the same spirit, Ulbricht promulgated a year later the "planned building of Socialism", the details of which were set out in a series of five-year-plans. This meant above all giving priority to heavy industry at the expense of consumption, as well as the expropriation of the middle class through the nationalisation of enterprises and businesses and the collectivisation of agriculture. At the same time, the workers were pressured to work harder in order to reach the production quotas that had been set. Since the SED knew that these policies were against the wishes of the great majority of the population, they sharpened their control over the workplace and in other areas of their citizens' lives. Whoever opposed their orders was harshly punished. This was particularly marked in the case of tradesmen, who for a while had managed to escape the claws of the totalitarian state.

While an economic course for the future was being set in the Federal Republic with American assistance, which involved the removal of bureaucratic obstructions so that West German exports rapidly returned to world markets (which was the root cause of the "economic miracle" of the fifties), the SED was introducing the backward structures and practices of the

Stalinist Soviet Union into the GDR. In addition there was the burden of the extremely high reparations payable to the Soviet Union, valued at some 10 million dollars.

All this, together with the short rein on which the planned economy was run, robbed most people of initiative and pleasure in their work. Through the over-emphasis on heavy industry from 1952 onwards, as well as the substantial state expenditure on defence, the living standards of the population deteriorated further and remained significantly below that of the Federal Republic. In view of this miserable situation, most workers were not prepared to accept a tightening of industrial discipline to bring about a ten per cent increase in productivity, coupled with reductions in wages, a package proclaimed in state propaganda as an "achievement of the working class". Already in 1953 there were strikes in several factories. Ever more people fled to the West.

THE PEOPLE'S REVOLT OF 17 JUNE 1953

After Stalin's death in March 1953, the Politbüro of the SED briefly switched to a "new course" on the orders of the new leadership in Moscow. Ulbricht now promised a resentful population that their needs as consumers would be met, price increases would be rescinded and the pressure on the church, the peasantry and the middle class would cease. On the other hand, the previously announced measures designed to increase the productivity of industrial workers was expressly re-emphasised. The result was that the long suppressed dissatisfaction of the workers exploded into industrial action in East Berlin, which spread on 17 June 1953 to all industrial centres of the GDR, finally leading to open popular rebellion in several hundred places. Demands for free elections and the removal of the Ulbricht regime followed hard on the initial calls for economic reform. In Berlin, rebels hauled down the red flag from the Brandenburg Gate. Government buildings were stormed, prisoners freed, policemen arrested, and SED posters torn down. Without the backing of Soviet tanks, the SED and its government would quickly have been defeated. However, on the orders of the leadership in Moscow, the Soviet army stationed in the GDR used their weapons against the demonstrators and put down the revolt with bloody severity. Over 100 people were killed.

The SED described the rebellion in its propaganda as a "Fascist putsch" organised by the West. This was a lie, an attempt to distract attention from the government's own responsibility for the first popular revolt in the area of Communist hegemony. To the great disappointment of many in the GDR, the Federal Republic and the Americans deliberately refrained from supporting the uprising and studiously avoided getting involved in the conflict, because the risk of military escalation was too great. Some 16,000 demonstrators were arrested, and 1500 were condemned to long periods of imprisonment by the SED-dominated judiciary. Ulbricht was later able to emerge victorious from an internal party power struggle with reform-oriented members of the Politbüro. He enjoyed the support of the Moscow leadership, which (after some uncertainty) once again began to see him as the guarantor of their power in East Germany.

Ulbricht consolidated his grip on power thereafter by making a few material concessions to the population (for example, lowering prices), but chiefly by means of renewed purges of the Party and the expansion of the security apparatus, as well as a series of organisational measures designed to exert further discipline and control over the population. The people of the GDR had to face up to the bitter reality that resistance against an SED regime propped up by the bayonets of the Soviet army was pointless, as long as the Moscow government regarded the SED as an essential pillar of its influence in East Central Europe.

From 1955, the Soviet Union had officially recognised the sovereignty of the GDR on paper, yet its dependence on the will of Moscow remained. In practice the GDR was bound into the Eastern Bloc militarily (through the Warsaw Pact), economically (through the Council for Mutual Economic Assistance) and politically. From now on, two highly armed military blocs confronted each other on German soil.

ULBRICHT ENTRENCHES HIS POWER

The "destalinisation" introduced in 1956 by the new strong man in Moscow, Party chief Khrushchev (which theoretically meant a retreat from the brutal methods used by Stalin to dominate the state and the economy), did not bring about any noticeable improvement of the situation in the GDR. Ulbricht limited himself to largely cosmetic compliance with the Moscow line: he released some ten thousand political prisoners early, while at the same time rendering impotent a number of reform-minded members of the Politbüro, who might have endangered his position. He also had long prison terms handed down to prominent members of an internal opposition faction. The suppression of the Hungarian revolution by the Soviet army in the autumn of 1956 also underlined how the post-Stalinist Soviet Union was no more prepared to tolerate any undermining of the dominance of the Communist Party than it had been under Stalin. To this extent Ulbricht was regarded by Moscow as totally reliable. Protests in universities and factories were strangled at birth.

A close confidant of Ulbricht, Erich Mielke, now took over the much expanded security services, the so-called "shield and sword of the Party". From late 1957, the SED made political persecution even more merciless, in order to root out more systematically those not prepared to toe the line, all of whom were defamed as "agents, spies and saboteurs". Attempts to flee the GDR (*Republikflucht*), or to assist anyone in doing so, were now declared to be crimes.

Economically the situation now began to improve for the population of the GDR. The range of consumer goods on offer began to expand. Cooking fat, meat and sugar were no longer rationed. Wages rose substantially. For a while, even the number of refugees to the West declined. However, that was soon to change when Ulbricht, as a result of the Berlin crisis engineered by Khrushchev, reverted once more to enforced measures to consolidate "socialism" in the GDR, naturally against the will of the people.

KHRUSHCHEV'S BERLIN ULTIMATUM

Almost exactly ten years after the unsuccessful Soviet blockade of Berlin, Party boss Khrushchev once more attempted to drive the Western powers out and to compel them by means of threats and blackmail to recognise the SED regime. The Soviet Union had now caught up with the USA in space technology (Sputnik 1), as well as in terms of military capability (intercontinental ballistic missiles). The Moscow leadership saw an opportunity with the dissolution of the four-power status of Berlin to close the last open flank of their empire. Khrushchev delivered an ultimatum to the Western powers in November 1958 demanding that West Berlin be transformed into a demilitarised "Free City". This demand was in effect one for the withdrawal of the Americans from Berlin. Khrushchev threatened to make a separate peace treaty with the GDR, whereby the latter would achieve control over all the access to, and exits from, Berlin. Khrushchev calculated that this would lead to an immediate and serious worsening of relations between East and West, but he wanted thereby to test the will of the Western powers to defend Berlin, while not actually intending to follow up his verbal threats with actions.

The stand-off in Berlin dragged on until 1961. However, despite the support of Khrushchev, the Communists under Ulbricht were unable to achieve their main aim. Nevertheless, Khrushchev could claim that his brinkmanship had influenced John F. Kennedy, the US President since 1961, who now showed himself willing to compromise with his Soviet opponents on the basis of the status quo in Europe, which implicitly meant accepting the division of Germany and Berlin.

Mass Flight and the Building
of the Wall, 1961

For many people in the GDR, the crisis engineered by Moscow represented an existential challenge, since they were now forced to decide whether to flee to the Federal Republic while this was still actually possible. For many, Ulbricht's renewed drive to subordinate everything to Communist ideology made their decision that much easier. The Party leadership, against all reason, held to its course of the "completion of socialist construction" in the GDR and in 1959–60 forced through the collectivisation of agriculture, an aim which had been pursued with greater or lesser intensity for years. Craftsmen and traders were also put under pressure to join the parastatal production co-operatives. Independent craftsmen or tradesmen who resisted could expect all manner of retribution or to be criminalised by accusations of tax evasion.

There was now a new wave of refugees from the GDR to the Federal Republic and West Berlin (1960: 200,000 refugees). The provision of basic supplies for the remaining population was no longer guaranteed and once again the GDR slid into a dangerous crisis. Because many feared that the flight route across East Berlin to the West would soon be closed, several tens of thousands left their homeland in the months up to August 1961. Almost all were of working age and every second refugee was under the age of 25.

In order to prevent economic collapse with predictable consequences for the SED, the Soviet Union finally allowed Ulbricht to do what he had long been pressing for, namely to seal off the GDR and to build the Berlin Wall. After President Kennedy had indirectly indicated in July 1961 that the closing of the GDR border would be accepted by the Western powers, but that at the same time the freedom of West Berlin had to be militarily guaranteed, the "People's Police" and the "National People's Army", under the direction of Erich Honecker erected barbed wire and stone walls along the sectoral border in Berlin on the night of 12th to 13th August, 1961. This makeshift affair was soon replaced with a wall, which later became a substantial beton construction that was to remain until 1989 as a symbol of the lack of freedom and repression under Communism and of the division of both Germany and Europe.

CHRONOLOGY

1950

8 February 1950	The Ministry for State Security (responsible for the control of the people and the monitoring of opponents of the SED) begins its activity.
26 April 1950	The "Waldheimer Trials" begin: in rushed trials, over 3300 real or imagined Nazis are condemned in special courts without the benefit of any of the legal norms of the rule of law. 32 death sentences are handed down, of which 24 are carried out.
6 July 1950	In the Görlitz Agreement with Poland, the GDR recognises the Oder–Neisse Line as the "Peace and Friendship Border".
25 July 1950	Following the Stalinist model, Walter Ulbricht becomes "General Secretary" of the Party at the Third Party Congress of the SED. Immediately a purge of the SED to eliminate "Social Democrats" is set in motion.
15 October 1950	The first sham elections to the People's Assembly are held on the basis of the SED-dominated unified list and mostly without benefit of secret voting. Protests against the unified list are treated as "incitements to boycott" and are severely punished. The result is a vote of 99.7% for the SED.
30 November 1950	The SED begins a propaganda campaign for "Germans at a single table".
15 December 1950	With a "Law for the Protection of Peace". oppositional figures and critics of the SED regime are criminalised and become the objects of legal persecution.
31 December 1950	In the course of 1950, 197,788 people have fled to the Federal Republic and West Berlin.

1951

1 February 1951	The SED demands the creation of ideological schools and high schools dedicated to Marxist-Leninism.
1 November 1951	The first five-year plan envisages the doubling of industrial production and a rise of 60% in productivity; also the expansion of basic and heavy industry.
31 December 1951	In 1951, 165,648 people have fled to the Federal Republic and West Berlin.

1952

9 January 1952 — Prime Minister Grotewohl rejects a proposal for the monitoring of all-German elections by the UNO.

8 May 1952 — The GDR regime announces the expansion of its "national military forces".

26 May 1952 — As reaction to the signing of the Germany Treaty, the GDR begins to seal the internal German border. Along the 1382-kilometre border, a five-kilometre exclusion zone is instituted, which can only be entered with special permission. A start is made on the forcible resettlement of the more than 12,000 people who live in the border area.

9–12 July 1952 — At the Second Party Congress of the SED, Ulbricht proclaims the "systematic expansion of Socialism" in the GDR.

23 July 1952 — Dissolution of the GDR *Länder* (Provinces) to be replaced by 14 Districts (*Bezirke*).

6 November 1952 — The Ministry of the Interior orders that in all dwelling houses and apartment blocks "logbooks" must be kept of the comings and goings of tenants and their visitors, and such logbooks must regularly be presented to the police for their inspection.

31 December 1952 — In 1952, 182,393 people have fled to the Federal Republic and West Berlin.

1953

5 March 1953 — Death of Stalin, described by the Central Committee of the SED as "the greatest man of our time". State mourning in the GDR.

28 May 1953 — The SED leadership announces a raising of work quotas by at least 10%.

1–5 June 1953 — The SED leadership visits Moscow. Soviet criticism of the speed of Ulbricht's Socialist transformation.

9 June 1953 — The Politbüro of the SED conforms to the "New Course" demanded by Moscow, but nevertheless sticks to the planned raising of work quotas.

17 June 1953 — The strike of the Berlin construction workers of the previous day expands into an uprising against the SED regime. Tanks of the Soviet army suppress the uprising, which is untruthfully described by the authorities as a "counterrevolutionary Fascist Putsch" organised from the West.

24 July 1953	Ulbricht renders his internal Party opponents impotent and remains as Moscow's stooge at the head of the Party. The Central Committee of the SED orders an increase in the production of food, luxuries and consumer goods.
31 December 1953	In 1953, 391,390 people have fled to the Federal Republic and West Berlin.

1954

1 January 1954	The Soviet Union foregoes further reparations from the GDR.
25 March 1954	The Soviet Union declares the GDR to be a sovereign state.
31 December 1954	In 1954, 184,198 people have fled the GDR.

1955

27 March 1955	First "youth initiation ceremony" held in East Berlin.
1 May 1955	First appearance of the Workers' Militia at the May Day parade, marching under the slogan: "Ready for work and the defence of the homeland."
14 May 1955	Founding of the Warsaw Pact by the East Bloc states, including the GDR.
31 December 1955	In 1955, 252,870 people have fled to the Federal Republic and West Berlin.

1956

18 January 1956	The 110,000 strong "People's Police" (*Volkspolizei*) is transformed into the National People's Army (*Nationale Volksarmee*).
15–16 February 1956	The FDGB (*Freier Deutscher Gewerkschaftsbund*—Association of Free German Trades Unions) becomes the sole provider of social security in the GDR.
14–25 February 1956	At the 20th Party Congress of the Communist Party of the Soviet Union, Khrushchev condemns the excesses and crimes committed by Stalin. A little later Ulbricht declares that Stalin was "not a classical Marxist figure".
24 October 1956	Revolution in Hungary against the Communist regime and the Soviet occupation. It is put down in two weeks by Soviet tanks. To quell protests by students at the East Berlin Humboldt University, SED forces and police are deployed.
22 November 1956	Opening of the Olympic Summer Games in Melbourne. An all-German team participates.

31 December 1956   Ulbricht suggests a confederation of German states.
In 1956, 279, 189 people have fled to the Federal Republic and West Berlin.

1957

18 January 1957   A law is passed determining the gradual introduction of a 45-hour week.

16–19 October 1957   Ulbricht overcomes internal Party opponents; the Stalinist Erich Mielke becomes the new boss of the security services from the beginning of November. The collectivisation of agriculture is to be vigorously implemented.

December 1957   Illegal departure from the GDR is in future to be punished as "flight from the Republic".

31 December 1957   In 1957, 261,622 people have fled to the Federal Republic and West Berlin.

1958

24 May 1958   Food rationing of meat, cooking fat and sugar is ended.

10–16 July 1958   Fifth Party Congress of the SED: it is decided that by 1961 the living standard of the Federal Republic must be exceeded.

14 September 1958   The former concentration camp at Buchenwald is inaugurated as an international memorial.

27 October 1958   Ulbricht states that "all Berlin belongs to the sovereign territory of the GDR".

27 November 1958   The Soviet Union announces that there is no longer four-power control of Germany and Berlin. West Berlin should become a "demilitarised Free City". The Soviet Union threatens to make a separate peace treaty with the GDR.

31 December 1958   In 1958, 204,092 people have fled to the Federal Republic and West Berlin.

1959

15–17 January 1959   The SED introduces ten-class polytechnic comprehensive schools.

24 April 1959   Bitterfeld Conference: Art and literature are to celebrate the "heroism of labour", workers are to be active in literature: "Seize your pen, workmate, our national literature needs you!"

3 June 1959	Law regulating the agricultural cooperatives; the remaining independent farmers are to be terrorised into "voluntary participation" in the cooperative.
31 December 1959	In 1959, 143, 917 people have fled to the Federal Republic or West Berlin.

1960

10 February 1960	Creation of a "National Defence Committee" under the chairmanship of Walter Ulbricht.
8 September 1960	Obligatory permits for visits by Federal German citizens to East Berlin.
12 September 1960	Ulbricht becomes Chairman of the newly created "State Council"; following Pieck's death (7 September), the office of President of the Republic is abolished.
15–17 December 1960	Alteration of the economic plan for 1961, since the aims of the original plan cannot be achieved.
31 December 1960	In 1960, 199,188 people have fled to the Federal Republic or West Berlin.

1961

28–29 March 1961	Warsaw Pact Conference: Ulbricht urges the sealing of East Berlin.
12 April 1961	Yuri Gagarin is the first man in space. The People's Assembly passes the "Book of Laws Relating to Work"; everybody has the right to a job, but there is no right to strike.
30 May 1961	Moscow allows the GDR a credit of two billion DM, and also supplies it with machines and food.
3–4 June 1961	Meeting of Kennedy and Khrushchev in Vienna. Kennedy indicates that the USA will not interfere in the Soviet sphere of influence.
15 June 1961	At a press conference in East Berlin, Ulbricht claims: "Nobody intends to build a wall."
3–5 August 1961	Conference of the Party leaders of the member states of the Warsaw Pact in Moscow. Ulbricht is given the green light for building the wall to prevent the economic collapse of the GDR.
13 August 1961	The GDR seals the border with West Berlin and begins building the wall.

5. From Stagnation to Take-Off, and from Ludwig Erhard to the Grand Coalition, 1963–1969

CHANCELLOR OF TRANSITION

One of the most popular politicians of the post-war period became Chancellor of the Federal Republic when Ludwig Erhard took over. However, during his period of office, he was unable to replicate the success of his time as Economics Minister in the cabinets of Adenauer. This was partly due to personality defects, but also because of the external circumstances that affected his short period of office.

Erhard was no power-politician like Adenauer. The latter knew how to carry through his political aims against the resistance of his party and coalition partners, and he had shown that he was not always choosy about how to achieve this. Erhard relied on the power of his arguments, was something of a populist, and believed that by reaching out directly to the people over the heads of parties and interest groups he could achieve his aims. However, his appeals to citizens that they should demand less and achieve more remained ineffective, since such urgings were not bound to any political vision. His criticism of the "backscratching democracy", and of the egoism of individual groups such as the federations and the unions, were mocked rather than heeded, because all too often he merely made rhetorical demands that he was unable to enforce through the political process. His critics in the coalition of CDU/CSU and FDP often accused him of weak leadership; not a few leading politicians in the Union hoped to succeed Erhard in the near future, which did not exactly strengthen their loyalty to the Chancellor. Nevertheless, as long as he proved a vote-winner among the federal citizens, and as long as his party could achieve a government majority as at the election of 1965, when the CDU/CSU obtained 496 seats in the Parliament with 47.6% of the vote, the party leaders were prepared to let him continue.

AMERICAN–SOVIET DÉTENTE AND THE GERMAN QUESTION

The Federal Republic under Chancellor Erhard was faced with new challenges, especially in the field of foreign policy, problems which provoked disagreements in the government camp and allowed the Social Democratic opposition to achieve a higher profile.

After the Cuba crisis of the autumn of 1962, which brought the world to the brink of nuclear war, the USA and the Soviet Union decided on a policy of détente and arms limitation. The precondition of this policy, which eventually freed both sides from the race for nuclear parity and the amassing of weapons of mass destruction, was the recognition of the status quo in Europe and therefore in Germany. The German question, which had so long been at the centre of world politics, thus lost a good deal of its significance for both sides. Erhard sought in vain to persuade the Americans to put the reunification of Germany on the international agenda. Instead, Johnson warned him from Washington that he should align himself with the American policy of détente. From that moment onwards, it was clear that no policy initiative for Germany would be possible without recognition of the interests of the GDR.

NEW POSITIONING IN BONN

In the Social Democratic opposition and amongst some of the Liberals, the message from Washington was welcome. These groupings felt that the human problems caused by the division of the country should be solved through negotiations with the GDR authorities, without however recognizing the latter's democratic legitimacy. This concept of "change through rapprochement" (Egon Bahr) was put into practice by the Social Democratic leader and Mayor of West Berlin, Willy Brandt, through temporary visiting permits for West Berliners travelling to East Berlin, which were negotiated by the West Berlin Senate with the agreement of the Federal government. In the election campaign of 1965 Brandt, now a candidate for the Chancellorship, announced that, if elected, he would pursue a policy of "step by step" rapprochement with the GDR, designed to bring about "alleviation of humanitarian problems". This policy, at first controversial, soon proved to be the most attractive approach for the future.

POLICY ON THE GERMAN QUESTION
RUNS INTO A CUL-DE-SAC

Chancellor Erhard insisted that he would do nothing that could be seen as upgrading the GDR. He held fast to the claim that West Germany represented all Germans, in accordance with the so-called Hallstein Doctrine of 1955. This basic principle of foreign policy meant that the Federal Republic broke off diplomatic relations with any country that recognised the GDR.

However, that did not hold for the Soviet Union, which, as one of the four victorious powers, shared responsibility for the division of Germany. The Chancellor was reluctant to recognize that this policy, particularly in regard to Poland and to other countries of the Eastern Bloc, was leading to a worrying isolation, and persisted with it despite the fact that the Americans made their disapproval of the policy abundantly clear. An attempted normalisation of the relations with the East Bloc countries through the setting up of trade missions in 1963–64, and the offer of non-aggression pacts with these countries (1966) came to nothing because the Foreign Minister, Schröder, expressly excluded the GDR from the proposed deal.

The result was that Erhard's policy on the German question ran into a cul-de-sac. But also in other areas of Federal foreign policy the attempt to isolate the GDR internationally proved to be counter-productive, because the Federal Republic could so easily be placed under economic or political pressure as a result of it. This became evident in the Near East. Despite intensive economic assistance to Arab countries, the Federal Republic could not prevent the GDR from gaining a foothold, particularly in Egypt. The SED leader was shrewd enough to exploit the difficult positioning of the Federal Republic between Israel and the Arab states. Bonn's initiation of diplomatic relations with Israel in August 1965 was partly intended as way of punishing the Egyptians, but this move greatly limited the influence of the Federal Government in Arab countries. The resultant debacle indeed diminished respect for Erhard in the ranks both of his coalition partners and his own party. The fact that he also failed to avoid the extra burden of costs ("currency stabilisation payments") for American troops stationed in Germany, demanded in short order by President Johnson to assist him with the Vietnam war, also discredited his leadership in the Party and among the public, although it is doubtful if even Chancellor Adenauer could have done any better on this issue.

On top of these foreign policy failures came the first economic crisis of the young republic, harmless enough in hindsight, but enough to end Erhard's chancellorship abruptly.

Economic Crisis: Signals of Dissatisfaction

The economic boom that had lasted for years now began to run out of steam, growth was slower and the citizens, long accustomed to rising wages and full employment, began to become anxious and blamed the Chancellor for doing too little to remedy matters. The mood of the people became significantly worse than the economic situation actually warranted. A few weeks before

Erhard's resignation in 1966, there were only 100,000 unemployed and 600,000 unfilled positions. Nevertheless, the economic dynamism of the previous years had unmistakably begun to slacken. Private and public investment was diminishing. More was produced than was sold, workers were laid off, inflation drove up prices and wages. At the same time, there was a full-blown crisis in the mining sector. The time when coal was the most important source of energy was already over and cheaper oil from the Arab countries was beginning to dominate the energy sector. In the Ruhr area, mines were closed. Supported by a warning strike right across the country, the miners took to the streets. Against this background, the CDU did badly in the provincial elections in Nordrhein-Westfalen in the summer of 1966, and the SPD only just failed to achieve an absolute majority. The senior politicians of the Union blamed the Chancellor for the decline in support, especially as he had expressly and unwisely described these elections as a judgement on the government's performance. Furthermore, the increasing economic insecurity among certain layers of the population gave a boost to a new extreme rightwing party. This party (NPD, *Nationaldemokratische Partei Deutschlands*—National Democratic Party of Germany), with its marked nationalistic programme, was led by former Nazis and aroused a good deal of anxiety at home and abroad when, after failing in the parliamentary elections of 1966, in November of the same year it got elected to the Hesse and Bavaria parliaments.

ERHARD'S OVERTHROW: THE SPD'S OPPORTUNITY

In the autumn, the Christian–Liberal coalition finally fell apart in a dispute over the planned budget for 1967, which threatened a black hole of seven billion DM. The tax rises planned by the CDU/CSU fraction were rejected by the Liberals, who accordingly left the government.

Behind the scenes senior politicians of the Union such as the CSU Chairman, Strauss, and the CDU leader in Rheinland-Pfalz, Kohl, had already set a course for the removal of Erhard and cooperation with the SPD. In the ranks of the latter it was particularly the Chairman of the Parliamentary Party, Herbert Wehner, who worked towards a political alliance with the Union. He was concerned to demonstrate the ability of the SPD to govern at national level. Urgent domestic political reforms (the emergency laws, finance), which would require a majority sufficient for constitutional change, but above all their own political interests, encouraged the Union to cooperate with the SPD. However, the SPD activists at first showed little understanding for the coalition politics of the Social Democratic leadership.

At the behest of his party, Ludwig Erhard made way at the beginning of November 1966 for the long-standing Prime Minister of Baden-Württemberg, Kurt Georg Kiesinger. The Union then adopted the latter as their candidate for the Chancellorship in a Grand Coalition. On the 1st of December 1966 Kiesinger was elected Federal Chancellor.

THE GRAND COALITION UNDER CHANCELLOR KIESINGER: A CABINET OF CONTRASTS

The leading politicians of the coalition parties—nine SPD ministers, seven CDU, four CSU—sat in the cabinet. The latter included Willy Brandt (Foreign Minister and Vice-Chancellor), Franz Josef Strauss (Finance Minister), Karl Schiller (Economics Minister), Gustav Heinemann (Justice Minister) and Gerhard Schröder (Defence Minister). The architect of the Grand Coalition, Herbert Wehner, also sat in the cabinet as Minister responsible for matters concerning Germany as a whole. Helmut Schmidt (SPD) and Rainer Barzel (CDU) became leaders of their respective parties in Parliament responsible for coordinating the government's programme.

The high-ranking politicians who built a Grand Coalition for crisis management, a "temporary alliance" as the government declaration put it, also represented a kind of reconciliation with the German past. Kiesinger had entered the NSDAP (*Nationalsozialistische Deutsche Arbeiterpartei*, the Nazi Party) very early on, a typical young sympathiser who was later posted to the Foreign Ministry under Ribbentrop and worked there as "scientific assistant" for radio propaganda. Wehner had been a leading functionary of the German Communist Party during the Weimar Republic, working closely with Walter Ulbricht. He spent several years of exile in Moscow, where he experienced the Stalinist terror at first hand and also had to come to terms with the dubious options that had to be embraced if he was not himself to become a victim. Towards the end of the war he broke with the Communists in Sweden, becoming a Social Democrat and subsequently the right-hand man of Kurt Schumacher in the Bundestag. The Social Democrat, Willy Brandt, was obliged to flee from the Nazis in 1933, first to Norway, then to Sweden, but reacquired German citizenship in 1948 and advanced rapidly through the ranks to the leadership of the Social Democratic Party in Bonn and Berlin, finally becoming his party's most voter-friendly figure and candidate for the Chancellorship. Franz Josef Strauss, whose career in Bonn appeared to have been ended by the *Spiegel* affair and his enforced resignation, now saw himself as rehabilitated in the eyes of his former political opponents. Together with Karl Schiller, the brilliant Economics Minister from the

SPD, he created a formidable partnership for dealing with the recession and the structural problems of the economy.

Acting as "a mobile negotiation committee", the humorous designation for Kiesinger, the publicity-minded Chancellor managed to balance the very different temperaments of his ministers, not to mention the contrasting political positions of the coalition parties, so that a homogeneous policy emerged. Where this was not possible, for example in the question of the majority voting system favoured by the Union but rejected by the SPD, the issue was put on ice.

Reform of the Market Economy:
Overcoming the Economic Crisis

The most important aim that the Kiesinger/Brandt government had set itself was reached in a surprisingly short time, namely the overcoming of the economic crisis. Economics Minister Schiller and Finance Minister Strauss joined forces to create a market economy basis for positive economic development, with the aim of achieving price stability, economic growth, full employment and a positive trade balance. One aspect of this "concerted action" was the voluntary discussion forum set up between representatives of the Federal States, the unions and the Employers' Federations. This forum was intended to bring wage demands into line with the realities of the economic cycle. However, this succeeded only in the initial period. As the economy began to boom again, the employees began once more to pursue their individual interests vigorously. In a short time, the government brought order into state finances, spurred economic activity with a series of investment measures (thereby creating debts that were later to be written off) and in this way managed to return to full employment. Already in 1968, GNP grew by 7.1%, unemployment receded by 1.5% and wages climbed by 6.2%. The economic crisis was over. The economy now began a new advance and the citizens of the Federal Republic once more looked optimistically to the future, at least as far as their economic security was concerned.

Modernisation

The Grand Coalition also ushered in a modernisation of society through further legal reforms, many of which anticipated the new attitudes of the seventies. The following government was able to build on this beginning. The most important area of reform was the liberalisation of the criminal law. The state retreated from the bedrooms of its citizens: adultery and adult homosexuality were no longer crimes. In general, previously harsh sentences were now more often commuted to probation periods. The reintegration of perpetrators into society (resocialisation) became the aim of the judiciary, together with an encouragement of remorse for the damage done to victims. In the political area there was also liberalisation, whereby contact with SED functionaries no longer had to be approved by the Attorney General. The founding of a new German Communist Party (DKP) followed in 1969. This too was a novelty of some significance, in view of the ban on the KPD by the Constitutional Court in 1956.

EMERGENCY LAWS AS
A DOMESTIC POLICY ISSUE

The economic successes of the Grand Coalition could not, however, prevent the Federal Republic from simultaneously plunging into a phase of domestic political turbulence. The democratic spectrum was polarised to the right and to the left. The extreme right NPD managed to get elected to state parliaments at numerous elections. In 1969 it only just failed to gain seats in the Bundestag, but thereafter rapidly lost its significance and influence. Discontent of quite another kind was articulated by the student movement, which characterised itself as the "Extraparliamentary Opposition" (APO). The latter protested against the "power cartel" of the government and the putative threat to democracy posed by the emergency laws of the Grand Coalition, a main policy aim of the Christian–Social Democratic alliance.

In contrast to all other Western states, the Federal Republic's Basic Law made no provision for emergency measures in cases where national defence was urgently needed, or in the event of serious domestic unrest or catastrophes. In the Parliamentary Council a new formulation of the notorious Article 48 of the Weimar constitution was being contemplated. This, inter alia, would have enabled the President of the Republic to set aside the constitution for temporary periods. Such a provision was indeed long overdue— and all the parties were agreed on this—because the Allies had hitherto reserved for themselves the right to intervene in the event of such a crisis and to overrule the powers of the Republic, as long as there existed no adequate provisions in Federal Law. The Grand Coalition now wanted to achieve what none of its predecessors since 1960 had managed, namely a compromise, whereby the Parliament would retain sufficient controls on the executive during an emergency, thus avoiding the danger of abuse of power. In this way, an emergency should not be exploited as an excuse for unilaterally strengthening the executive at the expense of democratic process.

THE REBELLION OF THE STUDENTS AND THE
EXTRAPARLIAMENTARY OPPOSITION

The struggle against the emergency laws in the spring of 1968 united the student movement, trades unions, writers and intellectuals at the time the relevant laws were being laid before Parliament. The public protest of the opponents of the emergency laws did not particularly interest the public at large, insofar as trusted democrats like Willy Brandt expressly supported the measures; on the other hand it laid the basis for a widespread hostility among part of the younger generation towards the established parties and the democratic institutions of the Federal Republic's political system.

The roots of the student protest movement lay deeper, however. It represented an inter-generational conflict that was observable in all the industrial nations. The *Zeitgeist* worked across all borders. The attitudes of the younger generation in San Francisco, Paris, London, Frankfurt or Berlin clashed with the conventions observed by their elders. The bourgeois virtues of diligence, order, cleanliness and reliability were regarded as "square", and were mercilessly mocked while enjoying a good smoke of hashish. Long hair, untidy clothing and new forms of cohabitation were the external signs of the youthful rebellion against authority in the family, at work, at school and in the state—in short, against the establishment.

The youth rebellion emanated from America, where students demonstrated for civil rights for blacks and against the Vietnam War. From the student protests against high schools unwilling to reform, and against authoritarian professors, there developed in France and Germany in the late sixties a political movement that defined itself as the "New Left", which vowed to oppose western capitalism and the consumer society. Further, it propagated an elitist form of Marxist interpretation of world events and took its heroes from the revolutionaries of the Third World, such as Fidel Castro, Mao Zedong and Ho Chi Minh. It was fashionable to be anti-American, but also the "beton ('concrete') Socialism" of the Soviets was held to be a model of society that had no future. In the Federal Republic, there was an added ingredient, namely the confrontation of the new generation with the often suppressed Nazi past of their elders.

The leading figure of the movement in Berlin was Rudi Dutschke, who had come from the GDR, and who propagated an idealistic Marxism-inspired programme of an authority-free society, embellished with revolutionary gesture-politics, which proved attractive to many students. The attempts of the older generation of reconstruction, who were dazed by the ferocity of the attacks on them, to defend their achievements were simply met by the children of the economic miracle with references to the Nazi past of their parents.

THE APOTHEOSIS AND DECLINE OF
STUDENT UNREST

In Berlin and other universities, the confrontations between demonstrators and police escalated in 1967–68. After the death of a student and an assassination attempt on Dutschke, the protests reached a high point in April 1968. In many cities there were street battles between police and demonstrators, which caused two deaths in Munich. The original rule that violence was to be directed only against installations, especially those of the Springer publishing house which produced the *Bild-Zeitung*, and that no violence was to be directed against persons, risked being lost in the activism of the streets. However, with the failure of the struggle against the emergency laws, the APO rapidly lost a rallying issue in the politics of the Federal Republic. In addition, the revolutionary rhetoric of the Republic's left-wing exponents lost its credibility when Soviet troops brutally crushed Prague's "socialism with a human face" in the August of 1968. Thereafter, the protest movement imploded. A small minority opted for terrorism, in order to carry on the struggle against the hated bourgeois society from the underground. Others joined the newly founded Communist Party, or various other groups with Communist aims, or took part in the spontaneous house-squatting movement of the 1970's. Yet others discovered ecology as the new social commitment. However, the great majority of the "sixty-eighters" turned their backs on the unrealistic utopias of the previous years and took up professional careers. In the reform politics of the SPD under Willy Brandt, they discovered their political home and not a few began to build their own political careers within its framework. The student revolt had not produced a cultural revolution; on the other hand it certainly was successful in breaking through the largely conservative basis of West German society.

TOWARDS A NEW POLICY FOR EAST GERMANY
AND THE GERMAN QUESTION

The Grand Coalition was less successful in its policy towards East Germany and the German question than it was in domestic issues. The announcement of the intention to come to an accommodation with the eastern neighbours and to "ease" (Kiesinger) the relationship with the GDR was the Federal Republic's answer to the American policy of détente. However, the attempt to achieve this foundered on the reaction of Moscow to the efforts of the new government to establish diplomatic relations with the countries of Eastern Europe. The Kremlin feared that this might lead to a sort of domino effect in the eastern alliance. The example of Romania, which established diplomatic relations with the Federal Republic at the beginning of 1967, was not a precedent they wanted others to follow. Hungary and Bulgaria wanted to do the same as Romania, but Moscow knew that reform Communists were only waiting their chance. Thus the Soviet leadership under Leonid Brezhnev decreed only a few weeks later that normalisation of relations between the East Bloc and the economically powerful Federal Republic could only follow the recognition of the GDR by Bonn. In addition, Moscow demanded the unconditional recognition of the Oder–Neisse border by the Federal Republic. In this way, the Soviet Union made sure that a restated foreign policy towards the East could not avoid the question of the GDR. Consequently, and despite an exchange of letters between Chancellor Kiesinger and the GDR Prime Minister, Willi Stoph, in the summer of 1967, there was no movement in the two governments' respective positions. The GDR demanded formal recognition as a sovereign state. The Federal government only wanted to negotiate on practical matters regarding the co-existence of the two Germanies and on closer economic cooperation.

Of course this question caused the first cracks in the governing coalition. The leadership of the SPD was prepared to go much further in the their policy towards East Germany and the German question than was the Federal Chancellor; indeed they were prepared to accept the realities of the status quo in Europe. Brandt and his closest adviser, Egon Bahr, were convinced that the key to any improvement in intra-German relations lay with Moscow and nowhere else. This view was shared by the left-liberal wing of the FDP, which had used its period in opposition in the Bundestag under a new party chairman, Walter Scheel, to develop a comprehensive new political programme and orientation. In view of the apparent failure of the reunification policy of previous governments, the main emphasis of the leading forces in the FDP was now placed on a policy of recognition of the existence of two states in Germany, in order to bring about for both of them a regulated relationship that would benefit the inhabitants in the East as in the West.

The Liberals Change Sides

At the election of the Social Democratic Justice Minister, Gustav Heinemann, as Federal President at the beginning of March 1969, the Liberals (FDP) voted en bloc for the Social Democratic candidate. This decision was the outward sign of the movement at federal level towards a new coalition, for which both party chiefs, Brandt and Scheel, had been working from May

1969, insofar as the result of the upcoming elections to the Bundestag would make it a practicable proposition. The possibilities for cooperation in the Grand Coalition were now exhausted.

CHRONOLOGY

1963

16 October 1963	Ludwig Erhard (CDU) is elected Federal Chancellor; continuation of the coalition consisting of CDU/CSU and FDP.
22 November 1963	Assassination of the American President, John F. Kennedy, in Dallas, Texas. His successor is Vice-President Lyndon B. Johnson.
17 December 1963	Agreement between West Berlin and the GDR on border transit: for the first time since the building of the wall, West Berliners can visit their relations in the East sector of the city between Christmas and New Year. Three further agreements follow up to June 1966; until 1972 there are then no further visits possible except in cases of extreme need.
20 December 1963	The mass trial of 22 functionaries of the Auschwitz concentration camp begins before the criminal court in Frankfurt am Main. The trial ends with convictions on 19 August 1965.
31 December 1963	The average unemployment rate in the Federal Republic during the year has been 0.8%.

1964

16 February 1964	Willy Brandt, the Mayor of Berlin, becomes Chairman of the SPD.
6 March 1964	Conclusion of a German–Bulgarian trade agreement. Similar agreements had already been made in 1963 with Poland, Romania and Hungary.
12 June 1964	Friendship Treaty between the Soviet Union and the GDR. The Treaty recognizes the existing borders of the GDR.
1 July 1964	Heinrich Lübke is re-elected to the Federal Presidency in Berlin.
7 August 1964	The US Congress approves intervention of the USA in the Vietnam War.
15 October 1964	Fall of the Soviet Party and Government boss, Khrushchev in Moscow. A new leadership takes over under Leonid Brezhnev (Party Chief) and Alexei Kossygin (Prime Minister).

2 November 1964   GDR citizens of pensionable age may make one annual visit to the Federal Republic.

28 November 1964   Founding of the extreme right wing National Democratic Party of Germany (NPD) in Hannover.

1 December 1964   Introduction of a minimum money exchange of 5 DM for western visitors to the GDR.

1965

25 March 1965   The Bundestag lengthens period of the statute of limitations for Nazi crimes, which can be punished with life imprisonment.

28 April 1965   Ulbricht demands 120 billion Marks compensation from the Federal Republic for the reparations for the whole of Germany paid by the GDR and the education costs of refugees ("cadres enticed away").

12 May 1965   The Federal Republic and Israel establish diplomatic relations. As a result, nine Arab states break off diplomatic relations with Bonn.

9 July 1965   In the election campaign, Chancellor Erhard labels prominent writers as "Philistines and conceited asses".

10 September 1965 The millionth *Gastarbeiter*, a Portuguese, arrives in Cologne.

19 September 1965 The fifth German parliament is elected: the CDU/CSU wins 47.6% of the vote (245 MPs); the SPD wins 39.3% (202 MPs), the FDP 9.5% (49 MPs); with 2%, the NPD fails to make it over the 5% hurdle into Parliament.

8 October 1965   The National Olympic Committee of the GDR is recognised by the International Olympic Committee; two separate German teams will be allowed to compete in the games in Mexico City in 1968.

15 October 1965   The German Lutheran Church publishes a memorandum that indirectly suggests the recognition of the Oder–Neisse border.

20 October 1965   Ludwig Erhard is re-elected Federal Chancellor and continues to lead a coalition consisting of CDU, CSU and FDP.

10 November 1965   Chancellor Erhard announces in a speech promulgating his government's programme that the German economic miracle is now entering "the natural phase of being tested in every respect and every day. We must either rein in our expectations or work harder."

5 December 1965	Correspondence between the German and Polish Catholic bishops emphasises their mutual desire for reconciliation.
31 December 1965	The average level of unemployment in the Federal Republic in the past year has been 0.7%.

1966

5 February 1966	Student protests in West Berlin against the American participation in the Vietnam War leads to serious clashes with the police.
7 March 1966	France leaves the NATO integration process.
11 March 1966	Countrywide strike against the closing of mines and to force the further subvention of coalmining.
23 March 1966	Ludwig Erhard is elected to the Chairmanship of the CDU.
25 March 1966	Note from the Federal Republic on German peace policy sent to 100 governments, including those of the Eastern European states (with the exception of the GDR), offering non-aggression pacts.
14 April 1966	The SPD welcomes the exchange of views offered by the SED, which however never takes place.
13 May 1966	The Bundeskongress of the DGB (the German Trades Unions Congress) rejects any form of emergency laws.
19 July 1966	The SPD emerges from the provincial elections in Nordrhein-Westfalen as the strongest party with 49.5% of the vote; CDU and FDP form a government with a majority of two votes; the coalition switch of the FDP leads on 1st of December to an SPD/FDP government under Prime Minister Heinz Kühn (SPD).
24 July 1966	In Brussels it is agreed to establish a common agricultural market from the middle of 1967.
27 October 1966	Resignation of the FDP ministers from the Erhard cabinet.
30 October 1966	Protest rally in Frankfurt am Main organised by the Committee for Democratic Emergency against the planned emergency laws.
6 November 1966	The NPD succeeds in getting elected to a State Parliament for the first time with 7.9% of the votes in the provincial elections for Hesse. In the Bavarian elections of 20th November, it wins 7.4% of the vote.

30 November 1966   Resignation of Chancellor Erhard.

1 December 1966   The Prime Minister of Baden-Württemberg, Kurt Georg Kies-inger, is elected Federal Chancellor. He forms a Grand Coali-tion of CDU, CSU and SPD, which commands 447 seats in the Bundestag against 49 seats for the FDP. Willy Brandt becomes Foreign Minister and Vice-Chancellor.

15 December 1966   The Council of NATO forms a committee concerned with nucle-ar defence, and a nuclear planning group, in both of which the Federal Republic has the right to be consulted.

31 December 1966   The unemployed figure is 300,000 and the average unemploy-ment for the year has been 0.7%. The gross domestic product has grown by only 2.8%. Short time working at Volkswagen.

1967

1 January 1967   The 40-hour working week is introduced in the metal industry.

31 January 1967   Diplomatic relations are established with Romania.

14 February 1967   Roundtable discussions take place as part of the "concerted action" proposed by the Economics Minister, Karl Schiller.

15 February 1967   673,000 are unemployed and the average unemployment figure for the year is 2.1%, or around half a million people out of work. GDP falls to 2%.

9 May 1967   NATO replaces the doctrine of "massive retaliation" in the case of attack with "incremental response", whereby in the event of conflict it is hoped that the Federal Republic will not automati-cally become a nuclear battleground.

10 May 1967   The Bundestag passes a law to stabilise growth in the economy ("Stability Law").

2 June 1967   A student named Benno Ohnesorg is shot by a policeman during a demonstration of about 3000 students in West Berlin against the visit of the Shah of Persia; about 100,000 students take part in demonstrations in other university cities.

13 June 1967   Chancellor Kiesinger proposes a non-aggression pact with the GDR. Recognition of the GDR is expressly rejected.

13 July 1967	A council concerned with state support for economic expansion is formed to advise the Federal Government on politico-economic questions; on the basis of its advice the government publishes an economic report each year which surveys the general economic situation of the country.
3 August 1967	Trade agreement signed with Czechoslovakia.

1968

31 January 1968	Re-establishment of diplomatic relations with Yugoslavia.
3 April 1968	Arson attack on two coffee houses in Frankfurt am Main; among those arrested and convicted are Andreas Baader and Gudrun Ensslin.
9 April 1968	The "Socialist Constitution" of the GDR comes into force. The exclusive "leading role" of the SED is thereby made permanent.
11 April 1968	Assassination attempt on the Chairman of the German Socialist Student Association (SDS), Rudi Dutschke, who is seriously wounded. In many German cities there is serious unrest.
10 May 1968	Commencement of talks in Paris between the Americans and the North Vietnamese with the aim of ending the Vietnam War.
13 May 1968	High point of the student demonstrations in Paris.
30 May 1968	The Bundestag passes a law covering states of emergency.
1 July 1968	Signing of the nuclear non-proliferation treaty in Washington, Moscow and London; the Federal Republic joins the treaty in November 1969.
21 August 1968	Violent suppression of the "Prague Spring" by Soviet troops and other forces of the Warsaw Pact; a serious setback for détente in Europe.
26 September 1968	Founding of a German Communist Party (DKP) as successor organisation of the forbidden KPD.
30 September 1968	Unemployment is running at 0.8% (174,500); the Federal Republic has overcome the recession.
12 November 1968	Promulgation of the Brezhnev Doctrine concerning the limited sovereignty of the East Bloc countries, and devised to justify the Soviet invasion of Czechoslovakia.

1969

24 January 1969   The FDP proposes a draft treaty with the GDR, which is reject-
                     ed by the Union and the SPD in the Bundestag.

26 February 1969   State visit of US President Nixon to the Federal Republic and
                     West Berlin.

5 March 1969   On the third round of voting, the joint sessions of Parliament
                     elect Justice Minister, Gustav Heinemann, to be the first Social
                     Democratic Federal President. Heinemann describes his election
                     as "a shift of power".

28 April 1969   Resignation of French President, Charles de Gaulle; his succes-
                     sor is Georges Pompidou.

8 May 1969   Cambodia recognizes the GDR as a sovereign state; a number of
                     other states in the Near East follow suit.

9 May 1969   Two reforms of the criminal law are passed in the Bundestag: one
                     concerns modernisation and liberalisation of the criminal law;
                     the other makes the concept of resocialisation a primary aim of
                     the justice system.

20 July 1969   The US astronauts, Armstrong and Aldrin, are the first people to
                     land on the moon: "A small step for a man, a huge step for hu-
                     manity." (Armstrong)

4 August 1969   Extension of the statute of limitations for murder from 20 to 30
                     years; Nazi crimes of violence can therefore still be prosecuted
                     after 1969. It is also laid down that there shall be no statute of
                     limitations for genocide.

2 September 1969   Unofficial strikes to back up wage demands; the Federal Republic
                     is enjoying an economic boom with growth of almost 12%.

28 September 1969   The sixth election to the Bundestag takes place: CDU/CSU
                     46.1% (242 mandates); SPD 42.7% (224 mandates), FDP 5.8%
                     (30 mandates), NPD 4.3%. The SPD and the FDP form a social-
                     ist–liberal coalition under Chancellor Willy Brandt.

6. After the Building of the Wall: Stabilisation of the SED State by Means of Force under Walter Ulbricht, 1961–1971

The Barricaded "Socialist Community of People"

The threatened economic collapse of the GDR meant that the Communist party leader in the East, Walter Ulbricht, was given the green light for a measure of extreme inhumanity, even though the building of the wall was tantamount to open admission of the total failure of the SED regime. This admission, however, seemed to be the lesser evil in the eyes of the Moscow leadership and its satellites, in view of the fact that the crisis in the GDR could lead to a serious threat to the Communist hegemony in the neighbouring Eastern European countries. It was thought also that the loss of face it engendered before the whole world could somehow be counteracted by vigorous propaganda.

It was also the case that the policy of "negotiation only from strength" that had for years been pursued by western governments had not been able to prevent the entrenchment of the SED dictatorship. The USA had for some time been signalling that it would avoid any provocation that might lead to unrest among the population of the GDR, and thereby perhaps to a direct military conflict with the Soviet Union. The East and West Germans had to realise that the division of their country was now a side issue in the larger context of a polarised confrontation between two highly armed superpowers.

The Dictators and Their Subjects

The international situation thus provided the Communist leadership in East Berlin with an opportunity finally to stabilise their hegemony. Walter Ulbricht, as First Secretary of the SED, and Chairman both of the State Council and of the National Defence Committee, disposed of an unprecedented amount of power, which he was determined to use quite ruthlessly in order to achieve his aim of securing Socialism in the eastern part of Germany. At the same time, he showed that he was flexible enough to use a variety of methods, as seemed appropriate in any given situation. Particularly in the field of economics (for example with the NÖSPL, or "New Economic System of Socialist Planning and Guidance") he appeared astonishingly willing to experiment, at least by comparison with most of the other members of the Politbüro. Of course this openness lasted only so long as the desired independence and individual responsibility of the workers and managers in factories and the administration did not develop into any threat to the leadership of the Communists. Ulbricht was a curious mixture of technological rationalism and uncompromising ideological stubbornness. He interpreted his role as that of the hatchet man of a Communist revolution steered from above, but at the same time attempted to pose as the father of his people, deeply concerned for their well-being. The people were regarded by him as his subjects, who needed to be brought into line with the deeper insights vouchsafed to the leadership, using the stick or the carrot as the circumstances required. Such freedoms as were allowed in the economic or cultural field were supposed to energise all layers of society, workers and intellectuals, women and young people, in order that the aims of the Party (namely the participation in the development of a modern industrial society, as in the West) should be achieved as soon as possible. This had nothing to do with democratisation in the GDR. Any new approach could be reversed at any time.

OPPRESSION OF THE POPULATION

Immediately after the building of the Wall, the authorities launched a campaign against so-called provocateurs in order to intimidate the population. Several thousand people were removed from the border area and resettled against their will. The newspapers reported on "agitators" and "saboteurs" who had to be taught a lesson by "the workers". Members of the youth movement (*Freie Deutsche Jugend*—FDJ) destroyed TV aerials that were positioned to receive broadcasts from the West. In the universities, the students had to sign a declaration that they would voluntarily take up arms in defence of Socialism. Anyone who refused was dismissed from the university and sent to work in a factory.

FLEEING THE REPUBLIC BECOMES A
CRIME AGAINST THE STATE

Up to September 1961, around 6000 people had been arrested for "agitation against the state" and condemned to periods in gaol. By the end of the year, a further 15,297 had been arrested. These so-called "state criminals" had done nothing more than criticise the policies of the SED, or had been caught trying to flee to the West. In order to deter others, the GDR judiciary handed down long prison sentences for "attempted flight from the Republic". Up to 1989, some 60,000 people met this fate. Those who knew of someone's plans to flee, but did not report it to the police, also had to reckon with punishment. In this way a climate of fear was created. Professional advancement, the individual's own future and the future of his or her children were all at stake.

Nevertheless, over 50,000 people still succeeded in fleeing to the West in the first months after the wall was built. Yet their flight was now especially dangerous since, only a week after the Wall was in place, the order was given for a shoot-to-kill policy for "border infringements". In the following years, the number of people fleeing sank to as little as 1100 by 1984, since border security was continually being improved. After that date, there were again an increasing number of refugees who often were able to leave the GDR simply by not returning from a permitted journey to the West. Some 1000 citizens of the GDR were killed while attempting to flee, while thousands of others suffered serious injury.

THE PRESSURE TO CONFORM

The propaganda of the SED celebrated the "anti-Fascist protection", as the Wall was officially designated, which was said to symbolise the success of the Socialist camp against the "militarists and imperialists" in Bonn and Washington, as well as being a victory for the forces of freedom that had forestalled West German aggression. However, only the loyal foot soldiers of the SED paid lip service to this claim. The great majority of the population could easily see through its falsity. Bitter jokes did the rounds, as in exchanges like the following: "Did you know Meier has taken his own life?" To which the reply was: "Well of course, everyone gets out if he can." Many felt as if they were the slaves of the state, but saw no alternative to that of conforming to "real existing Socialism", the cosmetising description of life under the SED which the GDR authorities soon became fond of repeating.

Most people lived a double existence that was only outwardly conformist. So far as possible, people tried to get round the unreasonable ideology of the State, and paid lip service to Party dogmas, while talking quite differently with friends or within the family. Thus they created a private sphere for themselves where they tried to live out their lives as normally as possible, although in fact it was difficult to escape the arm of the state even in the most intimate sphere. They dreamed of the West, which they continued to know through the TV or from the accounts of visiting relatives. The absolute ban on travel to the West for GDR citizens was loosened only several years later, first for pensioners, then also for "pressing family reasons", until in the 1980's permits for travel abroad at any time were theoretically available. Many hundreds of thousands sought to take advantage of these, often in vain, since applicants still had to reckon with endless chicanery and prevarication by the authorities.

The Arbitrary Behaviour of Officials

Notwithstanding the forced compromises that the population was obliged to make with the regime, there was in fact no reconciliation between citizen and state. The Stalinist bureaucratic apparatus of the SED and its daily encountered techniques of spying and oppression remained omnipresent, so that the citizen was entirely at the mercy of the arbitrary behaviour of officials. Cosmetic gestures, such as that propagated by Ulbricht in 1963, when he proclaimed that "the Republic needs everyone, everyone needs the Republic", which was supposed to instil some affection for the Communist regime in people's minds, did nothing to alter people's feelings about it.

A leitmotif of the regime was the unpredictability of the authorities; indeed it was the defining experience of two entire generations. In order to keep the population quiet politically, the Party leadership swung between reform and harshness, the swings often dictated by the way the wind was blowing in Moscow at any given moment.

After the building of the Wall, Ulbricht briefly loosened the chains on literature and art and the party renewed its efforts to win over youth. The security services took up a more relaxed stance and suddenly the young were even allowed to decide how they would like to dance. In this way the SED made its contribution to the de-Stalinisation still being pursued by Khrushchev in the Soviet Union. However, already in the middle of the sixties, this brief opening up had become a thing of the past for writers, filmmakers and songwriters; such things as beat music, jeans, the twist and jazz were forbidden to the young on the grounds that they represented Western decadence. The State mobilised massive police contingents against the beat movement: musicians and fans were criminalised as "rowdies" and designated enemies of the state. Many writers and intellectuals imposed self-censorship either out of loyalty to the Socialist state or in order to avoid conflict with the Party. Others, like the songwriter Wolf Biermann, were forbidden to perform or were unable to publish. Everywhere the SED authorities detected "damaging tendencies that were alien to Socialism" (Honecker, 1965) in artistic production. New films and stage-plays were routinely forbidden. The final years of the Ulbricht era became a cultural ice-age.

ECONOMIC REFORMS:
ONE STEP FORWARD, ONE STEP BACK

The economic reforms of 1963 were designed to make the factories more efficient by introducing incentives and more personal responsibility, this in the hope of increasing productivity and curing the general economic malaise of the GDR; but the reforms were withdrawn only a few years later, because the Party apparatus feared for its power. With the proclamation of economic reforms the population had hoped for a certain degree of general liberalisation. Now the disappointment and dissatisfaction was all the greater, since everyone had to face the truth that the SED was only interested in "reform" insofar as it might consolidate its power. Instead of threats and compulsion, Ulbricht now wanted to make Socialism impregnable through economic success.

Because so many artisans had fled to the West before the Wall was built, the young generation now had theoretically the best chances for prospering by taking their place. The attempt of the SED leadership to introduce economic reform was coupled with a reform of the entire education system, and indeed the education on offer in schools and for apprentices noticeably improved. Science and research was encouraged. The Party leadership wanted the results of the latter to be put into practice more quickly and to be exploited for the promotion of economic progress.

Notwithstanding Ulbricht's supposed enthusiasm for innovation, he left no doubt about the undivided monopoly of competence and leadership claimed by the Party. As a result, the initiatives for modernisation soon came up against the self-imposed limits of an authoritarian state. Anyone who had hoped for greater individual freedom to result from the reforms (which were in fact mostly well-received by the people) soon learned his mistake.

Although the "new economic levers" had unmistakably led to an improvement of living standards, a group in the Politbüro centred on Erich Honecker and Willy Stoph, which was hostile to reform, ensured that from 1967 there was a reversion to strict central leadership and control. This return to reaction was certainly also a response to directions from Moscow. Since the fall of Khrushchev (1964), Leonid Brezhnev had emerged as leader of the Soviet Communist Party, and he was by no means in favour of Ulbricht's experiments with reform, in which he saw a danger for Socialism. In addition, he rejected Ulbricht's aim of bringing about relative economic independence for the GDR, since this could only be achieved at the expense of Soviet economic requirements. Right up to the demise of the GDR, its economic policy was therefore determined by people like Günter Mittag, the "economics dictator" and protagonist of the centralised command economy.

MODEST PROSPERITY, UNKEPT PROMISES

Ulbricht failed in his ambitious plan to make the GDR the shop window for Socialism and to overtake the Federal Republic in terms of economic success. What was proclaimed to be "scientific and technical progress", namely the promotion of modern technology in the form of microelectrics, turned out to be a gigantic misdirection of investment, which was correspondingly lacking in areas such as construction and consumer goods, where it was urgently needed. Ulbricht's planned economy never did reach the "world level" officially claimed. However, it should not be overlooked that, by comparison with the fifties, the GDR economy did make progress from the middle of the sixties. The same was true of the other countries of the East Bloc.

A modest prosperity was now widespread. Televisions, refrigerators and washing machines were added to households. More and more families could afford a car, even if the cars were only built to the modest local specifications. Saturdays were holidays from 1967 onwards, and the citizens of the GDR certainly regarded that year as a time of breakthrough. On the other hand, this merely underlined the stark contrast that most people observed between their country and the Federal Republic. It was clear that, despite the improvement mentioned above, the planned economy of the GDR was unable to deliver parity with the living standards of its western neighbour, or to offer competitive products on the world market. Moreover, there were still difficulties of supply for the most basic articles on an almost daily basis.

ISOLATION POLICY AND THE DESPERATE
NEED FOR HARD CURRENCY

The cautious attempts of the Grand Coalition in Bonn to ensure that their policies regarding reunification and East Germany took account of the de facto reality, and especially to deepen their economic and political contacts with the countries of the East Bloc, caused a U-turn in the reunification policy of the SED. Ulbricht had hitherto directed his reunification appeals to the Federal Government and the Bundestag in the full knowledge that they would be rejected. Of course all these suggestions for reunification were coupled to conditions that would have led to a Socialist order in the reunified state, and to that extent were little more than crude propaganda ploys.

When Chancellor Kiesinger first offered to negotiate with the GDR over a declaration of non-aggression and a number of other technical issues, Ulbricht answered by obstructing Berlin transit traffic and introducing obligatory passports and visas, with accompanying fees, for transit travellers between the Federal Republic and West Berlin. However, he showed himself less uncompromising where the basic economic interests of the GDR were involved. Thus, at the same time as he created obstructions, the old agreements on inter-zone trade were renewed, with corresponding arrangements for the delivery of capital goods to the GDR. At the same time, the level of the GDR overdraft credit guaranteed by Bonn was also raised.

After the election of the Grand Coalition in West Germany, the East Berlin government tended to stress the de facto division of Germany into two parts. Ulbricht now pursued a more vigorous policy of isolation in respect of the Federal Republic. In 1967, the People's Assembly instituted citizenship of the GDR, which of course was never recognised by the Federal Republic. The currency in the eastern part of Germany was renamed the "the GDR Mark" in the same year, although the old bank notes and coins were legal tender until well into the seventies.

The consolidation of its own power required the recognition of the GDR by the Federal Republic and the other Western countries. This did not prevent the autocratic Ulbricht from making agreements for so-called "humanitarian relief" with the Bonn government (which he otherwise defamed as the "stronghold of imperialism"), in order to get hold of urgently needed reserves of Deutschmarks. In the Honecker era, these transfer payments from West to East played an even greater role. Nevertheless, they began covertly in the Ulbricht period, often made through middlemen, and from the beginning were vital to the economically weak and currency-starved GDR.

On the basis of one such top secret agreement, the Federal Republic bought the freedom of 33,755 political prisoners between the end of 1962 and 1989 for a sum of 3.4 billion DM. Millions of West Berliners were able, between the end of 1963 and 1966, to visit friends and relations in East Berlin (making use of the new border-crossing permits), and of course being obliged to pay a fee in DM for the privilege. West Germans could travel to the GDR once more from 1964, as long as they were prepared to exchange five DM per day (25 DM by 1980), a so-called "entry fee". Taken altogether, the state transfers from the Federal Republic to the GDR up to 1989 amounted to 21 billion DM. About half of this sum flowed to the GDR as income from Berlin transit, which grew rapidly from the seventies onwards (transit fees and motorway building).

None of this altered the fact that the SED leadership saw their main foreign policy aim as international recognition and attempted to hinder all attempts by the Bonn government to enter into normal relations with neighbouring states.

END OF THE ULBRICHT ERA

The Soviet Union fundamentally supported the GDR in this aim, and had moreover concluded a friendship treaty with it in 1974 that guaranteed the inviolability of the GDR borders. Nevertheless, Brezhnev was irritated by Ulbricht's increasing presumption of economic and ideological independence, with his tendency to present the GDR as a model to be followed by the other East Bloc states, and to highlight all too convincingly their relative backwardness. In addition, Ulbricht stubbornly rejected the Soviet policy of coming to terms with the social-liberal coalition under Chancellor Brandt. Yet the Soviet Union, after the brutal suppression of the Prague Spring and the marginalisation of Reform Communism (1968) was now interested in an improvement of relations with the West and the reactivation of détente with the USA, so vital to the economic prospects of the Moscow regime. In the end, Ulbricht, now 78 years old and for years the true vassal of the Soviet Union, who had faithfully followed every twist and turn of Moscow's line, lost the confidence of Brezhnev for the reasons mentioned above and had to make way in 1971 for the crown prince he had long promoted, Erich Honecker.

CHRONOLOGY

1961

15 June 1961   At an international press conference Ulbricht demands the neutralisation of West Berlin and declares: "Nobody intends to build a Wall."

25 July 1961   President Kennedy proclaims in a televised address the determination of the USA to defend the viability and freedom of West Berlin.

13 August 1961   The sectoral borders in Berlin are sealed and the building of the Wall begins. Closure of the GDR border with the Federal Republic.

16 August 1961   Proclamation of the Central Committee of the FDJ (*Freie Deutsche Jugend*): "The Fatherland calls! Defend the Socialist Republic!" More than 285,000 young people subsequently pledge themselves, though often under pressure, to serve in the armed forces.

24 August 1961   The Ministerial Council of the GDR issues an order limiting rights of settlement in specific areas of the GDR; thousands of

citizens living within the five kilometre border area with the Federal Republic must leave their homes in September ("Action Cornflower").

25 August 1961	For the first time a refugee (the twenty-four-year-old Günter Litwin) is shot by the People's Police while attempting to swim to West Berlin through the Humboldt Harbour.
5 September 1961	FDJ action to remove the TV aerials oriented to receive broadcasts from the West.
20 September 1961	Erich Honecker, the Central Committee's Secretary for Security, spells out on behalf of the Politbüro the order for shooting down "border infringers". The People's Chamber passes the "Law for the Defence of the GDR", which gives the State Council virtually unlimited emergency powers.
27 October 1961	American and Soviet tanks confront each other at the Friedrichstrasse sector crossing ("Checkpoint Charlie"); the Justice Ministers of the Federal States set up a Central Investigation Point, with its seat in Salzgitter, to record acts of violence by the GDR authorities.

1962

24 January 1962	The GDR introduces national service.
25 March 1962	In a so-called "National Document", the SED commits itself to the reunification of Germany. However, the pre-condition is to be the "victory of Socialism" in the GDR and in the Federal Republic. Ulbricht later speaks of a possible "German confederation" consisting of the GDR, the Federal Republic and "West Berlin, which lies in the territory of the GDR".
5 May 1962	12 GDR citizens flee to West Berlin through a 32-meter long tunnel under the Berlin Wall.
17 August 1962	The 18-year-old construction worker, Peter Fechter, is shot while attempting to flee across the Berlin Wall and allowed to bleed to death.

1963

12 January 1963	Cuba and the GDR establish diplomatic relations; the Federal Republic breaks relations with Cuba.
24–25 June 1963	The SED introduces an economic reform under the title of "New Economic System of Planning and Performance for the People's

Economy" (NÖSPL). It foresees an increase in the personal responsibility of individual enterprises at the expense of central planning, and also espouses performance wages, cost consciousness and the encouragement of the "material engagement" of the workers.

13 August 1963   Up till now 65 deaths on the Berlin Wall have been recorded. Politbüro member Albert Norden, responsible for Agitation and Propaganda, justifies the "shoot-to-kill" policy of the border guards.

17 December 1963   The first agreement on transit permits is signed between representatives of the West Berlin Senate and the GDR and treated by the GDR as de facto recognition of itself.

1964

2 January 1964   New identity cards are issued with the rubric: "Citizen of the German Democratic Republic".

13 March 1964   Robert Havemann, a Marxist critic of the regime, loses his professorship at the Humboldt University.

4 May 1964   A "youth law" is passed obliging the youth of the GDR to participate in the "comprehensive building of Socialism".

12 June 1964   Friendship Treaty with the Soviet Union. Guarantee of the inviolability of the GDR borders.

1 August 1964   New banknotes issued ("Mark of the German Central Bank").

1 September 1964   Refugees who had fled the GDR before the building of the wall and who want to return on a visit are guaranteed freedom from prosecution.

7 September 1964   Introduction of "non-military national service" for construction duties.

8 September 1964   Pensioners are allowed to visit the Federal Republic and West Berlin for up to four weeks at a time.

24 September 1964   Following the death of Otto Grotewohl, Willi Stoph, a member of the Politbüro, becomes Chairman of the Ministerial Council. New agreement on transit passes for West Berlin visitors to East Berlin.

10–24 October 1964	The Olympic Games are held in Tokyo. This is the last time (until 1992) that an all-German team takes part.
15 October 1964	Khrushchev falls from power in Moscow. His successor as Party chief is Leonid Brezhnev.
25 November 1964	Introduction of a minimum currency exchange for visitors to the GDR.
28 December 1964	The census records 17 million inhabitants of the GDR—1.3 million fewer than in 1950. 41,866 people leave the GDR in 1964 as refugees or settlers abroad; some 10,000 return to, or settle in, the GDR.
31 December 1964	Ulbricht demands negotiations at government level with the Federal Republic.

1965

24 February 1965	First State Visit by Ulbricht to a non-Socialist country (Egypt).
25 February 1965	Educational reform with the aim of achieving a "rounded and harmonious development of a Socialist personality".
20 March 1965	The Soviet Foreign Minister, Andrei Gromyko states during a visit to Great Britain that the reunification of Germany is no longer possible because the two states have become too dissimilar.
5 May 1965	The State Council, the Council of Ministers and the National Front jointly proclaim that a reunification of Germany can only take place under Socialist auspices.
17–28 September 1965	The SED leadership visits Moscow: it is decided to establish a "Governmental Parity Commission for Economic and Technical-Scientific Co-operation".
3 December 1965	Erich Apel, Chairman of the State Planning Commission and an economic reformer, commits suicide following internal party intrigue. His successor (until 1989) is Gerhard Schürer.
15–18 December 1965	The SED revokes part of the economic reform and again strengthens central planning. End of the cultural thaw: the "small freedoms" in cultural matters are again removed; artists such as Stefan Heym and Wolf Biermann are curbed and the close binding of art to the Party and the State is decreed.

1966

28 February 1966	The GDR applies to join the United Nations.

26 March 1966   The SED suggests an exchange of views with the SPD to take place in Karl-Marx-Stadt and Hannover. Although this is agreed in May (for June) it never takes place, after the Moscow leadership bans the meetings and the SED anyway decides that the appearance of prominent Social Democrats like Willy Brandt, Fritz Erler and Herbert Wehner in the GDR would be too risky.

6 July 1966   The Warsaw Pact member states sign an undertaking not to negotiate with the Federal Republic without obtaining recognition of the European post-war borders and the GDR. Romania does not keep to this agreement and establishes diplomatic relations with the Federal Republic at the beginning of 1967. On the 10th of February 1967, the Foreign Ministers of the Warsaw Pact agree on the so-called Ulbricht Doctrine: no normalisation of relations with West Germany without the recognition of the GDR as a sovereign state.

1967

20 February 1967   The isolation policy against the Federal Republic is made more acute: the law on GDR citizenship is passed; in December it is agreed that a "Socialist Constitution" will be worked out for the GDR and the local currency is renamed the "Mark of the GDR".

17–22 April 1967   At the Seventh Party Congress of the SED, Ulbricht declares that reunification of the two German states can only take place in the context of Socialism; he states his willingness to engage in negotiations on the basis of equal status with the Federal Government; the SED proclaims the development of a "Socialist community of people" in the GDR and "corrects" the economic reforms of the last few years by reverting to a centrally planned command economy.

10 May 1967   The first exchange of correspondence between the two Germanies at government level begins with a letter from the Prime Minister of the GDR, Willy Stoph, to Chancellor Kiesinger. Stoph requests "legal agreements". Kiesinger says he is willing to negotiate over a "normalisation of relations" through intermediaries appointed by each side. The correspondence ends in September without any concrete results.

28 August 1967   Introduction of the five-day work week.

1968

12 January 1968	Various new punishments aimed at the opponents of the SED are announced by the regime.
9 April 1968	The new "Socialist constitution" of the GDR comes into force, shortly after being submitted to a referendum at which 94.49% voted in favour in a turnout of 98%; the GDR is described in the Constitution as "the Socialist State of the German Nation".
10–11 June 1968	The GDR introduces passport and visa controls for travel between the Federal Republic and West Berlin.
20–21 August 1968	Warsaw Pact troops march into Czechoslovakia to crush the reforms of the Czech Communist Party under Alexander Dubcek, who is defamed as a "counter-revolutionary"; the GDR supports the military action with propaganda. Isolated protests in the GDR.
10 September 1968	The "Association for Sport and Technology" is given the task of preparing those not yet of an age to bear arms for subsequent military service.
12–27 October 1968	At the Olympic Games in Mexico City, two separate German teams are represented for the first time, although they appear under a joint flag and national anthem; the IOC decides on the 13th October that the GDR should be accepted as a member with equal rights to other members. Consequently, the GDR takes part in the Olympics from 1972 onwards under its own flag and playing its own national anthem.
21–28 October 1968	Seven GDR citizens, including two sons of Robert Havemann, who had protested against the invasion of Czechoslovakia are convicted of "agitation against the state".
12 November 1968	Brezhnev justifies the invasion of Czechoslovakia and stresses the limited sovereignty of the Socialist states if there is a danger of them breaking away from the Soviet Union's hegemony (the Brezhnev Doctrine).

1969

1 January 1969	Visas are required for journeys to the GDR from the Federal Republic: the host in the GDR must apply for a visa for a West German visitor at the People's Police.
22–23 January 1969	In view of the collapse of the economic reforms, a "pacemaking" conference of old activists is held in Halle that declares the virtues of "Socialist competition".

2–20 March 1969	Military clashes between the Soviet Union and China on the Ussuri border river.
8 May 1969	The GDR is recognised by the non-Communist state of Cambodia; this triggers "a wave of recognition" by countries of the Third World.
10 June 1969	The eight Lutheran churches of the GDR provinces separate, as demanded by the SED, from the all-German Lutheran Church (EKD) and form the Association of Lutheran Churches of the GDR.
10 July 1969	The Soviet Union declares its willingness to take up NATO's suggestion of four-power negotiations over Berlin.
30 July 1969	A new statute places the responsibility for state security at home and abroad with the Ministry of the same name under Erich Mielke.
16 September 1969	First negotiations between Ministers of the GDR and the Federal Republic over traffic and transit problems.
18 December 1969	Ulbricht sends an outline Treaty to Federal President Heinemann that would recognise the GDR as a German state with equal rights.

1970

28 July 1970	Erich Honecker presses the Moscow leadership to replace Ulbricht, who is seen as an opponent of the Soviet détente policies.
13 August 1970	The GDR and the Soviet Union agree the coordination of their economic planning up to 1975.
8 September 1970	Strong criticism of Ulbricht's economic policy in the Politbüro: his ambitious plans for modernisation are thrown out as costly and unrealistic.
December 1970	Mines are laid along the internal German border on the GDR side.
17 December 1970	Ulbricht describes the GDR as a "Socialist German National State".

1971

3 May 1971	Resignation of Ulbricht as First Secretary of the SED. His successor is Erich Honecker.

7. The Republic in Transition:
The New Policy Towards the East and Commitment to Reform in the Brandt Era, 1969–1974

FEDERAL ELECTIONS, 1969

The election campaign of 1969 was characterised by a new mood. Under their new leader, Walter Scheel, the Liberals promised to "cut off the old pigtails" (i.e. to make a new start). The slogan of the Social Democrats was somewhat similar, namely "we will create the new Germany". The result of the 1969 election held on the 28th of September considerably altered the political landscape in West Germany. However, the electoral mathematics left open the possibility of various coalitions. The strongest party remained the CDU/CSU union with 46.1%. The SPD won 42.7 %, an increase of 3.4%. On the other hand, the FDP was faced with serious losses. A large part of their supporters in business, together with the more nationally minded bourgeois voters, rejected them; with only 5.8% of the vote, the party representing left-liberal reform policies was thus the undoubted loser in this election. Because of this, many in the SPD leadership were inclined to continue the Grand Coalition. Herbert Wehner, the most influential political strategist of the Social Democrats, made no secret of his distaste for the "toppling over" party (*Umfallerpartei*), as he designated the Liberals. The ruling Chancellor, Kiesinger, also believed strongly that he should continue in office.

"WE WILL MAKE IT WORK" (BRANDT) — DECISION TO FORM A SOCIAL–LIBERAL COALITION

However, the normally hesitant Chairman of the Social Democrats, Willy Brandt, showed that he was determined to exploit the chance of forming a government under his leadership. Only in partnership with the Liberals could he see any possibility of bringing about a substantial change in the policy on reunification and East Germany, change which had hitherto been blocked by opposition in the Union. Basing his policy on the actual situation in Europe as it had developed in the twenty-five years since the war, and in close cooperation with the Western Allies, Brandt wanted to normalise relations with the Soviet Union and the other states of the Warsaw Pact, in order to win room for manoeuvre in the question of reunification.

He quickly came to an agreement with Walter Scheel that they would take the risk of forming a small coalition with only a 12-seat majority over the Union. Many FDP Members of Parliament were sceptical from the beginning of the new course taken by their Party leadership and even at the vote for the Chancellorship in October 1969, only 251 of the 254 combined MPs of the SDP and FDP voted for Brandt (the minimum necessary would have been 249 votes). The ability of the Social–Liberal coalition to govern was therefore in no way guaranteed. Nevertheless, in the euphoria of the SPD's electoral success, such reservations counted for little.

THE UNION IN OPPOSITION

For the first time in the history of the Federal Republic, the Christian Democrats had to get used to being on the opposition benches. The party "born to rule" suddenly found itself deprived of power. It was not only the former Chancellor Kiesinger who felt that this fate was undeserved; most of the leading politicians of the Union immediately set about trying to engineer a change of government. Their indignation was all the greater when the newly elected Chancellor Brandt summed up the spirit of renewal in his first keynote speech at the end of October 1969 with the words: "We stand, not at the end of our democracy, but at its beginning." Government and opposition were to remain bitterly opposed for years. However, the critics who spoke of a "CDU state" were proved wrong and no serious crisis ensued. The change-over seemed to work and the Bonn democracy withstood its first test.

The mood in the country was positive and hopeful. The new cabinet with experienced, and in some cases brilliant ministers such as Karl Schiller (Minister for Economics), Alex Möller (Minister for Finance), Helmut Schmidt (Defence Minister), Hans-Dietrich Genscher (Minister for Home Affairs), and of course the Vice Chancellor and Foreign Minister, Walter Scheel, conveyed an impression of competence and solidity. As Minister in the Chancellor's Office, a Professor of Law, Horst Ehmke proved himself a dynamic and reliable facilitator for Brandt; Herbert Wehner, no friend of the incorrigibly cheerful Chancellor, kept the party off the government's back in his capacity as Chairman of the Parliamentary Fraction.

A NORMAL CHANGE OF GOVERNMENT

What the SPD basis over-dramatically described as a "shift of power" was in fact a normal change of government. All the same it did mark a caesura with the past.

For the first time since 1930, a Social Democrat, in the person of the 55-year-old Willy Brandt, headed the German government; not only that, but the government was now headed by a man who had been active in the resistance to the Hitler dictatorship, a fact which was not judged positively in the national conservative camp of the Republic and which led to repeated malicious calumnies against him.

A POPULAR CHANCELLOR

Brandt had charisma and knew how to appeal to the younger generation of voters. Many saw in him a German version of John F. Kennedy and the voter strategy of his party played heavily on this image. The apprentice years of his political career had been spent in the Berlin SPD during the most critical period of the Cold War between East and West. As a member of the inner circle of the legendary Mayor of West Berlin, Ernst Reuter, he was among the strongest opponents of the Communist regime in East Berlin at that time. On the other hand, he had no illusions about the fact that there would be no end to the division of Germany in the near future. As Mayor of West Berlin from 1957, he soon became one of the best-known politicians in Germany. Abroad, above all in the USA, Brandt was esteemed as an open-minded and eloquent representative of the "other" Germany, and (even better) one without a Nazi past. For the SPD, he soon became the focus for those who wanted a party willing to modernise itself; with him at its head (Chairman from 1964), and then as candidate for the Chancellorship (from 1961), it could appeal to new layers of voters and develop into the second great centrist party of the Federal republic. The two electoral defeats against Adenauer (1961) and Erhard (1965) had cost him dear, and he had even wanted to give up his political career in federal politics. However, the Grand Coalition, with which at first he had little sympathy, initiated his rise to become the second great strategist of the Republic's foreign policy after Adenauer, and subsequently enabled him to realise that strategy as Chancellor.

PROMISES OF REFORM

The new government presented itself as dedicated to reform. With slogans such as "we want to risk greater democracy", it expressed the feeling of the hour and in particular won over the younger generation, as well as artists and writers. The "renewal" of society became a key phrase in political propaganda. Changing social values in areas such as marriage, the family, the criminal law and sentencing were to be reflected in a slew of reforms that had partly been prepared under the previous government; at the same time, specifically Social Democratic or left-liberal aims were pursued, such as the reform of education, especially for the High Schools, the lowering of the voting age to 18, the expansion of consultation rights, and above all the expansion of social security. More successful than these projects, of which some only came to fruition years later, and others could only partially be implemented, was the Brandt/Scheel foreign policy, which ushered in an historic change of course.

INTERNATIONAL DÉTENTE

The situation in world politics was favourable to the policy of normalisation of relations with the East that Brandt had long espoused. Moscow and Washington were holding talks over the limitation of strategic arms, and NATO had made suggestions for mutual troop reductions. At the end of November 1969, the Federal Republic signed up to the Nuclear Non-Proliferation Treaty. Both super-powers were pursuing a course of détente. The Soviet leadership under Leonid Brezhnev hoped to profit economically from such a course and to stabilise the Soviet Union's sphere of influence in Europe. US President Nixon wanted to reduce America's overstretch in the world, above all in Vietnam, and had redefined the national interest of his country as one of maintaining parity between the super-powers.

CHANGE THROUGH CLOSER COOPERATION

The building of the Wall and the extremely cautious reaction of the Western powers at the time had convinced Brandt and his closest adviser, Egon Bahr, that the situation of the inhabitants of the GDR could only be improved if the bitter reality of the division of Germany was accepted and legally binding agreements were made with the SED regime. The pre-condition for such agreements, however, was the recognition of the GDR by the Federal Republic. Waiting for the collapse of the SED regime meant being condemned to political inactivity and impotence. The leading politicians of the Berlin SPD were all convinced of this.

Recognising the de facto situation in the other part of Germany, in order to overcome it, thus became the paradoxical formula for the new policy in regard to reunification, which Bahr had already sketched out in 1963: "The [East] zone must be transformed with the agreement of the Soviets. When we have achieved that, we will have made a great step forwards to reunification." The new Bonn government wanted to fix the borders in Europe, in order to make them more penetrable; the GDR should be recognised as a second German state, in order that fellow-Germans "over there" should not be left in the lurch; negotiations with the SED were necessary to achieve humanitarian aims.

THE KEY ROLE OF MOSCOW

The key to all this lay in Moscow—and the chances for a Soviet–German rapprochement were not at all bad. As later in the 1980's, the precarious economic situation of the Soviet Union played an important role in persuading the Moscow leadership to open up cautiously to the West. Party Chief Brezhnev wanted above all a guarantee from the West that the status quo in Europe would not be disturbed, and fixing the existing borders was a vital aim of his security policy. Western economic assistance should help the Soviet Union to progress, above all in technology. In this context, the Soviet Union was particularly interested in better relations with the Federal Republic, in the hope of profiting from West German economic strength.

These perspectives were more important for Brezhnev than the obstinate defence of maximalist aims in the foreign policy of his allies in Warsaw and East Berlin, who demanded from Bonn the unconditional recognition of the Oder–Neisse border, or the likewise unconditional recognition of the GDR as a sovereign state, as well as the virtual severance of West Berlin from the Federal Republic. Notwithstanding his willingness to reach some sort of accommodation with the East Bloc in order to keep the peace in Europe, Chancellor Brandt had nevertheless made clear in his first policy statement as Chancellor where the limits of his accommodation lay: he was ready to recognise the fact that there existed "two states in Germany"; but, in order to maintain the unity of the nation, the recognition of the GDR "according to international law" was impossible.

The new Federal Government therefore had a chance, in view of the ongoing super-power détente, to test the willingness of Moscow to compromise. But first a community of interest with the Kremlin needed to be formed, on the basis of which it might be possible to improve internal German relations. This proved to be more difficult than anticipated, as long as the German ambassador in Moscow conducted the preliminary discussions. It was only when Brandt entrusted the negotiations to Egon Bahr, his closest adviser and the architect of the new policy towards the East, that progress could be made.

The simultaneous meetings, on Brandt's initiative, with Prime Minister Willi Stoph in Erfurt (March 1970) and Kassel (May 1970) were considered a sensation at the time. For the first time the heads of government of the two German states were sitting at the same table; and in Erfurt the GDR security services were unable to prevent the crowds that assembled from greeting the Federal Chancellor with evident and optimistic jubilation. However, this "policy of one step at a time" did not at first produce any results, because the SED leadership under Ulbricht stubbornly held to its position of demanding recognition, decisively rejecting every reference to the continuity of the German nation.

DIFFICULT NEGOTIATIONS IN MOSCOW

The Federal Government saw in this a confirmation of their view that the detour via Moscow was necessary, if anything was to change for the better in the German question. In Bonn nobody had any illusions about the real situation: the Soviet Union would only allow the East Berlin rulers as much leeway as did not infringe on Soviet interests.

Egon Bahr, now State Secretary in the Office of the Federal Chancellor and Brandt's official negotiator, tested the water in numerous talks held with Foreign Minister Andrei Gromyko from the end of January 1970. The Bonn opposition accused Brandt's confidant of conducting secret diplomacy that bypassed Parliament, and later suspected that he had not fought vigorously enough in Moscow for the unification of Germany. This was untrue, but Bahr's preference for secret channels and informal discussions—including some with representatives of the Soviet secret service, about which only Brandt and Scheel were informed—fed speculation in the West German press. Refugee associations accused the government of "appeasement", while the CDU/CSU opposition lamented the looming permanence of the division of Germany as a consequence of the coalition's policy. The passionate debates in the Bundestag polarised the public.

THE MOSCOW TREATY AS MODEL

Notwithstanding the controversy, the two coalition partners held fast to the course upon which they had embarked. In August 1970, Bonn and Moscow agreed a non-aggression treaty following delicate negotiations by the German Foreign Minister. The core of this Treaty was a de facto recognition of the existing borders and power relations in Europe by the Federal Republic, which nevertheless expressly left open the possibility of a later reunification of the two German states. No other option was anyway allowable under the Republic's Basic Law. At first the Soviet Union was adamantly against such a formulation. It was only through tough negotiations that the Federal Government was able to get its position agreed by the Soviets, namely that the borders of Europe were "inviolable" but not "immutable". The option of reunification was laid down in the especially controversial "Letter on German Reunification" sent by the German Foreign Minister to Gromyko and accepted by the Soviet side. The Moscow Treaty was seen by both sides precisely as a framework and model for subsequent agreements with Poland (1970), the GDR (1972) and Czechoslovakia (1973). These treaties, together with the Berlin Four Power Agreement (1971), formed a complicated network of negotiated settlements that all hung closely together in terms of time-scale and content.

BERLIN FOUR POWER NEGOTIATIONS

Of particular importance was the Four Power Agreement over Berlin. The Bonn government had made clear to the Kremlin leadership that the Treaty with the East would not be passed by the Bundestag without security guarantees for West Berlin, since Berlin was seen as the litmus test of Soviet willingness to pursue détente.

After long negotiations, the four victorious powers drew a line under the decades-long dispute between East and West over the status and allegiance of West Berlin and the freedom of movement of its citizens. Their deliberations were incorporated in the Berlin Agreement of September 1971. What was at stake was nothing less than the future viability of the city. The Soviets now agreed to the strengthening of ties between West Berlin and the Federal Republic; in return, the Western powers accepted the Soviet reading that the three western sectors of Berlin did not actually belong to the Federal Republic. The agreement by no means encompassed all that the West wanted, but on the other hand it made the life of the West Berliners more bearable. Although there were later repeated disputes about the interpretation of specific heads of the agreement, it was clear that the Soviet Union had made substantial concessions, which above all benefited the West Berliners. These included safer transit to West Germany, permission for visits to East Berlin and the GDR, and even (after twenty years) the opening of telephonic communication between the two zones of the city. The dangerous crisis-point of Berlin, which had brought the world several times to the brink of war, was now finally defused and the Four Power Agreement proved a catalyst for the improvement of East–West relations inside and outside Germany.

THE CHANCELLOR FOUNDERS

After the Four Power Agreement was concluded, the East Treaty was put before the Bundestag for ratification. The diplomatic negotiations over this treaty had been hard enough and several times were in danger of collapse; but now in February 1972 it landed in choppy waters once again. The ruling coalition feared for its majority after several MPs from the FDP (among them the party's former chairman, Erich Mende) and from the SPD changed sides and joined the Union. The loss of the majority in the Bundesrat (Upper House) after the victory of the CDU in the provincial elections in Baden-Württemberg (April 1972, which ended the Grand Coalition here) was a further disturbing factor.

The two Union fractions, which wanted to obstruct the East Treaty in its existing form, saw their chance to return to government and moved a motion of no confidence under Article 67 G against the Federal Chancellor. The overthrow of Brandt seemed to almost all observers to be all but certain. Rainer Barzel, the Chairman of the CDU and the Parliamentary Party, already imagined himself Chancellor of the Federal Republic of Germany. Millions of citizens followed on radio and television with bated breath the vote taken in the Bundestag on 27th of April 1972. The result, however, proved a severe shock to the opposition: Barzel achieved only 247 votes, two less than was required. At least two MPs from his own side had refused to follow his lead. In fact one of them, a backbencher from Baden-Württemberg named Julius Steiner, had received 50,000 DM from the GDR Ministry of Security, although this only came to light after 1989.

RATIFICATION OF THE EAST TREATY

Although the opposition had failed to dislodge Brandt, the coalition no longer disposed over a majority, as was revealed in a vote on the Chancellor's budget one day later. Government and opposition therefore agreed on early elections to be held on the 19th of November 1972, to break the deadlock in the Parliament. In order that the East Treaty should not be allowed to fail at the last minute, Brandt and Barzel agreed on a common formula, whereby the Bundestag would attach a provision to the Treaty concerning reunification which was so phrased that the Union fraction would be able to vote for it. Barzel committed himself to this, but influential politicians of the Union, such as Franz Josef Strauss, failed to follow his lead. To avoid splitting the Union, it was agreed among the opposition simply to abstain on the relevant vote. On this basis, the Bundestag was able to approve the Treaty with the Soviet Union on the 17th of May 1972, when 248 votes were cast for it.

RECOGNITION OF THE GDR

Although the coalition in Bonn was practically a lame duck administration, the main protagonists of the new approach towards the East nevertheless managed to set the desired policy course rather quickly. The Transit Treaty of May 1972 effectively meant that the recognition of equality of status demanded by the GDR was already conceded; as a quid pro quo, a number of measures were instituted that made travel in either direction considerably easier. As it later turned out, such measures proved to be important in reinforcing the sense of Germans, both in the East and in the West, that they shared a common destiny. However, these were only isolated questions. A comprehensive regulation of intra-German relations was to follow in the Groundwork Treaty (*Grundlagenvertrag*), which Egon Bahr was negotiating with Michael Kohl, the GDR representative, from June 1972 onwards.

After the Bonn politicians had agreed on early elections, the Federal Government showed itself determined to bring the Treaty with the GDR to a successful conclusion before the election in November. This provoked the accusation from the opposition that unnecessary concessions were being made to the GDR purely out of electoral calculations. However, Brezhnev also put pressure on Honecker to be flexible in negotiations, in order to improve the electoral prospects of the Social Democratic–Liberal coalition. Both sides were therefore prepared to weaken some aspects of their initial negotiating positions. Nevertheless, every comma of the Treaty was vigorously fought over. The end result of tough negotiations over many months was that the East Berlin side achieved recognition of the GDR as a sovereign state (*Hoheitsgewalt*), while the Federal Republic fought through the reunification option (*Selbstbestimmung*), that was stipulated in an accompanying letter ("Letter on the Unity of Germany") similar to the one that had accompanied the Moscow Treaty. In order to underline the special nature of the relationship between the two German states (and as a result of determined pressure by the West Germans) it was agreed that "Permanent Representation" should be established in each state, rather than Embassies. The continuation of the four-power responsibility for Germany as a whole was also fixed in the Treaty. The continuity of a single Germany was referred to as a disputed point between the two sides, and thus at least received documentary recognition.

The GDR government had achieved its aim. It was now recognised by 132 states, including the three Western powers. The GDR authorities believed that recognition would serve in the long run to compensate for the regime's lack of internal legitimacy in the absence of democratic elections. The Federal Republic, on the other hand, hoped that the extraordinarily intricate

Treaty with its annexes, supplementary letters and commentaries would provide a lever to achieve an improvement in the humanitarian situation of the GDR, and also a means of binding the two nations closer together. Whether that would really turn out to be the case was impossible to say at that moment in time, and accordingly the Union was strongly critical of the Groundwork Treaty. Yet it became clear over the years that the SED regime had paid a high price in order to achieve its so urgently desired inclusion in the community of sovereign nations. The obligations under the Treaty (easing of travel restrictions, allowing families to be reunited, lifting of restraints on journalists, as well as cooperation in the technical, scientific and cultural fields) meant that the wall gradually became more penetrable. Even though the SED leadership in the following years perfected its control mechanisms for surveillance and oppression of its own people, the policies of the bunker mentality were no longer so effective and the bacillus of freedom could not be eradicated.

THE VOTERS SIGNAL THEIR AGREEMENT

A few days before the Federal elections for the Bundestag, the two leaders of the negotiations agreed on a final text for the Groundwork Treaty in Bonn. The subsequent spectacular victory at the polls for the Social Democratic–Liberal coalition on 19 November 1972 demonstrated that a significant majority of Federal citizens approved the new policies of Willy Brandt's government towards the East and with regard to reunification. Following a highly emotional campaign and a uniquely high turnout of over 91%, the SPD achieved 45.8% of the vote, a result they could hardly have dreamed of, and for the first time became the strongest fraction in the Bundestag. The FDP climbed to 8.4%, while the CDU/CSU opposition fell back to 44.9%, the losses being mostly at the expense of the CDU.

   Willy Brandt, winner of the Nobel Peace Prize (1971) and now an internationally respected statesman, had succeeded in capturing the sympathy of the voters above all because he made the election into a plebiscite on his East policy. The government now enjoyed a comfortable majority of 46 seats, so that the bitterly held objections of the opposition to the Groundwork Treaty were of little consequence.

   On the 11th of May 1973, 268 MPs voted for the Treaty and 217 against. After Bavaria appealed to the Constitutional Court, the latter ruled at the end of July 1973 that the Treaty was not in conflict with the reunification clause of the Basic Law. At the same time, the Court reaffirmed the duty of every Federal Government to direct their policies towards the goal of reunification and to abstain from any measure that might undermine this obligation. The Constitutional Court, by its interpretation of the Treaty, guaranteed the protective force of the Basic Law in respect of the citizens of the GDR. The moment they set foot on West German territory, if they so wished, all were to be treated as Federal Citizens, an important declaration, as it turned out, for the refugees and settlers of 1989–90. (The taking of German citizenship was subsequently to be eased in 1990 by bringing the GDR within the compass of Article 23 GG (old) of the Basic Law).

The Bavarian Provincial Government had meanwhile, through its appeal, helped to redefine the reunification question in respect of the two national states. The Federal Government was also satisfied with the court's judgement, because it saw its course of action justified by the Karlsruhe judges: the Groundwork Treaty was not to be seen as confirming the division of Germany, but simply as creating the preconditions for an improvement in intra-German relations.

THE REFORMS FALTER

Although the Social Democratic–Liberal coalition now enjoyed a stable majority in the Bundestag, Willy Brandt's second period of office was not successful and ended with his resignation in May 1974. The domestic reforms that had been announced progressed but slowly. Some of them, such as the increased consultation rights demanded by the trades unions, had already been watered down by the Liberal partners in the coalition. Others, such as the reform of Paragraph 218 concerning abortion (with the introduction of a time limit during which abortions were to be carried out), failed due to the resistance of the opposition in the Bundesrat, and then finally in the Constitutional Court. Yet other reforms that had been promised, such as the further development of the equality of men and women that was already anchored in the Basic Law, and in particular a new divorce law replacing the principle of blame with that of the irretrievable breakdown of marriage, could only be realised many years later. The ambitious plans for a comprehensive reform of education were already dependent on the political situation in the individual *Länder*, in whose area of competence education lay.

EXPANSIVE SOCIAL POLICIES

More successful was the extension of the welfare state, on which topic the government and the opposition were largely agreed. In the fields of pensions and health insurance, expensive improvements in benefits were made for pensioners, women, families with many children, the sick, war invalids, students and farmers; between 1970 and 1975 these measures led to a doubling of benefit and social security payments, which now totalled 334 billion DM. This in turn represented a rise over the period from one quarter to one third of the gross national product. Today such expenditure would be deemed extraordinary: the politicians in Bonn were at that time already planning to apply expected surpluses to the welfare budget and create further benefits, since they assumed that there would be a continuing economic boom. However, the economic crisis (oil crisis) of 1973–74 abruptly ended this phase of welfare expansion.

THE END OF ECONOMIC GROWTH

Two Finance Ministers in Brandt's first cabinet had already vainly fought against the reckless expenditure plans of the government and had subsequently resigned—Alex Möller in May 1971 and Karl Schiller one year later. It fell to Helmut Schmidt, the new Economics and Finance Minister, to explain to his colleagues that there was simply no more money in the pot for expensive reforms. The reason was that the economic position of the Federal Republic had considerably worsened since 1973. By the end of the Brandt era in 1974, inflation had climbed to 6.9%, economic growth had fallen from 7.5% (1969) to 0.5%, and the number of unemployed had trebled to 600,000. Despite a stabilisation programme, the government was unable to reverse this trend. Because of the steep price rises, the trades unions demanded and got higher wages, which only drove inflation higher. The government attempted in vain to persuade the unions to adopt a more moderate policy on wages. Brandt lost a great deal of his personal authority when Klunker, the Social Democratic leader of the Services and Transport Union (ÖTV), blithely ignoring the government's insistence on pay restraint for public service workers, managed to push through a wage rise of 11% for his members.

RESIGNATION OF THE CHANCELLOR

On this issue, as in too many other day-to-day matters, Brandt appeared indecisive and unengaged; he let matters take their course and displayed no inclination to strong leadership in cabinet. Brandt, and this was a view shared by many in the leadership of the SPD, had become detached, too much a monument to his own vanity. His resignation from the office of Chancellor came therefore as a surprise only to the public. Internally, resignation had long been a matter for speculation, especially after Herbert Wehner, the powerful Chairman of the SPD parliamentary fraction, had accused Brandt of weak leadership in autumn of 1973, inter alia because the improvements in intra-German relations did not seem to be materialising.

The actual trigger for Brandt's resignation a few months later was the so-called Guillaume affair. It was discovered that one of his personal advisers (since 1972) in the Bundeskanzleramt, Günter Guillaume, was an officer in the GDR's secret service. Brandt had allowed the suspect Guillaume to remain in his post when he was already under surveillance by the Office for Protection of the Constitution. In April 1974, Guillaume and his wife were arrested on charges of spying for the GDR and later condemned respectively to 13 and 8 years in prison for betrayal of their country. Even today it is not known whether Guillaume, who had a relatively minor position in Brandt's entourage, was really able to convey important information to East Berlin. Markus Wolf, Chief of the GDR's espionage service, later decisively downplayed his importance.

When Brandt was informed by the authorities at the beginning of May 1974 that Guillaume might well reveal real or invented stories about the Chancellor's love life in court, he decided to resign on the 6th of May 1974, since he did not wish his private life to become a matter for public scrutiny. However, most of those in the Party who knew Brandt well believed that this was really an excuse; the reality was that he had been weary of office for some time. The confrontations with Wehner and Schmidt over the direction of the government and the quarrels inside the Party between left-inclined reformers and conservative pragmatists played an equally important role in his decision, as did the realisation that he had little to contribute to the solution of the difficult economic problems. He suggested the Finance Minister, Helmut Schmidt, as his successor.

CHRONOLOGY

1969

21 October 1969	With the support of the SPD and the FDP, the Chairman of the SPD, Willy Brandt, is elected Chancellor by the Bundestag. The Chairman of the FDP, Walter Scheel, becomes Vice-Chancellor and Foreign Minister of the Social Democratic–Liberal coalition.
28 October 1969	In announcing his government's programme, Chancellor Brandt declares his willingness to recognise the GDR as a second state in Germany.
29 October 1969	The Federal Republic signs the Nuclear Non-Proliferation Treaty.

1970

13 February 1970	The German Educational Council presents a plan for the restructuring of education, which is designed to offer more equality of opportunity.
14 March 1970	Federal Chancellor Brandt and Prime Minister Stoph (of the GDR) meet in Erfurt.
14 May 1970	The violent liberation of Andreas Baader from detention marks the birth of the "Red Army Fraction" (RAF), the later notorious terror group.
21 May 1970	Like the first, the second meeting between Brandt and Stoph, this time in Kassel, produces no concrete results.
23 June 1970	Agreement with Poland on economic cooperation.
25 June 1970	The Federal and State Commission for Educational Planning is set up.
31 July 1970	The "active" voting age is lowered to 18 years, the "passive" age to 21.
12 August 1970	Signing of the non-aggression pact between the Federal Republic and the Soviet Union in Moscow (the Moscow Treaty).
8 December 1970	Over two million foreign employees are recorded in the Federal Republic.
13 December 1970	German–Polish Treaty signed in Warsaw (the Warsaw Treaty).

1971

19 July 1971	Law to promote city development.
1 September 1971	Federal Law for the Promotion of Education (Bafög).
3 September 1971	Four Power Agreement over Berlin signed by the ambassadors of the USA, Great Britain, France and the Soviet Union.
20 October 1971	Willy Brandt receives the Nobel Peace Prize.
17 December 1971	Transit agreement signed between the Federal Republic and the GDR.

1972

28 January 1972   "Ordinance against Radicalism": Brandt and the Prime Ministers of the individual Federal States (Länder) stress that every candidate for public service must guarantee that he or she will defend the basic values of a free democracy.

27 April 1972   The no confidence vote called by the CDU/CSU in the Bundestag against Chancellor Brandt just fails to unseat him. In a secret ballot, the Union's candidate for Chancellor, Rainer Barzel, fails to achieve an absolute majority by two votes.

11 May 1972   Terrorist attack against the Headquarters of the US Army in Frankfurt am Main; this is followed by further assassination attempts and bomb attacks against Federal judges, the Springer skyscraper in Hamburg, and the US army in Heidelberg, all subsequently attributed to the RAF.

17 May 1972   The Moscow and Warsaw Treaties are ratified by the Bundestag with the abstention of the CDU/CSU.

26 May 1972   A Transit Treaty is signed between the Federal Republic and the GDR.

1 June 1972   Arrest of several terrorists, among them Andreas Baader.

5–6 September 1972   During the Olympic Games in Munich, members of the Palestinian terrorist organisation "Black Hand" invade the Israeli team's quarters, kill two sportsmen and take nine further team members hostage. The attempt of the Bavarian police to free the hostages at Fürstenfeldbruck Airport fails: all the Israeli hostages are murdered and five of the eight terrorists, together with one policeman, are killed.

14 September 1972   The Federal Republic and Poland establish diplomatic relations.

19 November 1972   Early elections are held for the Federal Parliament (Bundestag): the SPD wins 45.8% of the vote, CDU/CSU 44.9%, FDP 8.4%. Willy Brandt is elected Chancellor for the second time.

21 December 1972   The Groundwork Treaty signed between the Federal Republic and the GDR.

1973

1 January 1973   Denmark, Great Britain and Ireland join the European Community.

27 January 1973	An agreement is reached in Paris between the USA and North Vietnam that ends the Vietnam War.
11 May 1973	The Bundestag ratifies the Groundwork Treaty with the GDR; the Union, however, votes against.
21 June 1973	The Groundwork Treaty comes into force.
3–8 July 1973	The Conference for Security and Cooperation in Europe (CSCE) begins its work in Helsinki.
31 July 1973	The Constitutional Court declares the Groundwork Treaty to be in conformity with the Basic Law, and stresses the constitutional obligation of each Federal Government to work for reunification.
18 September 1973	The Federal Republic and the GDR become members of the UNO.
1 October 1973	Deliveries of gas from the Soviet Union begin.
17 October 1973	At a crucial moment in the Arab–Israeli War (the Jom Kippur War, 6–25 October), the oil producing Arab states begin to raise the price of oil and to cut output. The result is the first serious economic crisis in the Federal Republic since 1949. A wide-ranging discussion over the "limits to growth" begins.
9 November 1973	Law on the safeguarding of energy supplies.
19 November 1973	Selective bans on Sunday travel and speed limits are imposed.
23 November 1973	The Federal Republic stops the recruitment of *Gastarbeiter*.
11 December 1973	The Prague Treaty between the Federal Republic and Czechoslovakia is signed.
19 December 1973	The number of unemployed climbs to over a million.

1974

22 March 1974	The legal age of majority is lowered to 18.
25 April 1974	Günter Guillaume, a personal adviser to Chancellor Brandt, is arrested and charged with spying for the GDR.
2 May 1974	The permanent representations of the Federal Republic and the GDR in East Berlin and Bonn begin their work.
6 May 1974	Willy Brandt resigns as Federal Chancellor.

8. The Crisis Years: Political Strains and Their Solutions During the Period of the Schmidt/Genscher Government, 1974–1982

THE NEW GOVERNMENT

Brandt's resignation from the Chancellorship did not weaken the Social Democratic–Liberal coalition. Their cooperation continued with the election of Helmut Schmidt to the Chancellorship on the 16th of May 1974. One day earlier, the Foreign Minister, Walter Scheel (FDP) was elected as successor to Gustav Heinemann (SDP) to the office of Federal President. The new Foreign Minister and the strong man of the FDP was Hans Dietrich Genscher, formerly Minister of Home Affairs, who shortly thereafter succeeded Scheel as Chairman of the FDP. Moreover, the new government's team and programme differed markedly from its predecessor. Its tone was set by stalwart Social Democrats with an unmistakably conservative tendency who saw themselves as political pragmatists. Typical of this type of politician were Hans Apel (Finance Minister), Hans-Jochen Vogel (Justice Minister), and Egon Franke (Minister for intra-German Relations). A conspicuous number of ministers came from the trades unions: Walter Arendt (Minister for Employment), Georg Leber (Defence Minister), Kurt Gscheidle (Traffic and Posts) and Hans Matthöver (Research); in this line-up it was not surprising that a free-thinking intellectual like Erhard Eppler resigned after only two months in office (as Minister for Economic Cooperation), to be succeeded by Egon Bahr.

THE END OF REFORM EUPHORIA

Even if the new Chancellor stressed the continuity with his predecessor, such continuity related chiefly to the policy towards the East and was largely a matter of courtesy. The core of his government programme was the abandonment of any kind of costly reform projects, and the eschewing of cloudy political visions for the future: "In a time of growing problems we must concentrate on fundamentals in the spirit of realism and soberness; we must apply ourselves to what is needed at this particular moment and the rest we should leave on one side."

THE PRAGMATIST AND
CRISIS MANAGER

Schmidt had originally envisaged becoming Brandt's successor somewhat later and in less dramatic circumstances. By his own account, he had considerable anxieties about the difficulties of office that awaited him. However, he was not afraid to take responsibility and his political opponents soon had to admit that the ship of state was now being steered by a remarkably strong Chancellor who was willing to give a firm lead to the country. Caution, good judgement and decisiveness characterised this Chancellor, qualities which the 56-year-old had developed over a long political career as Member of Parliament (since 1953), Hamburg Senator (1961 to 1965), Chairman of the Parliamentary Fraction of the SPD (1967 to 1969), Deputy Chairman of the Party (from 1968) and Minister in the Brandt governments (Defence Minister and Minister for Economy and Finance).

The new Chancellor saw himself as a realist and pragmatist, as "the chief employee of the Federal Republic of Germany", as he liked to style himself when characterising his view of the ethical and practical role that he saw as the hallmark of his office. He was not a man who developed political visions. He understood his job as one of problem-solving and political fixing within the limits imposed by political conditions, not as one of leading society intellectually and morally, which he thought a task more appropriate to the churches, to science and to the societal elite. Nor had the impatient "fixer" and convinced protagonist of the free market much time for the theoretical ideological debate and planning games carried on by the left wing of his party. He was much closer to the trades unions than most of the theoreticians. Unlike Willy Brandt, he never became the charismatic idol of the Party, nor did he seek the Party Chairmanship, which later proved to be a political and tactical error. On the other hand, throughout his time as Chancellor, he received approval ratings among the public that were far higher than those of the Party itself.

Hardly any other politician had so much political experience in questions such as defence, security, the economy and finance as did Helmut Schmidt, and it was precisely in these areas that the Federal Republic now faced new challenges. The era of reform was over. The feeling of renewal amongst the population of the previous years had been replaced by a sense of crisis and there were growing demands for security and stability.

THE OIL SHOCK AND ITS
ECONOMIC CONSEQUENCES

Schmidt had hardly assumed office before being tested in the art of crisis management. Economic conditions had sharply deteriorated since 1973. The first oil crisis in the autumn led a few months later to a downturn in economic activity that soon became a recession. The ban on Sunday travel ordered by the government at the end of 1973 symbolised the end of an era. The days of cheap energy were over, and the *"Limits to Growth"*, as proclaimed in the title of a best-selling and widely discussed book put out by the club of Rome at this time, seemed to have been reached.

For the first time, and in their fourth war against Israel, the Arab states exploited oil as a weapon to put pressure on America and Western Europe. They reduced oil production, so that the price of the most important energy source of the Western industrial states grew fourfold almost overnight. The result was a drastic reduction in the exports of the now more expensive German goods and a rise in unemployment. The second oil crisis of 1979–80 affected the Federal Republic and its partners even more harshly. After the revolution in Iran had driven out the Shah, who had been a reliable ally of the Americans, there was panic buying on the international oil markets. The OPEC cartel of oil producers exploited this situation and drove oil prices even higher. Between 1978 and 1981, the price of raw oil rose by 250%. This price explosion set off a chain reaction of negative economic consequences in the Federal Republic and elsewhere. These included inflation, sharp increases in wages, decline in production and exports, and a rise in unemployment. The worldwide recession began to take its toll.

ECONOMIC CRISIS AND
UNEMPLOYMENT

In 1973, the relatively full employment that had lasted since 1959 came to an end. The average growth of the German economy in the following years was now only modest. Inflation rose and at the same time many people became unemployed: somewhat over half a million in 1974, and one year later, over a million. By the end of the Schmidt era in 1982, 1.8 million people were out of work. Despite this, the economic situation in the Federal republic was relatively favourable compared to that of other industrial states, and the Chancellor got the credit for that. With numerous economic initiatives, the government succeeded in sporadically restarting the economy, although the price paid was a sharp increase in budget deficits. The government also reacted quickly and decisively with a series of state initiatives for energy conservation and in general developed an energy policy that made the country less dependent on oil (by exploiting nuclear energy, gas and coal), and on the Arab oil states (by importing oil from Great Britain and the Soviet Union).

To the irritation of many Social Democrats, the Chief Economist in the Bundeskanzleramt never tired of stressing that state expenditure should be redirected to encourage investment by enterprises. Nevertheless, the struggle to reduce unemployment, that seemingly insoluble problem of the late seventies, cost many billions of DM, so that tax cuts, or even saving, was in this situation unthinkable. On the contrary, the indebtedness of the state continued to rise sharply, from 47 billion DM (1970) to 309 billion DM (1982). The bone of contention between the coalition partners now concerned the best way of restoring state finances to health, and the ongoing disagreement between the Social Democrats and the Liberals (the latter favouring cuts in welfare) presaged the end of the coalition itself.

INTERNATIONAL ECONOMIC POLICY

Internationally, the Chancellor won great respect as an economic expert. It was on his initiative that yearly economics summits were held from 1975, in which the seven leading industrial nations took part (USA, France, England, Italy, the Federal Republic, Japan and Canada). The Chancellor was a star performer at these and could take credit for his leading role in the international agreements reached on energy and currency policies that helped to prevent even worse consequences arising from the worldwide recession. German–American relations suffered, however, because of the poor personal relationship between Schmidt and the US President, Jimmy Carter (1977–80), whom the Chancellor accused of complete ignorance of global economic relations. There was indeed no personal chemistry between the rationalist German protagonist of *Realpolitik* and the moralistic US President, and it proved very difficult for the Europeans to persuade the American government to alter its lax approach to energy policy.

While the differing economic interests of the Europeans and America were hard to reconcile in the Carter era, the Franco–German axis became stronger, with a consequently favourable impact on the European unification process. The French President since 1974, Valéry Giscard d'Estaing, himself a former Economics and Finance Minister, got along excellently with the German Chancellor: the two *Realpolitiker*, both with a gift for sharp intellectual analysis of problems, began to work well in tandem.

The two statesmen's wide economic and political horizons were demonstrated in 1978 when they launched their initiative for a European Monetary System. With the introduction of the EMS, the currencies of the member states of the European Community were effectively chained together (a deviation of 2.25% upwards or downwards from the benchmark being allowed), in order to forestall the dangerous economic turbulence unleashed by sharp and sudden changes in relationships between currencies (currency parities). This was an important orientation towards, and trial run for, the decision taken in the nineties to introduce a common European currency (Euro) for the European Union.

CONTINUITY IN REUNIFICATION POLICY

Schmidt opted for continuity in intra-German relations. A series of technical agreements were now added to the Groundwork Treaty. These included the building of a motorway from Berlin to Hamburg, making the railway between Berlin and Helmstedt two-track, and widening part of the Mittelland canal. Further cooperation was achieved in areas such as transit, road use and posts, as well as the extension of trading agreements, including an interest-free credit facility of up to 850 million DM, which the GDR badly needed.

Taken together, these agreements were very costly for the Federal Republic and represented yearly debts of several hundred million DM. However, with its cool calculation and quietly pursued policy of "money for humanitarian relief", the Republic proved to be on the right track, as was later to be demonstrated.

Internal German tourism from West Germany and West Berlin into the GDR, and also from the GDR to the Federal Republic, began to boom, and even the periodic attempts of the SED leadership to hinder it with the chicanery of border controls and the raising of the minimum sum of obligatory currency exchange, had little obvious dampening effect. The SED leadership under Honecker had an urgent interest in trade with the West, Western currency and credits, and economic cooperation with the Federal Republic in order to maintain internal stability. The Schmidt/Genscher government, taking advantage of this, was able to wring concessions on such matters as ease of travel, resettlement, the reuniting of families, and buying the freedom of political prisoners. In this continual bargaining Schmidt, supported by the leader of the SPD Parliamentary fraction, Wehner, and making discreet use of an intermediary, the lawyer and confidant of Honecker, Wolfgang Vogel, was able to establish a direct line to Honecker that could be activated whenever impasses occurred in bilateral relations.

THE EAST BLOC AND THE POWER OF
THE WEST GERMAN ECONOMY

These arrangements were useful above all to help discreetly tens of thousands of people who had got caught up in the machinery of ideological confrontation on German soil. Nevertheless, the telephone diplomacy of Schmidt and the mediation of Honecker's confidant, Vogel, could only work as long as the contacts of Bonn with the hegemonial power in the East were free of complications. For this reason, relations with the Soviet Union always had priority for the Schmidt/Genscher government. At the heart of these relations lay trade and economic matters, since the Federal Republic was the most important trading partner in the West for the Soviet Union. A series of long-term economic agreements, such as the deal on Soviet gas deliveries to Germany concluded in 1978 and valid until 2000, entrenched the bilateral relations between the two countries, which survived even the revival of confrontation between the two super powers.

The West German economy also functioned as a door-opener for Poland and contributed to better relations. The Chancellor and the Polish Party boss and head of state, Gierek, agreed a swap in 1975 of a type that was common at the time. The Polish side received credits to the tune of a billion DM on favourable terms and in return was prepared to allow 100,000 Germans to leave Poland in the coming years. However, for these resettlements a further payment of "blood money" (*Kopfgeld*), set at 10,000 DM per person, was payable.

DAMAGE LIMITATION POLICY IN
RESPECT OF THE GDR

Schmidt and Honecker first met at the CSCE in 1975 in Helsinki and used the opportunity to hold personal discussions. Subsequently, both remained in contact by letter and by telephone, even at the end of the seventies, when another ice age threatened to descend over East–West relations. On the one hand the Chancellor stood by his view that the NATO states must raise their defence capability to cover the gaps in the West's defences against the Soviet Union; on the other he was at pains to limit any fallout that this might cause with respect to intra-German relations.

Simply the fact that the two politicians remained in contact through informal channels, and indeed were planning an official meeting in East Berlin, was considered a political success at that time. However, Honecker was obliged to cancel the meeting on instructions from Moscow.

Dubious Aspects of the
Intra-German Summit

It was only in December 1981 that the Soviet "friends" gave the green light for a meeting and the Chancellor travelled to the GDR. However, the talks failed to bring about any substantial change in the reunification policy of the East Berlin Communists. The talks were anyway overshadowed by the introduction of martial law in Poland. The SED were extremely alarmed at the protest actions of the Polish trade union movement *Solidarność*. The ever louder demands in Poland for economic reform, personal freedom and disarmament were considered by the East German regime as nothing less than "counterrevolution" against the hegemony of the Communist Party. Within the Warsaw Pact, Honecker was a hardliner who urged a military intervention with the participation of GDR troops, although in the event it never came to this. The new Party boss in Poland, General Jaruzelski, regained control of the situation for the time being by the simple expedient of throwing the leaders of the protest movement into prison, among them Lech Wałęsa, later the first President of democratic Poland.

The main concern of the East Berlin Politbüro was therefore that the Polish virus should not take root in the GDR. For this reason, Honecker stuck to his obstinate isolation policy in respect of the Federal Republic, typified by his reiterated demand for recognition by the Federal Republic of a separate GDR citizenship. The continuation of "good neighbourly relations" between the two German states, to which Schmidt and Honecker committed themselves at an intra-German summit in December 1981, was thus merely a diplomatic form of words lacking any real substance. Indeed, Schmidt's visit to the town of Güstrow in Mecklenburg demonstrated the extent to which the SED leaders were determined to place the GDR population in a sort of permanent quarantine. The Chancellor wanted to visit the workshop of the famous sculptor Ernst Barlach. The GDR feared nothing more acutely at this time than an uncontrolled show of sympathy by the Güstrow population for a Helmut Schmidt who was also greatly admired in East Germany. There should be no repeat of the embarrassing scenes at Erfurt. This, therefore, was the finest hour of the State Security Service under Erich Mielke. All "hostile or negatively inclined persons" were kept under close watch and the inhabitants of Güstrow were not allowed out of their homes. Their place in the streets was taken by police and members of the security and secret services.

Despite the success with which the GDR evaded its responsibilities under the Helsinki Agreement, which obliged them and the other East Bloc states, in return for recognition of their sovereignty by the Western states, to respect the human rights and basic freedoms of their citizens, it nevertheless slid into virtual economic dependence on the Federal Republic. The apparent stability of the Honecker regime noted by contemporaries rested in reality on feet of clay. It was not the Bonn policy of dialogue and economic cooperation pursued at that time with East Berlin that stabilised the SED regime, but a military guarantee supplied by the Soviet Union. Nothing would have altered this essential fact, whether or not the Bonn government had put more distance between itself and the SED regime.

THE CHALLENGE TO THE STATE POSED BY TERRORISM

Few political events that occurred during the government of Chancellor Schmidt incensed contemporaries more than acts of violence committed by mostly very young terrorists against the elite of the Federal Republic's state and society. These events therefore need a more extended analysis here.

From the beginning of the 1970's, terrorism and combating dominated much of domestic politics. As never before, the civil order of the young Bonn democracy appeared to be endangered. The renaissance of Marxist and anarchist ideas supplied the intellectual backdrop for the student protest movement (APO) of the late sixties, out of which grew a small group of leftish revolutionary activists, who proclaimed the need for an armed struggle against the state. Out of the widespread criticism of existing capitalist society and the demand for its modification, radical activists developed an image of the enemy that was to justify the use of brute force.

THE RED ARMY FRACTION

Terrorism began in the Federal Republic with arson attacks on two department stores in Frankfurt in 1968. These were followed by bomb attacks against installations of the police or the US army. Among those arrested for the Frankfurt arson attacks was Andreas Baader, later the main player on the German terror scene, together with the student daughter of a pastor, Gudrun Ensslin. Their defence was undertaken by the Berlin barrister, Horst Mahler, while journalistic support was supplied by one Ulrike Meinhof, who wrote sympathetically of the arson attacks as demonstrations against so-called "consumer terrorism". Both Mahler and Meinhof later joined Andreas Baader's group. Baader and Ensslin were condemned to three years in prison, but used their temporary liberty while their appeal was being heard to go underground. Baader could be re-arrested in April 1970, but a few weeks later he was violently freed by sympathisers, one bystander being killed in the course of his break-out. The Baader–Meinhof Group now began to build a terrorist organisation to which they gave the name the *"Rote Armee Fraction"* (Red Army Fraction—RAF). Following the model of Latin American revolutionaries ("urban guerrillas"), the highest representatives of state power were to be targeted for assassination and prominent personalities were to be taken hostage, in order to destabilise the state and mobilise the masses to "armed struggle against their 'oppressors'". These confused ideas had nothing to do with the actual situation in the Federal Republic. This however didn't prevent the self-appointed revolutionaries, after a paramilitary training in the Near East, from making preparations for armed struggle in the Federal Republic. They obtained money from bank robberies and break-ins, which involved several deaths and many wounded, and also obtained weapons and false passports. In the summer of 1972, the hard core of the RAF in Frankfurt was arrested.

SYMPATHISERS AND ACTIVISTS

These arrests by no means meant that the problem of terrorism was thereby solved. The terrorists directed the first generation of those dedicated to the struggle against West German society from prison. With the assistance of their lawyers they organised hunger strikes in the gaols and made contact with another underground organisation known as *"Bewegung 2"* (Movement 2). In addition, they enjoyed support from a large number of sympathisers ("Committees for the Assistance of Prisoners"), mostly of middle class origin, who rented accommodation and automobiles, provided safe houses and organised public protests. From the ranks of these sympathisers the second generation of terrorists was recruited. It included, for example, 32 of the 69 members of the "Heidelberg Socialist Collective of Patients" (an organisation known to the police), who graduated to the terror scene of the RAF.

ATTEMPTED LIBERATION OF
ARRESTED TERRORISTS

By means of spectacular kidnappings and robberies, the new RAF attempted to blackmail the authorities into freeing their comrades. After the death of one of the members of the Baader–Meinhof Group following a hunger strike, there were demonstrations all over the Federal Republic against the police and the judiciary. One day later, members of the RAF shot the President of the Berlin Superior Court, Günther von Drenkmann, who had resisted an attempted kidnap. In February 1975, a terror group called the "Movement of the 2nd of June" kidnapped the Berlin CDU President, Peter Lorenz, and forced the release of five of their comrades, who were flown to South Yemen. Crisis meetings were held in Bonn and Berlin under Chancellor Schmidt and the Mayor of Berlin, Klaus Schutz (SPD); despite serious misgivings, the government decided to give in to the terrorists and Lorenz was freed. The kidnappers were later given long prison sentences. The terrorists who had blackmailed their way to freedom returned later to the Federal Republic and committed more crimes of violence.

Two months after the kidnapping of Lorenz, a terrorist group attempted to secure the release of the entire leadership of the RAF by occupying the German Embassy in Stockholm. When the Bonn crisis committee this time refused the kidnappers' demands, two of the hostages were killed. The Swedish police was able to free the other hostages; two terrorists were killed during the action and the rest were arrested.

INTERNAL SECURITY ENDANGERED

So-called revolutionary cells managed to keep the population in a state of anxiety and fear by means of bomb attacks on people in public life, or on busy terminals like the Hamburg main railway station (eleven wounded), and also on company buildings or barracks of the US army. The successful break-outs of several terrorists from a Berlin prison unsettled the public no less than the suicide of Ulrike Meinhof in her cell in the Stuttgart-Stammheim prison in May 1976, which led to demonstrations against the state by her sympathisers all over the Federal Republic. It also became evident that there were links between the Germans and international terrorism, as revealed after the attack on oil ministers attending the meeting of OPEC in Vienna in 1975 (three casualties), and also after the hijacking of an aircraft to Uganda by Palestinians in 1976. The action to free the hostages by a special services division of the Israeli army resulted in the death of 31 people, including two German kidnappers. In the summer of 1976, citing protection of the constitution, the Federal Government declared terrorism to be the greatest danger for the internal security of West Germany. With the introduction of new crimes onto the statute book, among others that of the "formation of terrorist associations", the government attempted to mobilise against these developments.

ASSASSINATION AND KIDNAPPING:
BLACKMAILING THE STATE

In 1977, the terror of the RAF reached its bloody apotheosis. At the beginning of April, the Attorney General and his two companions were assassinated on the open street in Karlsruhe. At the end of July, a terrorist group murdered a member of the board of the Dresdner Bank, Jürgen Ponto. And finally, at the beginning of September, the most senior figure of the German economy, the President of the Employers' Association and the BDI, Hans Martin Schleyer, was abducted in Cologne, his driver and two policemen being shot in the process. An RAF section demanded the release of eleven condemned terrorists, including Baader and Ensslin, and threatened to murder Schleyer. The emergency committee summoned by Chancellor Schmidt, which included leading members of the opposition, agreed not to give in to the terrorists' demands, in order to prevent a situation where the state became an easy prey for blackmail.

Schmidt played for time, in the hope that Schleyer could be rescued by a secret police operation. The government also agreed a voluntary news blackout with the media, in order not to endanger the weeks' long police operation, which, however, was unsuccessful. At the beginning of October 1977, the Bundestag rushed through a highly controversial law forbidding "contact with the outside world" to the imprisoned terrorists, which chiefly affected their access to legal defence. Although much criticised at the time, the law was later approved by the Constitutional Court. Various ultimatums from the kidnappers expired. To support the terrorists' demands, four Palestinian hijackers seized a Lufthansa airliner with 91 people on board en route from Majorca to Frankfurt on the 13th of October 1977. After a wild journey with many interim stops, during which the airliner's captain was murdered, the machine landed in Mogadishu. The Chancellor decided to attempt a rescue action in distant Somalia, after the Somalian President, Siad Barre, personally approved the deployment of a division of the special forces of the Federal Border Protection Unit (*Bundesgrenzschutz*—GSG 9). Shortly after midnight on the 18th of October 1977, these commandos stormed the airliner and freed all the hostages. Three terrorists were killed in the action and a female kidnapper was seriously wounded; she was later captured in Norway in 1994 and convicted in Germany. A few hours later the three leading terrorists in the Stuttgart-Stammheim prison, Ensslin, Baader and Raspe, all committed suicide by shooting themselves after they had somehow learned of their comrades' failed action, despite the ban on contact with the outside world. A few days later the police, following up information supplied by the kidnappers, discovered the body of the murdered President of the Employers' Association, Hans Martin Schleyer, in a car near Mühlhausen in Alsace.

No Solidarity Effect in Society at Large

In a very difficult situation the state had shown that it could not be blackmailed. It had also not exhibited the "ugly Fascistic features" (*faschistische Fratze*) that were constantly claimed to exist in the propaganda leaflets of the RAF; instead it had responsibly applied the levers of power, which had been extended in range through anti-terror legislation passed in 1978. Chancellor Schmidt stood at the apex of his reputation both inside and outside Germany. While the majority of the population supported the determination with which the government had acted, the latter was confronted by the accusation from some of the left-leaning intelligentsia, at home and abroad, that the Federal Republic was on the way to becoming a police state. However, the deciding factor was that the terrorists were unable to achieve any solidarity with society at large. The success of police operations after 1977 contributed to this. Many of the RAF terrorists who had been sought in vain for years could be arrested and brought before the courts. The successors of the RAF were similarly isolated in society in the 1980's and at the beginning of the 1990's, as they continued their campaign of violence with undiminished brutality, targeting the US military, high-level officials and (increasingly) the top managers of industry. Victims included a board member of the Deutsche Bank, Alfred Herhausen, in November 1989 and the President of the Detlev Trust Company, Carsten Rohwedder, in April 1991. It was only with the collapse of the GDR in 1989 that it became known that some of the most wanted RAF terrorists of the 1980's had sought refuge and received covert assistance there, the Stasi providing them with new identities. They lived inconspicuously in the GDR until their arrest in 1990.

The terrorists of the RAF also provided a model for the extreme right in the 1980's. In fact the number of victims of assassination by people with an extreme right background actually exceeded that of the RAF victims. A bomb attack by a loner with contacts to right-wing extremist groups killed 13 people at the Munich October Festival in 1980 and wounded 219, some of them gravely. But the rightist terrorists were no more successful than those on the left in building a base in society that was strong enough to endanger democracy in the Federal Republic.

THE BUNDESTAG ELECTIONS IN
1976 AND 1980

Notwithstanding that Chancellor Schmidt enjoyed respect that extended well beyond the rank and file of the SPD, the coalition increasingly lost the support of the voters from 1974 onwards. In particular, the SPD leadership apparently failed to convince the country, which was unsettled by the economic crises, of their ability to manage these problems. A sign of this was the constant loss of votes to the CDU in the provincial elections.

After a fiercely fought campaign, with the CDU/CSU slogan of "Freedom instead of/or Socialism" pitted against the SPD's "The better man must remain as Chancellor", and in which the reform of pensions was a significant issue, the Union and its chancellor candidate Helmut Kohl (Chairman of the CDU since 1973 and the successful Prime Minster of Rheinland-Pfalz since 1969) achieved its best election result since 1957 with 48.6% of the vote. The SPD sank to 42.6%, and only the respect in which Schmidt was generally held had prevented it from falling even further. The FDP just about held onto its voters with 7.9%. Since the continuation of the FDP–SPD coalition had been previously agreed, the re-election of Helmut Schmidt to the Chancellorship was as good as certain. However, this was suddenly made uncertain by the fact that Schmidt now wanted to cancel a rise in pensions that had been promised during the election campaign. The general indignation amongst the public over this move, which the Union immediately dubbed "the pensions swindle", also had its effect in the ranks of the coalition backbenchers. Schmidt was in fact elected on the 15th of December 1976 with 249 votes, but by the tiny and precarious margin of only one vote, on which rested his absolute majority. Three MPs from the coalition had refused him their support.

His re-election four years later was in much more favourable circumstances. Schmidt had in the meanwhile demonstrated strong leadership in combating terrorism in the Federal Republic. Internationally, he was viewed as an exceptional political personality among the western heads of government and also as the European spokesman in questions of military strategy. The new protest and alternative movements at home were concerned with opposition to nuclear reactors, with environmentalism, women's rights and pacifism. These issues had partly coalesced in 1980 under the banner of "The Greens", a movement that was having a destabilising effect on the traditional landscape of political parties. Nevertheless, the most salient aspect of the Bundestag elections was the relative weakness of the opposition. The lengthy conflict between the CDU Chairman, Kohl, and the Chairman of the sister party in Bavaria, Franz Josef Strauss, that had almost led to a breach between the two parties in 1976, culminated in the choice of Strauss as chancellor candidate for the 1980 election, whereby he was supported by a considerable number of CDU MPs against Kohl.

During the election campaign, the Union attacked the Chancellor as the "pensions swindler". Schmidt countered by casting doubt on the "capacity" of his Bavarian opponent, who was indeed a figure who tended to polarise the electorate, "to work for peace". Although the Union achieved in the October vote its worst result since 1949 with 44.5% of the vote, unlike in 1972 it nevertheless was ahead of the SDP. The latter received 42.9%, while the FDP took 10.6%, a significant increase. The re-election of Helmut Schmidt to the Chancellorship at the beginning of November 1980 went through with 266 votes, a firm majority. In the Bundestag the Social Democrat–Liberal coalition under Schmidt now faced a weakened opposition. However, this positive election result could not prevent the victor from losing the support both of his own party and of his Liberal coalition partner much more quickly than might have been expected.

DÉTENTE IN CRISIS

One of the greatest controversies of the Schmidt era, and the one which indeed precipitated its end, was NATO's security policy in respect of the Soviet Union. The change in the politics of energy and the problems of energy-related economic stability since the middle of the seventies had left its mark on Western European society. The result was a strong impulse to continue the policy of détente with the East, particularly since the United States was preoccupied with internal matters after the disgrace of President Nixon (Watergate affair) and the trauma of defeat in Vietnam. Only gradually did the western governments realise that the Soviet leadership under Brezhnev was using the relative weakness of the United States to expand its influence in numerous countries of Africa, the Middle East and the Caribbean, and above all had used the opportunity to increase its military capability considerably. Soviet–American relations worsened markedly, a situation that was unhappily not as productive of a community of interest between Europe and America under the erratic US president, Jimmy Carter, as it should have been.

NATO's Decision
to Increase Armament

The two super powers had agreed on limitation of their intercontinental nuclear weapons through long drawn out negotiations on arms control (SALT I, 1972; SALT II, 1979). However, the nuclear balance that was thus agreed between the two world powers did not automatically mean more security for Europeans. In Europe, the superiority of the Soviet Union in conventional and tactical nuclear weapons was clear. Above all, the new Soviet medium range rockets (SS20) were a growing threat to Western Europe. Chancellor Schmidt was one of the first western heads of government to point out to his allies the dangers posed by the Soviet armaments policy in respect of medium range rockets at a meeting in London in October 1977. He argued for an increase in Western European armament, if it should prove impossible to persuade the Soviets to undertake concrete armament reductions (specifically, the discontinuation of the SS20).

On a visit to Bonn in May 1978, the Soviet party leader, Brezhnev, signalled a willingness to negotiate over what Schmidt told him was a weapons systems that represented a serious threat to western security interests. However, in practice nothing changed. The Soviet Union continued to deploy its highly manoeuvrable SS-rockets, because the USA and the Europeans could not at first agree on a common political line. It was only in December 1979 that the Foreign and Defence Ministers of NATO could agree on a double-track policy. This was to consist of the deployment of their own medium range rocket system, accompanied by simultaneous negotiations with the Soviet Union over disarmament in this field. By the end of 1983, a modernisation of the West's deterrent was to be completed through the deployment in Western Europe of Pershing II middle range rockets and ground-based cruise missiles, in case the negotiations with the Soviets over medium range rockets should produce no results.

The last leader of the Soviet Union, Mikhail Gorbachev, described the positioning of the Soviet middle range rockets in retrospect as "unforgivable adventurism". But the Soviet leadership of the day thought it saw a realistic opportunity of scoring points off the USA under Carter in a way that would enhance its influence in the world. Brezhnev also apparently believed that the NATO states would be incapable of responding in kind because of critical public opinion. Notwithstanding numerous warnings from Washington, two weeks after the NATO decision, Soviet troops marched into Afghanistan to keep the Communist regime there in power. At the same time Moscow showed no interest in opening negotiations with the West. A temporary end to détente between East and West now ensued.

THE PACIFIST MOVEMENT IN
THE FEDERAL REPUBLIC

Whether the two-track NATO policy, which was substantially worked out by Helmut Schmidt was really a "blunder", as the historian Hans-Peter Schwarz has claimed, because it opened the door for the East Bloc to exercise both propagandist and financial influence on the West German pacifist movement, is a moot point. Certainly, without the offer of negotiation, however delayed, Schmidt would have had even less support for the decision to upgrade armaments than he actually received. The fact was that the imminent prospect of having atomic medium range weapons deployed in the Federal Republic led to harsh criticism of the Chancellor. The psychological effect of NATO's double-track decision, the second component of which was continually overlooked by its critics, had certainly been underestimated by Schmidt.

From 1980 onwards, critics who argued from a standpoint of security policy joined with the originally environment-oriented protesters of the young generation in a media-effective mass peace movement. One group of critics disputed the necessity of a western armament upgrade; others accused America of having an interest in carrying on a nuclear war limited to the confines of European territory; yet others demanded the unilateral withdrawal of nuclear weapons from the Federal Republic. A horror at the possibility of the extinction of mankind through nuclear war determined much of the thinking and the protests of what were otherwise very heterogeneous groups within the pacifist movement. The German word *"Angst"* entered the French and English vocabularies at this time.

EMOTIONS INSTEAD OF POLICIES

The pacifist movement in the Federal Republic managed to win over many who were hesitant or undecided with its mass demonstrations, human chains and innumerable debates in churches, universities and public institutions. The gigantic sums spent on armaments both in the East and the West, and the heaped up destructive capacity on both sides, made it difficult for the government to sell a policy based on realistic considerations of deterrent and military balance in Europe. In some circles, and also within the ruling SPD, the planned deployment of American rockets was considered just as dangerous as the already deployed Soviet arsenal of weapons. The radical change of security policy in Washington when the new Republican President, Ronald Reagan, took office in 1981, and his announcement that he would "out-arm the Soviet Union to death", attracted ever more activists and sympathisers to the peace movement from all layers of the population, people who were above all critical of American policy.

The anti-American pacifist orientation of the West German peace movement was obvious, as was also their extremely sparing criticism of the Soviet military apparatus. Today it is known that the GDR and its secret service were active in the West German peace movement with a net of agents and organisations financed out of East Berlin. Nevertheless it was not directed by these elements, and at best influenced by them only in a few instances such as the "Soldiers for Peace". What was more important was that this mass movement, with its strong appeal to the emotions and chiefly involving idealistic young people, found increasing support within the Social Democrats, who found the rational and technocratic style of Helmut Schmidt increasingly alien.

ALIENATION WITHIN THE SPD/FDP COALITION

Opponents of weapons upgrade on the left wing of the SDP, such as Erhard Eppler and Oskar Lafontaine, created a growing momentum with their ever more openly expressed attacks against their own chancellor. The fact that the latter insisted that Reagan would come away successful from disarmament negotiations with the Soviet Union was simply ignored. The result was that the SPD experienced a stand-off between supporters and opponents of the government course, something which at the same time caused friction with the FDP coalition partner. By contrast, the CDU/CSU opposition under Helmut Kohl portrayed itself as the party which supported the NATO double-track policy and the security policy of the USA without qualification. The growing hostility between the FDP and SPD was closely watched by the leader of the Christian Democrats. Behind the scenes private discussions were held with the Foreign Minister, Genscher, who was a personal friend of Kohl's.

THE FALL OF THE CHANCELLOR

The actual reason for the departure of the Liberals from the governing coalition with the Social Democrats was a difference concerning economic and social policy. For Genscher and the Economics Minister, Otto Count Lambsdorff, the cutbacks in spending on social policy, only half-heartedly supported by the SPD, but designed to cover a hole in the budget that ran to 7.8 billion DM in 1982, did not go nearly far enough. In August Lambsdorff criticised the prevailing mentality of "entitlement" and in an internal paper demanded a "new course" in finance policy, in order to reduce the high level of government debt. This was the moment the opposition had been waiting for. Throughout 1982 Chancellor Schmidt tried in vain to set the coalition on a mutually agreed course in financial and economic policy. In February the governing fractions promised him support in Parliament, and two months later the Chancellor demonstrated that he still had the will to continue by shuffling his cabinet. However, he could not take his own party with him when he tried to woo it away from an employment programme that could not realistically be financed, and to which the Liberals had not agreed. In any case there was now no longer a majority of mutual understanding in either party.

Lambsdorff and Genscher prepared to break away and join the Union, something which a considerable number of their colleagues still did not want to do. Lambsdorff wrote a memorandum urging drastic cuts in social spending in order to consolidate the budget, a paper that Helmut Schmidt described as the coalition's "letter of divorce". The four FDP ministers anticipated their dismissal by resigning and Schmidt continued in office for two weeks with a minority government. On the 1st of October 1982, for the first time in the history of the Federal Republic, the Chancellor was toppled as a result of a vote of no confidence moved by the CDU/CSU and the FDP in the Bundestag. The hitherto leader of the opposition, Helmut Kohl, was elected to be the new Chancellor. So ended the rule of a Chancellor of considerable stature, whose main achievement, in the words of Hans-Peter Schwarz, had been "to bring the Federal Republic unharmed through a pretty turbulent era".

CHRONOLOGY

1974

15 May 1974   Walter Scheel (FDP) is elected to the office of Federal President.

16 May 1974   The Bundestag elects Helmut Schmidt (SDP), the former Finance and Economics Minister, to the Chancellorship; the coalition of Social Democrats and Liberals continues with Hans-Dietrich Genscher as Vice-Chancellor and Foreign Minister.

10 November 1974   Terrorists of the so-called "Movement of the 2nd of June" assassinate the President of the Berlin Superior Court.

1975

18 February 1975   The building site of the planned nuclear power station at Wyhl in Südbaden is occupied by anti-nuclear activists. This marks the beginning of the anti-nuclear movement in the Federal Republic.

27 February 1975	The Chairman of the Berlin CDU, Peter Lorenz, is kidnapped by terrorists and freed six days later, after the conditions for freeing him have been met.
21 May 1975	The Baader–Meinhof trial begins before the Supreme Court in Stuttgart-Stammheim.
19 June 1975	The Chairman of the CDU, Helmut Kohl, is nominated as candidate for the Chancellorship by the parties of the Union.
1 August 1975	The final agreement of the CSCE is signed in Helsinki; signatories include both the GDR and the Federal Republic.
15–17 November 1975	First world economics summit in Rambouillet (France).
11 December 1975	The Bundestag passes a new law on marriage and the family. For divorce, the principle of "blame" is replaced by that of the "irretrievable breakdown of a marriage".
31 December 1975	In 1975 there had been 7.7 million journeys from the Federal Republic and West Berlin into the GDR and East Berlin (in 1971 the figure had been 2.7 million).

1976

31 January 1976	1.35 million are unemployed (5.9%); this is the highest figure since 1954.
4 May 1976	Consultation rights introduced for workers in enterprises with more than 2000 employees (parity of consultation).
18 August 1976	The "founding of terrorist associations" becomes a new crime.
3 October 1976	Bundestag elections result in the CDU/CSU getting 48.6% of the vote; the SPD gets 42.2%, the FDP 7.9%. Helmut Schmidt is once more elected Federal Chancellor on the 15th of December and continues with the Social Democratic–Liberal coalition.
13 November 1976	Serious clashes occur between demonstrators and police because of the planned nuclear reactor at Brokdorf.

1977

27 January 1977	The Federal Law on Data Protection comes into force.
7 April 1977	The Federal Attorney General and his driver are assassinated by RAF terrorists in Karlsruhe.

28 April 1977   The terrorists Andreas Baader, Gudrun Ensslin and Jan-Carl
                         Raspe receive life sentences.

30 July 1977   The Chairman of the Board of the Dresdner Bank, Jürgen Ponto,
                         is assassinated by terrorists.

 5 September 1977   The President of the Employers' Association, Hans Martin
                         Schleyer, is abducted by terrorists in Cologne and his compan-
                         ion murdered.

29 September 1977   The Bundestag rushes through a law preventing contact between
                         terrorist prisoners and the outside world.

18 October 1977   A special commando group (GSG 9) of the *Bundesgrenzschutz*
                         frees the hostages of the Lufthansa airliner *Landshut* in Moga-
                         dishu (Somalia); the airliner had been hijacked by Palestinian
                         terrorists five days earlier when flying back from Majorca. The
                         hijackers intention was to blackmail the Federal Republic into
                         releasing imprisoned members of the RAF. The successful oper-
                         ation is followed by the suicide in Stammheim prison of the ter-
                         rorists Baader, Ensslin and Raspe. On the following day, the
                         body of the murdered Schleyer is found at Mühlhausen (France).

1978

4–6 May 1978   State visit to the Federal Republic by the Soviet Head of State
                         and Party boss, Leonid Brezhnev. An agreement is signed con-
                         cerning long-term economic cooperation.

 6 November 1978   The CSU Chairman, Franz Josef Strauss, becomes Prime Minis-
                         ter of Bavaria.

16 November 1978   Intra-German agreement over the building of an *Autobahn* bet-
                         ween Berlin and Hamburg.

1979

2–27 January 1979   The Third Programme of the ARD broadcasts the American TV
                         series on the Holocaust, detailing the Nazi crimes against the
                         Jews.

13 March 1979   The European Monetary System comes into force.

25 May 1979   The two houses (Bundestag and Bundesrat) elect Karl Carstens
                         (CDU) to the Federal Presidency.

 2 July 1979   Franz Josef Strauss is nominated as the Chancellor candidate for
                         the Union.

3 July 1979	The Bundestag passes a law suspending the statute of limitations for murder and genocide.
7 October 1979	First direct elections to the European Parliament. The Greens enter local government for the first time, winning seats in the Bremen City Parliament.
12 December 1979	The NATO states agree in Brussels on NATO's "double-track policy".

1980

13 January 1980	Founding congress of The Greens in Karlsruhe.
5 October 1980	Bundestag elections: the CDU/CSU achieves 44.5% of the vote, the SPD 42.9% and the FDP 10.6%. Helmut Schmidt is again elected Chancellor, leading a Social Democratic–Liberal coalition.
4 November 1980	The Republican Ronald Reagan is elected President of the USA.

1981

11 May 1981	The Economics Minister of Hesse, Hans Herbert Karry (FDP), is shot by terrorists.
10 October 1981	300,000 supporters of the Peace Movement demonstrate in the Hofgarten in Bonn against the NATO decision to upgrade its armaments.
11–13 December 1981	Chancellor Schmidt visits the GDR for "constructive talks" with Honecker at a town on the Werbellinsee. At the same time martial law is declared in Poland.

1982

24 February 1982	Leading Bonn politicians are investigated in the "Flick" affair concerning irregular payments to political parties.
10 June 1982	350,000 supporters of the "Movement for Peace and Disarmament" demonstrate in Bonn during the NATO summit being held there.
1 October 1982	Helmut Schmidt is toppled in the Bundestag in a vote of no confidence and the Chairman of the CDU, Helmut Kohl, is elected Chancellor with the votes of the Union and the FDP.

9. The Dictatorship's Deceptive Facade of Normality: GDR under Honecker from the 1970's Onwards

THE TOPPLING OF ULBRICHT

From May of 1971, a completely reliable servant of the Moscow leadership was once again leading the GDR, in the person of the 58-year-old Erich Honecker. Although Walter Ulbricht had himself always loyally toed the line, towards the end of the sixties the autocratic SED boss began to show signs of deviance from the Soviet Union in ideological and economic matters. This deviation stemmed from his determination to make the GDR the model and glorious example for all the other East Bloc Communist states, with himself acting as the great schoolmaster. He also aroused hostility in Moscow because he placed too much emphasis on the GDR's individual interest in economic cooperation with the Federal Republic, and on its recognition by Bonn as a sovereign state, against the wishes of Brezhnev, who was concerned to reach a rapid accommodation with the Brandt/Scheel government.

Most of the members of the Politbüro in East Berlin also came to see the stubborn Ulbricht as a liability and accused him of failing to judge the economic potential of the GDR correctly. They complained to Brezhnev that he had become convinced of his "infallibility", to the detriment of the regime. Meanwhile Honecker kept close contact with the Soviet Party boss and positioned himself as successor.

At the beginning of 1971, Brezhnev gave the green light for the replacement of the overweening Ulbricht, who announced his "resignation" on the 3rd of May. His deposition was total. The two token functions that he was awarded or allowed to keep (Chairman of the State Council and of the SED) came without any substantive power at all. The 78-year-old founding father of the GDR became in fact a non-person: after his death in 1973, he even disappeared from official photographs in the history books. In this way, the leading role of Moscow in GDR politics was once again secured. For a decade and a half, Honecker held loyally to the course that Brezhnev had already warned him he should stick to in the summer of 1970: "Erich, I tell you openly, never forget this: the GDR cannot exist without us, without the Soviet Union, which is the source of its power and strength. Without us, there would be no GDR." It was only when the Moscow "friends" under Mikhail Gorbachev urged internal reforms on the GDR in the late eighties that Honecker failed to follow the Soviet line and promptly suffered the same political fate as Ulbricht.

NEW ERA, OLD AIMS

However, Honecker's rise to power did usher in a new era in the history of the GDR, which many contemporaries in the East, and even more in the West, were to experience as a period of economic growth, political stability and normalisation of relations between the two German states. This was nevertheless only one part of the contemporary reality, and it primarily dominated the perspective of the West. In the GDR, this reality was experienced only by the functionaries of the regime and a small minority of its most loyal supporters. The majority of the East Germans soon realised that the generational change at the top of the SED did not mean any change in the system. The dictatorship altered its methods, but not its aims.

Ulbricht was hated amongst the population. It could only get better under Honecker, or so most GDR citizens hoped. Although he had belonged to the innermost circles of the SED from the very beginning, he was still a largely unknown quantity at the time he took over.

HONECKER: A GERMAN CAREER

Born the son of a miner in the Saarland, Honecker had been a responsible functionary of the KPD (German Communist Party) since the age of 18. He never completed his apprenticeship as a roofer, a fact that he later concealed. Due to illegal activity in the Communist Party during the Third Reich, he was condemned to ten years in prison in 1937. Among his co-prisoners he was considered a loner who, in March 1945, was assisted by a female warden to flee from a forced labour detachment. After the war, he began his meteoric rise in the Soviet occupation zone, acting as a close confidant of Ulbricht, whose benevolence he earned through his unswerving loyalty. As Chairman of the Free German Youth from 1946, he transformed this body into a Communist-steered mass organisation, which he was able to use as a springboard for his own advancement. Authoritarian, slavishly loyal to the Party line, he led this so-called "battle reserve of the Party" until the middle of the 1950's. Ulbricht later transferred several important Party functions connected with security and personnel questions to the competence of this most reliable of apparatchiks. As Secretary of the Commission for Security of the Central Committee of the SED, he became responsible for the armed forces, the police, the border guards and the Stasi, all of which made him the single most powerful man in the GDR.

When it became necessary in the late fifties, Honecker could be relied on to ensure the removal of prominent internal critics of the old Stalinist,

Ulbricht, and generally to strengthen the latter's power base. Honecker became a full member of the Politbüro, the central power of the SED, in 1958, and from 1960 he also acted as Secretary of the National Defence Council. In this capacity he gave full satisfaction to his mentors as the organiser of the building of the Berlin Wall on the 13th of August 1961, a decision that he continued to justify until the collapse of the GDR. Later, his relationship with Ulbricht cooled, when the intellectually underpowered foot soldier, Honecker, began to be increasingly irritated by the old man's changes in economic policy and technological dreams for the future. Still, Honecker had now stepped out of the shadow of his patron. Totally lacking in charisma, but tactically astute, he had managed to build up a considerable following within the Party apparatus. What was even more important from the point of view of Moscow was that he was seen as a reliable and devoted partner of the Soviet Union, for whom the overriding priority was the retention of power by the Communist Party. In the summer of 1971, the new Party boss, who had borne the title of "General Secretary" since 1976, also took over the Chairmanship of the National Defence Council, the body which decided over the deployment of weapons in defence of the dictatorship at home and abroad. In 1976 the People's Assembly elected him to the Chairmanship of the State Council. From this point onwards, Honecker had all the important offices in his hand.

CONSUMER SOCIALISM AND RELAXATION IN DOMESTIC POLITICS

The new strong man of the SED wanted the GDR to develop a Socialist welfare state. Honecker hoped to win over the people to himself and the Party by providing social benefits. The grandiose plans and proclamations of the Ulbricht era disappeared into the bottom drawer, and the new Party leadership now proceeded more pragmatically to improve consumer supply and the living standards of the average citizen. He also showed a little more generosity in the field of culture and appeared to be more open to the aspirations and wishes of the younger generation. However, it was typical of his dictatorship, as of any other, that its underlying strategy was to distract attention from fundamental lack of freedoms by the concession of small ones. Despite this, many GDR citizens viewed the first years of the Honecker regime as positive and hopeful. Many artists and writers, but above all young people, tended to take this view. Western beat music could now be played, the much desired blue jeans could be imported and eventually were even available from local production. The SED also discontinued its campaign against long hair and short skirts and generally appeared to spend less time interfering in the private life of individuals. Western television could now be watched.

BETWEEN OPENNESS AND OPPRESSION

Unfortunately, this liberality was only a facade. Honecker, who liked to portray himself as the benevolent father of his people, was concerned to demonstrate openness abroad, but was equally determined to show that he had everything strictly under control at home. An early example of this double strategy was the "World Festival of Youth and Students" held in the summer of 1973, when tens of thousands of young people travelled to East Berlin from diverse countries, both in the East and the West, as well as from the Federal Republic and every corner of the GDR. The GDR authorities posed as generous and tolerant, allowing the young people to make music, dance and discuss as they wished. What appeared to a world audience, and also to the participants, as a demonstration of the SED regime's willingness to reform was in reality a carefully staged sham, controlled down to the smallest details by the authorities. For months, under the codename "Action Banner", the security services had taken every possible precaution to ensure that order and security was guaranteed. Thousands of GDR citizens were not even allowed to travel to the festival. The rest enjoyed a comprehensive "guest care" courtesy of the authorities. Almost 20,000 police, several thousand members of the security services in blue FDJ (Youth Movement) shirts, as well as countless functionaries of the latter organisation and of other mass organisations, were continually on duty to protect the East German citizens from the class enemy. The double strategy of apparent openness and actual hidden repression worked well on this occasion and was to remain a favoured means of those in power for deceiving the West and their own population into believing in the stability of the GDR.

THE CONSTRUCTION OF THE SURVEILLANCE STATE

The SED clung to its claim of absolute hegemony in politics, economic matters and society. The dictatorial elite tried to portray itself as more modern, more liberal and more responsive to the people than many had been accustomed to think, yet at the same time was constructing an apparatus of boundless surveillance. This apparatus was chiefly the handiwork of Erich Mielke, who had entered the Politbüro at the same time as Honecker. Together, these two Communists, both of them functionaries of total ideological conviction, put in place the unrivalled apparatus of control and discreetly applied terror that characterised the later years of the GDR.

Anxious to build a more liberal reputation abroad, the state now eschewed open displays of violence in favour of a comprehensive system of spying on its own citizens. Opponents of the regime were not to have the remotest chance of making a public protest or of committing crimes under the repressive laws of the GDR (such as, for example demanding freedom of speech, making preparations to flee the Republic, demanding freedom to travel outside the GDR or making an application for the same, which for a long time was itself counted as a crime).

In order to neutralise the supposedly "hostile" influence arising from contacts of GDR citizens with the West, a comprehensive system of surveillance was set up and carried on with ever more refined methodology. All "hostile and negative" groups, forces and persons (as all the critics of the regime were indiscriminately labelled), were to be "undermined", intimidated and forced to give up their opinions and plans. In particular, anyone who was involved in church groups was automatically suspect. However, the paranoia of the authorities also extended to all those who had regular visits from West German relatives, especially if the latter were members of environmental groups, the peace movement or similar; more generally, all those who had been openly critical of conditions in the GDR, as writers, artists or simply normal citizens, were equally suspect, and of course all of them soon became objects of the Stasi's attention. There were even lists compiled of the names of GDR citizens who counted as enemies of the state and who were to be arrested and placed in isolation camps in the event of unrest or tension. Appropriate plans for these camps were being drawn up until 1989 and the lists were constantly being updated. However, the plans were never actually put into operation.

THE STASI:
SHIELD AND SWORD OF THE PARTY

Under Honecker, the personnel of the headquarters of the Stasi (State Security Service) doubled to 91,000 employees, all of whom bore weapons and had military rank. The Stasi became increasingly the cure-all for dealing with "counter-revolutionary" activity and every kind of "hostile influence", to which the dictators imagined they were exposed. Even at school level, suitable future personnel for the Stasi would be singled out.

Also in the Honecker era there developed an ever more closely meshed net of spies and informers, the so-called unofficial workers (*Inoffizielle*

Mitarbeiter—IM), who became the most important means whereby the Ministry for State Security (MfS) could fulfil Mielke's ukase that "we must know about everything". From the middle of the seventies, give or take an annual fluctuation of about 10%, 170,000–180,000 people were collaborating with the Stasi. This implies that around every hundredth citizen was prepared to assist with the "struggle against the enemy". In great secrecy, the IM would meet with their contact officers in the Stasi and supply oral or written reports on their friends, neighbours, colleagues at work and even members of their own family. These people were traitors, yet considered themselves to be valuable supports for the Socialist state. In most cases, such people were politically committed; less often they were motivated by financial gain, and only a few were actually blackmailed by the MfS. Even under-age persons, about one per cent of all IMs, were recruited by Mielke's secret service officers, all to satisfy the dictatorship's unquenchable thirst for information.

The aim of the surveillance organs was the total control of the population at all times. These organs considered themselves to be the "shield and sword of the Party", and they were ever-present, like the tentacles of a huge octopus extending from the centre in East Berlin to every district and parish of the land. Erich Mielke was determined that there should never be another "17th of June". A total of 600,000 "unofficial workers", the shadow army of the MfS from the foundation of the GDR onwards (since 1990 only about a sixth of its members have been unmasked) contributed to the fear, dissembling and conformance that characterised the behaviour of so many people in East Germany, and for so long.

THE INDIVISIBILITY OF ECONOMIC AND SOCIAL POLICY

At first, Honecker's double strategy seemed to work quite satisfactorily. The security services showed an ever higher degree of alertness, in the manner already described, against the "class enemy" in the West and among the GDR's own citizens. Simultaneously, the SED leadership attempted to ingratiate itself with the population by means of social concessions and improvements in the standard of living. Wages and pensions were raised and the long neglected construction of new homes was driven forward with energy (albeit in the drearily standardised form of panel housing—while the fabric of older houses in the inner cities continued to fall apart). The "baby year" off and other sweeteners for working mothers was introduced, the supply of kindergartens and créches greatly expanded. Workers could also enjoy shorter working hours. The availability of electrical and white goods for homes (refrigerators, televisions, washing machines) and of cars greatly expanded in the seventies. Although GDR citizens had to wait at least twelve years for delivery of a Trabant motor car, the number of households with their own car increased to 38 % between 1970 and 1980.

Storing up Future Trouble

The GDR boasted the highest living standards within the East Bloc. Its proclaimed "unity of economic and social policy" became the hallmark of Honecker's consumer Socialism. However, it proved to be a policy that stored up trouble for the future, as was soon to be demonstrated. The expectation of the SED leadership that improved and more various consumer goods, together with the free social benefits already mentioned, would spur the workers to greater productivity, was not fulfilled. Economic productivity did not rise and the costs of all the free benefits could no longer be covered by increasing exports to the West of goods that were of the standard required for the world market, since the GDR did not produce enough of them.

Undesirable Developments

An increase in quality exports could not be achieved because, under Honecker, the strict application of the centrally directed command economy still failed to provide any incentives for higher productivity. Productivity remained permanently stuck at around 33% of the West German level. Although incentive wages were introduced at the end of the seventies, in practice they were rapidly relativised to conform with egalitarian dogma. Factories were incredibly wasteful in their use of energy and raw materials, which could still be obtained cheaply from the Soviet Union, with the result that the modernisation of processes and buildings was neglected; many of the plants indeed dated to the pre-war period. Moreover, in 1972, about 11,000 remaining small and middle-sized private concerns were nationalised, precisely those businesses that were a significant presence in the consumer sector of the economy. With this action, the leadership could count on support based on the material envy of the broad mass of the population, since the expropriated owners of such enterprises had generally enjoyed net incomes four times larger than those of workers and employees. The private *"Mittelstand"* (middle class) was now finally sidelined, and all that remained of it was a small residue of about 2000 independent craftsmen, restaurant owners and sole traders. The ideology of a Socialist production that avoided the dissemination of capitalist values was now applied in full, but it lacked the economically dynamic element of a middle class.

Honecker's new economic and social policy was also built on sand, because the average GDR citizen was not inclined, not even as a quid pro quo for state benefits, to make a sclerotic planned economy more productive, in view of the fact that such a system stifled every individual initiative. The GDR citizen's yardstick for comparison was not the situation in the "brotherlands" in the East, but always and only that of the Federal Republic, a comparison that was unlikely to bring him any satisfaction.

THE DANGEROUS INCREASE IN DEBT

The calculation of the SED leadership foundered above all on the simple fact that the money paid out for consumption, social benefits and subventions for cheap rents, food, traffic tickets etc. was not covered by the GDR's earnings.

Between 1970 and 1988, subventions of various kinds grew from 11.4 billion Marks to 61.6 billion, which was equivalent to one quarter of the total state budget. The result was an increasing burden of debt owed to the West. Between 1970 and 1975, foreign debt rose from 2 billion DM to 13 billion; five years later (1980), the debt mountain had grown to 28 billion DM, and in 1989 the GDR's total indebtedness was 49 billion DM. Because of the huge subsidy required by the SED leadership to keep consumer prices stable, the internal budget deficit of the GDR also soared over the same period from 12 billion Marks to 123 billion. At the end of 1978, the debt mountain was so high that new credits needed constantly to be sought, simply in order to pay the interest on the old ones.

This vicious circle of debt and interest payments had already brought the SED state to the brink of bankruptcy at the beginning of the eighties. "Real existing Socialism" was living well beyond its means. This of course was well-known to the small circle of economic specialists in the Ministry of Finance, the State Bank and the State Planning Commission. Nonetheless, as later reported by Gerhard Schürer, the longstanding head of the Planning Commission, the admittedly extremely cautious warnings that these people gave to Honecker and other top functionaries like Günter Mittag, were met with obdurate incomprehension. To make the cuts in social expenditure of the severity merited by the economic situation was not acceptable to Honecker, as he thought it would be destabilising. There was also to be no change in the "policy of stable consumer prices for necessities, including rents, fares and services", which Honecker had decreed at the

Tenth Party Congress in 1981. That these permanent subsidies must eventually spell ruin to the state finances was not a notion that the first man of the SED state was willing to entertain. On the contrary, with a complacent ignorance of the technical issues, he confidently rejected the critical reports in the western media on what he regarded as the *pièce de résistance* of Socialist economic and social policy: "They talk as if only 'the free play of demand and supply' can lead to the correct price levels and a healthy economy," he remarked. "That is naturally a fairy tale." Henceforth, there was no question of implementing solid financial planning. From an economic point of view, the GDR was living off its capital. The East German economy now took an ever more precarious course, at the same time becoming ever more dependent on the Federal Republic.

DÉTENTE AND INNER ISOLATION

The international re-evaluation of the SED regime that followed the new policy towards the East adopted by the Federal Republic reached a high point with the incorporation of both states into the United Nations in 1973. In the following year, the USA established diplomatic relations with the GDR, and by 1978 a total of 123 states all over the world had recognised the Communist part of Germany as a sovereign state. Thereby, the SED leadership had achieved what it had been seeking since 1949. Its unelected hegemony was no longer questioned by the international community and its dignity was considerably enhanced. The complicated reservations still harboured by Bonn had become purely a matter for initiates and increasingly lost their significance for the rest of the world. Henceforth, the GDR was virtually seen as a fully-fledged state like any other.

Nevertheless, the dictators in East Berlin were aware that this development also held dangers for the regime. An increasing number of GDR citizens tried to assert their rights under international human rights conventions and applied for settlement in the Federal Republic. Above all, the CSCE final document, to which the GDR had signed up in Helsinki in August 1975, had two sides as far as the regime was concerned. The recognition of the inviolability of borders in Europe certainly corresponded to the political aims of the GDR. However, the simultaneously agreed "free exchange of people, information and opinions" between East and West, and the lifting of restrictions on visiting and travel, was seen by the Communist leaders as a threat to their power basis, against which they reacted with an ever more aggressive policy of demarcation from West Germany.

The raising of the sum of obligatory currency exchange was one means of keeping control of the stream of visitors. One result of the dictators' attempts at demarcation was the introduction of "military training" as an obligatory subject in the ninth and tenth classes at school, together with many other measures taken by the state that aimed generally to militarise GDR society, whose enemy was epitomised by the Federal Republic. Alertness against the "class enemy" in the West and preparedness to defend "Socialist achievements" with a weapon in the hand were both demanded of each GDR citizen by official propaganda. The propaganda began in the kindergarten and did not cease when the young adult finally joined the work force.

Honecker was also at pains to deepen the ideological divide between the GDR and West Germany by stressing at every opportunity the leading role of the Soviet Union, a role which was given very specific and even more emphatic form in the treaty of friendship and support signed with Moscow in 1975 and valid until the year 2000. The new constitution of 1974 finally abandoned the notion of a common German nation, which the GDR had still recognised in the first two decades of its existence, and thus deliberately established an even sharper fault line between it and the Federal Republic. This move was designed to make it clear to the GDR's own population that improvement of intra-German relations, if the SED had anything to do with it, would never end in a policy of reunification on a democratic basis. Honecker left no room for doubt on this, even if the contacts between Bonn and East Berlin during the Chancellorships of Helmut Schmidt and Helmut Kohl were conducted in a climate of constructive engagement that sought to extract maximum benefit from and for both sides. Honecker indeed did several things to reinforce this policy of demarcation: he demanded in a speech at Gera in 1980 that the Federal Republic should recognise GDR citizenship; he also demanded that the two Permanent Representations in the respective states should be upgraded to Embassies; and finally he demanded that the investigation centre in Salzgitter, charged with registering the politically inspired miscarriages of justice in the GDR, should be closed. Even the text of the GDR National Anthem by Johannes R. Becher incorporating the inconvenient phrase "...*Germany, the single fatherland*" was not allowed to be sung any more.

BORDER SECURITY

Lastly, the territorial demarcation between the GDR and the Federal Republic and West Berlin was to be made even more sophisticated and formidable in the course of the seventies. For some time, the border had not only consisted of the wall and barbed wire, but also of tens of thousands of self-firing devices and land mines, as well as a steeply echeloned kilometre-wide system of control points and security. A border troop of 50,000 men guarded the state borders of the GDR day and night. The Party leadership required that the soldiers should make "ruthless use of their weapons" (as Honecker ordered in 1974) and praised them effusively when they did exactly that. All those entering or leaving the country were exhaustively checked on the border by members of the Stasi, although these Stasi officials were not officially identified as such.

PERSECUTION OF REGIME CRITICS

The consequences of this physical and ideological policy of isolation could soon be felt by anyone who was not prepared to knuckle under to Communist propaganda, who saw through the official lies put out by the Party, and who insisted on the observance of human rights. Citizens of the GDR who applied to travel, citing the relevant clauses of the Helsinki Agreement, were threatened with punishment and criminalised as enemies of the state. Chicanery organised against them at their place of work was a common occurrence. Only later was this tactic altered and attempts were made to solve the problem by depriving "critical" applicants of their citizenship.

The authorities also came down harshly on those western journalists who became conspicuous through their critical reports on the situation in the GDR. There were constant expulsions on the grounds, as it was claimed, of "defamation of the people and the government". GDR writers, artists and intellectuals who dared to criticize the policies of the leadership were subjected to repressive measures, even if they were themselves members of the SED. This was the fate of the Marxist critic of the regime best known in the West, the former Professor of Chemistry, Robert Havemann, who was criminalised by applying methods of psychological terror and placed under house arrest. All of this was simply to prevent him from propagating within the GDR his idea of a Socialist democracy in which human rights would play a central political role. Havemann died in 1982 but long afterwards remained an inspiration for intellectuals protesting against the East German dictatorship of the Party.

In 1976, there was a full-blown confrontation between the Party and many prominent artists when Wolf Biermann, a long disgraced critical singer/songwriter, though still a convinced Communist, was arbitrarily deprived of his citizenship while on an officially permitted concert tour of the Federal Republic. The authorities ruthlessly persecuted the one hundred or so prominent and lesser known writers and artists who protested against this. Their privileges were removed, they were threatened with prison and attempts were made to isolate them politically and socially. Some (like the writer Reiner Kunze) were even expelled from the worker and peasant paradise (as it was proclaimed to be by the tireless official propaganda). Others (for example Manfred Krug, one of the GDR's best known actors) received permission to leave for the Federal Republic: it was the authorities' mistaken belief that, in getting rid of such "unruly elements", the remaining "makers of culture" could once again be harnessed to the interests of the Party.

THE CHURCH UNDER SOCIALISM

In 1978, Honecker reached an accommodation with the Lutheran Church, the only remaining institution that was substantially autonomous under the SED dictatorship. The church obtained more freedom for its social activities, for example in the area of peace initiatives, which at that time were still considered to be useful for exploitation by official Party propaganda. In return, the church leadership refrained from open criticism of the SED state, accepting the role of the "church in a Socialist context", which formally supported the regime but also wanted it to reform. Neither the Party leadership, nor that of the Church had any idea that this compromise would provide a basis for protest that ultimately hastened the demise of the GDR. Nevertheless, there were signs even then that the docility of the church so much desired by the SED was unlikely to last. Many church-based communities were formed at grass roots level and increasingly became rallying points for the opposition and for critics of the regime's infringements of human rights. Many groups of East German environmentalists and members of the peace movement also found shelter here and exploited that shelter to stage quasi-public demonstrations in support of their principles. Prayers for peace which, since 1981, were held every Monday in the Leipzig Nikolaikirche and elsewhere, had a particular symbolic significance in the repressive context of the GDR, providing a focus for alternative thinkers hoping to make common cause with people who might share their views; for this reason, of course, they provoked alarm amongst the security services.

PEACE CAMPAIGNERS AND ENVIRONMENTALISTS
VERSUS THE AUTHORITIES

After the failure of its campaign against the upgrading of NATO's armaments, the SED at once began to confront the peace movement at home, since the slogan of "swords into ploughshares" was now largely understood as criticism of the armaments policy in the East. In addition, the SED leaders well knew that these groups were demanding not only peace, but also freedom and democracy.

Under the mantle of the church, and mostly supported by courageous young priests, although not always with the approval of the bishops and the church administration, these alternative-thinking groups developed their activities, which automatically made them "enemies of the state" in the eyes of the dictatorship. Notwithstanding that the regime proceeded against them using all the brutal potential of its previously described surveillance system, and indeed arrested some protagonists in an attempt to intimidate the others (in 1983, for example Bärbel Bohley and Ulrike Poppe, founders of the initiative "Women for Freedom" the previous year), and also penetrated their discussion and activist groups with spies and subjected their members' private lives to surveillance, such groups increasingly managed to build contacts with each other. In this way an opposition movement was gradually formed, one that ultimately the regime was unable to crush.

MISTAKEN CALCULATIONS

At the end of the day, the advantages of the GDR's treaties and cooperation with Bonn and other Western states heavily outweighed the disadvantages, and the same was true in reverse. Without the West German economic and financial assistance already described, no improvement in the living standards of GDR citizens would have been possible and therefore Honecker would not have been able to entrench himself. The regime calculated that it could neutralise the possibly dangerous consequences of East–West contacts by arresting or expelling individual critics, while at the same time making it easier for others to apply for exit visas (30,000 in 1984), in the expectation (false, as it soon turned out) that this would produce a state of tranquillity. In fact this move acted as a detonator. It was not long before 40,000 to 50,000 GDR citizens were applying for exit visas each year, and by 1987 there were over 100,000, against whom the security service took harsh measures. In the end, the SED and MfS settled for a judicious mixture of repression and sporadic commutation of penalties, which they hoped would keep a lid on things.

This was a fatal misappreciation of the situation. It was not only sections of the younger generation and intellectual opponents of the regime who criticized the fossilised nature of the GDR state, and ever more boldly and demanded their civil rights. Millions of normal GDR citizens showed that, by the beginning of the 1980's, they were deeply unsatisfied with the so-called "real existing Socialism" that they were obliged to endure on a daily basis. There was also widespread disappointment over the many promises of emancipation made by the Party leaders, which were subsequently never kept. Of course, western television also played a role. It supplied East Germans with a virtual world of consumption in their own living rooms, in the light of which the everyday greyness of life in the GDR seemed to be even more drab than it was in reality. Nevertheless, the swelling dissatisfaction also had more concrete causes.

DISSATISFACTION GROWS

The GDR did provide social security and full employment. However, the obverse of this "socialist achievement" of the first "worker and peasant state on German soil", as the senile Politbüro never tired of presenting it, was obvious to virtually everyone. In the Socialist factories (*"Kombinate"* or "collective combines") investment was lacking for renewal of the often antiquated industrial processes. As a result, there was much inactivity and wastage; indeed, many working days were spent simply repairing the machines. The technological backwardness compared to the West was evident everywhere. Environmental protection was largely ignored and the despoliation of nature was correspondingly unrestrained. Another grievance shared by many was the fact that higher quality consumer goods from the GDR's own production (cameras, music centres and the like) were made exclusively for export, in order to earn hard currency, while GDR citizens had to be content with products of modest or indifferent quality. And finally, in the 1980's, there were ever more frequent shortages, even of staple foods. The long queues in front of the shops (satirically described as "Socialist waiting communities") became an everyday experience. Ever more GDR citizens retreated into the private sphere, more or less resigned to the apparently unalterable political dispensation; they paid the verbal tribute demanded by Party propaganda, but thought and spoke quite differently when amongst their friends. All they could do was attempt to live as normal a life as possible under the given circumstances.

ECONOMIC DECLINE BY INSTALMENTS

The Party dictatorship of the SED was as yet unchallenged. The Politbüro and Honecker's close circle, to which Erich Mielke, Willi Stoph, Egon Krenz and Günter Mittag belonged, presided over a disciplined army of some 100,000 Party secretaries, 44,000 other functionaries of the Party and about 100,000 higher ranking members of the military and security forces. The "Block Parties" paid homage to the SED leadership and accepted its "leading role", while the mass organisations, such as the Free German Association of Trades Unions (*Freie Deutsche Gewerkschaftsbund*), ensured that the millions of the "working population" remained bound to the Party and toed its line. Last but not least, the Party leadership could count on the support of the big brother in Moscow and the 380,000-strong contingent of the Soviet army stationed in the GDR. However, that began to change in 1981–82. The Soviet army remained the most important guarantee of Communist hegemony in the GDR, but the state lost a part of the economic support hitherto provided by Moscow. The Soviet Union abruptly reduced oil deliveries to the GDR by two million tons (about ten per cent of the supply hitherto), which it now needed in order to raise money urgently in hard currency. Oil sales on world markets were the only reliable means by which the Soviet Union could finance its huge military expenditure. Honecker's appeal to Brezhnev to reverse the cut, which threatened to destabilise the GDR, was ignored. Thereafter, the GDR economy stagnated at a low level of activity. The previously described massive debt that the GDR had built up with the West made the economic crisis into which the Party had manoeuvred the country even more acute. The GDR urgently needed more credits for its expensive imports, which were not balanced by sufficient exports. At the same time, its creditworthiness among the international bankers was in doubt, since Poland and Romania had just announced their inability to meet their liabilities.

BONN OFFERS A LIFELINE

In this catastrophic situation, that bore all the signs of the incipient demise of the GDR, the Party leadership was bailed out by two credits of a billion DM each in 1983 and 1984, an initiative of the Bavarian Prime Minister, Franz Josef Strauss, but undertaken with the agreement of the Federal Government. With this financial support propping it up, the GDR was again able to obtain the foreign currency that it so desperately needed from the international money markets. The Social Democratic opposition in the Bundestag also supported this initiative, since at that time (unlike in the Gorbachev era) all leading West German politicians believed that a collapse of the GDR would be likely to provoke an attack by the Soviet Union. The quid pro quo offered by the SED leadership was to make a few humanitarian gestures: the self-detonating devices on the border were removed at the end of 1983, the Federal Government was able to buy the freedom of more political prisoners, and the GDR approved more exit visas.

SECRET CURRENCY DEALS

An important role in setting up this intra-German "deal" (strongly criticised by the Soviet leadership) was played on the GDR side by Alexander Schalck-Golodkowski. In his dual capacity as Stasi Officer for Special Projects (OibE) and economic manager, he had for years been involved in the "commercial coordination" of the two areas under his control, with the aim of raising billions of DM in hard currency for the ailing state finances. Brass plate firms in the Federal Republic, armaments trading, the sale of blood plasma and of antiquities confiscated from their owners, all these were among the most important sources of income for this shady project, whereby Socialism would be stabilised by applying capitalist methods.

THE ENDURING IMAGE OF "THE ENEMY": INFILTRATION AND BUGGING

The SED regime by no means considered that the financial assistance provided by the Federal Republic justified any let-up in their decades-long struggle against democracy in the West, or in their attempts to infiltrate and undermine that democracy. As hitherto, the 500 to 1000 agents of the Ministry for State Security active in the Federal Republic were operated as "scouts for peace" by their controllers in East Berlin. Economic and industrial espionage now played an increasingly important role in their activities.

In addition, there were the many thousand West Germans (estimated to have been at least 20,000 between 1950 and 1989) who acted as unofficial accomplices of the Stasi in the Federal Republic's administration, businesses, universities, research institutes, political parties and other state institutions; and these continued with their work.

Naturally, the 500 most senior Stasi employees of *Hauptabteilung III* (Department III) of Mielke's Ministry received no order to cease their eavesdropping on western politicians. On the contrary, they diligently evaluated the recorded telephone conversations of western authorities and politicians of all parties and immediately reported to the top anything particularly explosive. For example, in 1984 they kept Honecker and eight other members of the Politbüro comprehensively informed on the internal discussions of the SPD leadership regarding the so-called "Flick donations affair" (*see next chapter*). According to the reports, the discussion mostly concerned the extent to which the CDU knew of the involvement of leading Social Democrats, and whether, in view of their opponents' probable knowledge of its involvement, the SPD should seek an accommodation with the Conservatives. Equally detailed were the Stasi reports on the telephone conversations of the CDU functionaries regarding political donations laundered through Switzerland. From the beginning of the seventies onwards, the Stasi were almost always able to listen in to the telephone calls of West German politicians. Some 100,000 telephone connections were permanently "targeted", i.e. bugged, including the car telephone of the Federal President, and those of several members of the Federal Government, and of course that of the Federal Chancellor. The Stasi noted the content of calls diligently in their lengthy bugging reports, 740 metres of which lie today in the archive of the Gauck authority; naturally they did not forget to pass on anything important to the Soviet secret service (KGB).

All in all, until the middle of the 1980's, Honecker succeeded once again in preventing the economic collapse of the GDR and in regulating intra-German relations with the Kohl/Genscher government on the basis of a "coalition based on good sense" (Honecker). Nevertheless, the tension between the leadership and the people in the GDR grew sharper, because the Communist Party insisted in maintaining its hegemony over every sphere of life and continued to defend its power with all the means at its disposal.

CHRONOLOGY

1971

3 May 1971 — Erich Honecker becomes First Secretary of the SED; Ulbricht remains President of the State Council.

15–19 June 1971 — The SED holds its Eighth Party Congress. It is decided that economic and social policy should be harmonised to take more account of people's needs. The first measures are encouragement of house construction and a price freeze on consumer goods and services.

24 June 1971 — Honecker adds Chairman of the National Defence Council to his other offices.

30 September 1971	Posts and telephone agreement between the two Germanies.

16–17 December 1971 Honecker announces in the Central Committee that cultural life is to be handled more liberally: "If one starts from a firm base of Socialism, I do not believe that there can be any taboos in the field of art and literature."

17 December 1971 State Secretaries Bahr and Kohl (GDR) sign the first intra-German agreement on transit traffic between the two states.

20 December 1971 The GDR and the West Berlin Senate agree on the easing of restrictions on transit travel.

1972

27–28 April 1972 The state decrees a rise in minimum pensions, reductions in rents, social measures to assist working mothers and families with many children, and interest free loans for young married couples.

18 May 1972 The last wave of nationalisation of small traders and craftsmen ends.

7 November 1972 The SED Politbüro decides to intensify surveillance of all contacts made with the West.

8 November 1972 The GDR joins UNESCO.

21 December 1972 Egon Bahr and Michael Kohl sign the Groundwork Treaty in East Berlin.

31 December 1972 During 1972, 17,164 people have left the GDR as refugees or officially for resettlement. By the end of the year, 20 states have established diplomatic relations with the GDR (among them Austria, Switzerland, Sweden and Belgium). In January and February 1973, fifteen more follow suit, including Italy, Great Britain and France.

1973

1 March 1973 Correspondents from ARD and ZDF and numerous West German newspapers are accredited to the GDR.

8 March 1973 The GDR rejects any form of compensation payment to Israel.

11 May 1973 The Bundestag ratifies the Groundwork Treaty, with the CDU/CSU Union voting against.

1 August 1973 Walter Ulbricht dies aged 80.

18 September 1973   The Federal Republic and the GDR become members of the UNO.

2 October 1973   The SED announces a programme of housing construction, designed to solve the housing problem by 1990.

5 November 1973   The sum to be compulsorily exchanged by western citizens visiting the GDR is doubled (to 20 DM per person at an exchange rate of 1 to 1 GDR Marks).

19 December 1973   GDR citizens holding hard currency are allowed to shop in the Intershops.

31 December 1973   During 1973, 16,189 people have left the GDR as refugees or officially for resettlement.

1974

1 January 1974   The GDR introduces the international car sign "DDR", in place of the "D" used hitherto.

9 January 1974   Egon Krenz becomes Chairman of the Free German Youth movement (FDJ).

2 May 1974   Permanent Representations of both German states are opened in Bonn and East Berlin respectively.

3 May 1974   The National Defence Council confirms that weapons are to be used in the case of "border infringements".

4 September 1974   Establishment of diplomatic relations between the GDR and the USA.

7 October 1974   All existing references to "the German nation" in the constitution of 1968 are removed. The "irrevocable" alliance with the Soviet Union is given constitutional rank.

26 October 1974   The sum of compulsory currency exchange for visitors is lowered.

31 December 1974   During 1974, 13,252 people have left the GDR as refugees or officially for resettlement.

1975

1 August 1975   Erich Honecker signs the Concluding Instrument of the CSCE for the GDR in Helsinki. Meeting between Honecker and Schmidt.

7 October 1975	Second Friendship Treaty with the Soviet Union. Part of the Treaty confirms the Brezhnev Doctrine of the limited sovereignty of the Socialist states.
31 December 1975	During 1975, 16,285 people have left the GDR as refugees or officially for resettlement.

1976

23 April 1976	The Palace of the Republic is opened in East Berlin. The building, irreverently dubbed by the locals "Erich's lampshop" and "the ballast of the Republic", has cost over one billion Marks.
18–22 May 1976	Honecker takes the title "General Secretary", after the Soviet model.
27 May 1976	Further welfare measures are implemented by the regime, including higher basic wages and pensions, more holiday time, and the gradual introduction of the 40-hour week.
18 August 1976	In Zeitz, the Lutheran pastor, Oskar Brüsewitz, burns himself to death in public as protest against the oppression of the church in the GDR.
16 November 1976	The songwriter Wolf Biermann is deprived of his citizenship during a concert tour of the Federal Republic. GDR artists and writers unite in protesting against this move by the dictatorship.
31 December 1976	During 1976, 15,188 people have left the GDR as refugees or officially for resettlement.

1977

17 February 1977	Writing in the *Saarbrücker Zeitung,* Honecker warns that without recognition of GDR citizenship, there will be no freedom for East Germans to travel in the West.
26 August 1977	The GDR expels several critics of the regime to the Federal Republic after they have served prison sentences, a tactic that will be employed ever more frequently to muzzle dissent in the future.
7 October 1977	Brawls among youths on the East Berlin Alexanderplatz results in three dead and many injured.
31 December 1977	During 1977, 12,078 people have left the GDR as refugees or officially for resettlement.

1978

6 March 1978	Meeting between Honecker and Bishop Schönherr, Chairman of the Administration of the Lutheran Church. A less tense relationship between church and state follows from this meeting.
26 August 1978	Sigmund Jähn goes into space aboard the Soviet space capsule "Soyus 31", the first German to go into space.
27 September 1978	Introduction of the new curriculum for Classes 9 and 10 in GDR schools. It includes "pre-military preparation and education" (military training), which is to be obligatory for all boys and girls.
31 December 1978	During 1978, 12,177 people have left the GDR as refugees or officially for resettlement.

1979

18 January 1979	An MfS (Stasi) officer, Wener Stiller, defects to the Federal Republic: a network of GDR spies is uncovered in West Germany as a result.
14 April 1979	Bureaucratic measures are enforced to prevent free reporting out of the GDR.
25 May 1979	Conviction of Robert Havemann for infringement against currency laws. He is fined 10,000 Marks. The trial is staged like a film script by the security service and judiciary, each phase carefully prepared in advance.
7 June 1979	The Writers Union expels nine writers who have criticised the GDR's cultural policies. Most of them are able to leave the GDR.
28 June 1979	Penalties for political crimes are increased as a measure to combat critics of the regime.
27 December 1979	Soviet troops invade Afghanistan.
31 December 1979	During 1979, 12,555 people have left the GDR as refugees or officially for resettlement.

1980

31 August 1980	Following mass strikes right across Poland, the Polish government is obliged to concede the formation of free unions and the right to strike.

13 October 1980	In a keynote speech in Gera (the "Gera Demands"), Honecker makes the improvement of intra-German relations dependent on the recognition of GDR citizenship, the transformation of the Permanent Representations into Embassies, the confirmation of the Elbe border (the border to be the middle of the river) and the closure of the Central Investigation Office in Salzgitter (monitoring GDR abuse of civil rights). The compulsory currency exchange for visitors to the GDR is drastically increased.
30 October 1980	Private travel of GDR citizens to Poland is made difficult.
31 December 1980	The GDR's debts reach 10 billion dollars. During 1980, 12,763 people have left the GDR as refugees or officially for resettlement.

1981

26–31 May 1981	State visit by Honecker to Japan.
1 September 1981	Pre-military training is now also made obligatory in the Extended High School (*Erweitererten Oberschul—EOS*).
11–13 December 1981	Federal Chancellor Helmut Schmidt meets Honecker at the Werbellinsee.
13 December1981	The Polish Prime Minister, General Jaruzelski, introduces martial law in Poland. The leader of the Solidarity trades union, Lech Wałęsa, is arrested.
31 December 1981	During 1981, 15,433 people have left the GDR as refugees or officially for resettlement.

1982

25 January 1982	The "Berlin Appeal": Pastor Rainer Eppelmann and the scientist Robert Havemann formulate a plan for "peace without weapons". It is the first time that the peace movement achieves wide resonance in the GDR.
9 February 1982	Honecker ceremonially hands over the two millionth home to its new owners. Later it turns out that the figures have been faked.
14 February 1982	A peace forum in the Kreuzkirche in Dresden attracts 5000, mostly young people.
18 June 1982	The GDR announces that it will consider easing travel restrictions.

20 November 1982	Opening of the transit Autobahn between Hamburg and Berlin.
31 December 1982	During 1982, 13,203 people have left the GDR either as refugees or officially for resettlement.

1983

29 June 1983	The precarious finances of the GDR are propped up by a credit of one billion DM from West German banks. This has been negotiated by Franz Josef Strauss, but with the approval of the Federal Government. This credit enables the GDR to return to the world financial markets to seek credits.
27 September 1983	The GDR begins to dismantle the self-firing devices on the internal German border.
24–25 November 1983	Egon Krenz becomes a member of the Politbüro and the Central Committee's Secretary for Security.
12 December 1983	Bärbel Bohley and Ulrike Poppe of the "Women for Peace" movement are arrested and only released after five weeks.
31 December 1983	During 1983, 11,343 people have left the GDR as refugees or officially for resettlement.

1984

14 March 1984	A delegation from the SPD meets the SED leadership in East Berlin.
6 April 1984	Günter Mittag, the member of the Politbüro responsible for the economy, meets Kohl and Strauss in Bonn.
25 June 1984	Provisional closure of the Permanent Representation of the Federal Republic in East Berlin, because 55 GDR citizens refuse to leave it until they are granted exit visas.
25 July 1984	The GDR receives a further credit of one billion DM from the Federal Government.
2 August 1984	The Soviet Party newspaper *Pravda* criticizes the relationship between the GDR and West Germany, and accuses Bonn of intervening in the internal affairs of the GDR by using economic leverage.
3 October 1984	Honecker writes in *Neues Deutschland*: "A union between Socialism and capitalism is just as impossible as one between fire and water."

31 December 1984   During 1984, 40,974 people have left the GDR as refugees or officially for resettlement.

1985

13 February 1985   The Semper opera house in Dresden, destroyed in 1945, is re-opened.

23–24 April 1985   State visit of Honecker to Italy, where he meets Pope John Paul II.

26 April 1985   The Warsaw Pact is extended by another twenty years.

27 November 1985   The GDR finishes removing landmines from the internal German border.

31 December 1985   During 1985, 24,912 people have left the GDR as refugees or officially for resettlement.

1986

9 February 1986   The GDR extends the possibilities for travel to the west in case of urgent family need.

1 March 1986   Extension of the automatic dialling service for telephoning between the Federal Republic and the GDR.

26 April 1986   The greatest civil nuclear catastrophe in history occurs at Chernobyl near Kiev.

26 June 1986   The independent peace and ecology movement of the GDR sends an appeal to the People's Assembly to change the information policy of the government concerning energy and economic policy.

18 September 1986   At the request of the Federal Government, the GDR limits the numbers of asylum seekers who enter West Germany via East Berlin.

31 December 1986   During 1986, 26,178 people have left the GDR as refugees or officially for resettlement.

1987

17 July 1987   The death penalty is abolished.

27 August 1987   SPD and SED publish their joint paper entitled "Ideological Dispute and Mutual Security" (*Der Streit der Ideologien und die gemeinsame Sicherheit*).

7–11 September 1987   Official visit by Honecker to the Federal Republic.

24–25 November 1987   The Stasi searches the ecology library of the Lutheran Community of Zion in East Berlin. Members of the church-based peace and ecology movement are arrested. There are further strikes against oppositional groups in several towns. Protest and solidarity rallies are held all over the GDR. Those arrested are subsequently released.

31 December 1987   During 1987, 16,958 people have left the GDR as refugees or officially for resettlement.

10. A Change of Government in Bonn: The Christian Democrat–Liberal Coalition under Helmut Kohl from 1982

KOHL BECOMES CHANCELLOR

On the 1st of October 1982, the thirteen-year rule of the Social Democrats ended dramatically. It was highly ironic that the internationally admired Helmut Schmidt, a politician who was hardly less respected by the opposition at home than he was abroad, became the first, and up to now the only, Chancellor to be unseated by a constructive vote of no confidence in Bundestag. He was replaced by the leader of the CDU/CSU Union, Helmut Kohl. The somewhat arrogant Schmidt indeed made no secret of the fact that he regarded the Chairman and Fraction Leader of the Union as a provincial politician who was unfit to hold the office of Chancellor. This was a view shared by Kohl's colleague and longstanding political rival, the Bavarian Prime Minister, Franz Josef Strauss. Many commentators in the press held the same opinion and were only to revise it when Kohl made history by his handling of the reunification of Germany. But that was long in the future.

The public experienced the no confidence vote in the autumn of 1982 as something of a suspense drama. It was not so long ago that a similar attempt to dislodge a sitting Chancellor had failed spectacularly in 1972. In the end, however, the change of government went smoothly, thus once again demonstrating that the parliamentary system incorporated in the Basic Law did indeed function. The fact that the newly ejected Chancellor, Helmut Schmidt, was obliged to vacate his study next to the lobby of the Bundeskanzleramt on the very next day after his fall, when Kohl grandly made a "technical appreciation" of the rooms, hardly improved his low opinion of his successor, which he maintained to the end. However, his scorn could not prevent the "duckpond owner" (*Ententeichbesitzer*), as Schmidt derisorily dubbed Kohl, from arriving at the head of a fleet of removals vans and moving in immediately. The official handover from Schmidt to the new Chancellor followed only several days later.

THE LIBERALS ARE PUT TO THE TEST

Had the Liberals (FDP) not changed sides, Kohl would not of course have become Chancellor. The plan to abandon the SPD that the Party leader and Foreign Minister, Hans-Dietrich Genscher, at first hesitantly, then determinedly, plotted from the middle of 1981 onwards ("A change is required"—Genscher, August 1981), originated with pressure from the Economy Minister, Otto Graf Lambsdorff. Many supporters of the Social Democratic-Liberal coalition regarded the move as a betrayal. Nevertheless, the coalition was undeniably no longer capable of action on important political issues, as had become clear at the latest by 1982. The FDP leadership feared that loss of power was imminent if they stuck with a Social Democratic Party that was deeply split on security and economic issues, and that had refused to back its own Chancellor in the question of NATO's double strategy. The opinion polls showed the Union leading the SPD by a wide margin, while in the Upper House it already enjoyed a majority of between 15 and 30 votes.

The change of allegiance that Genscher considered to be vital, although he lost the sympathy of many of his supporters as a result, really put the Liberals to the test. Of its Federal Committee, 18 members voted for the change, 15 against; and in the parliamentary fraction, 40% of the MPs voted against. In the long term however, this extremely controversial move turned out to be a guarantee of the FDP's survival, insofar as the economics-oriented wing of the Party henceforth called the shots on policy.

KOHL CARRIES THE DAY: STABILISATION OF THE COALITION AFTER NEW ELECTIONS

The Liberals found in Kohl a man well versed in the art of power politics, and one who saw eye to eye with them on most policy issues; more to the point, he never forgot to whom he owed his opportunity to become Chancellor. From the very beginning, the new Chancellor was anxious to consolidate his position by means of a popular vote, but not in the way envisaged by Strauss, who had by no means abandoned his political ambitions at federal level. The latter pressed for an immediate election, which seemed likely to produce an absolute majority for the Union, but which would have robbed Kohl of unfettered choice in forming his team (particularly for the Foreign Ministry) and of fixing his policies more with reference to the FDP than the CSU. Strauss's demand was therefore not at all in Kohl's interest, and he accordingly fixed a date for new elections in the early part of 1983. The time leading up to them was to be used by the new governmental team to achieve a high profile, before offering itself to the voters. This was a strategic decision that bore witness to Kohl's extremely acute political antennae and understanding of power. His rescue of the FDP laid the first brick of an edifice that was to become a 16-year-long chancellorship, and the pre-condition for the building of this edifice was to be Kohl's unchallenged dominance in the CDU.

Kohl's calculation proved to be correct. The elections brought forward to 6th of March 1983 were constitutionally controversial, because of the requirement that the Bundestag be dissolved by Federal President Karl Carstens (CDU); however, the dissolution was retrospectively approved by the Constitutional Court. The election resulted in a clear victory for the coalition and supplied Chancellor Kohl with the popular mandate that he required.

ELECTION TO THE BUNDESTAG, 1983

In a robust turnout of 89%, the Union parties increased their support by 4.3%, achieving 48.8% of the vote and 244 of the 498 mandates, a superb result by any standards. The FDP's vote went down 3.6% since 1980, but the party still achieved 7% of the vote and 34 mandates, a result that was better than expected in view of internal party disagreements. Helmut Schmidt no longer stood as Chancellor candidate, and was replaced by Hans-Jochen Vogel, the respected former Justice Minister and Mayor of Munich. Despite Vogel's political weight, he was unable to prevent the SPD from slipping under the 40% mark for the first time since 1965; the Party lost 4.7% of its support and achieved only 38.2% of the votes, 193 Bundestag seats. For the first time the Greens entered the Bundestag with 5.6% of the votes and 27 MPs. Their electoral success, which they later consolidated in the *Länder*, provoked a wave of interest in environmental issues in the Federal Republic, something which pressured the large parties to take the environment more seriously in future, in the hope of attracting concerned voters thereby.

GOVERNMENT POLICY BETWEEN
CONTINUITY AND CHANGE

The rhetoric of change and renewal espoused by the leadership of the Christian–Liberal coalition in 1982 and 1983 was not accompanied by any alteration of course on a wider front. Change was concentrated on economic and social policy. In foreign policy and security matters, continuity was the order of the day, and was epitomised by the figure of Hans-Dietrich Genscher, who remained Foreign Minister: Genscher regarded it as his life's work to continue and consolidate a German foreign policy that would be regarded as consistent from the perspectives both of the East and the West.

REFORM IN ECONOMIC AND
SOCIAL POLICY

The Kohl/Genscher government saw itself confronted with acute economic problems, including a financial crisis, mass unemployment, massive debt, inflation and weak economic growth. The new government was very much aware that they would only continue to have the support of the majority of voters if they performed well in tackling these problems.

In the following years, the Christian–Liberal coalition set about creating the conditions for a renewed economic upswing with considerable reformist zeal. In order to rid themselves of the "inherited burdens" of the previous government, both the Union and the Liberals applied themselves to the strengthening of the operation of market forces. Individual initiative, competition, tax breaks for enterprise and less interference of the state in the economy were all significant aspects of the new economic credo.

The Finance Minister, Gerhard Stoltenberg, after Genscher the most important politician in the cabinet, proved to be an active and successful cost-cutter. The "cool-headed intelligence from the North", who had been tested in various ministerial capacities right back to the Adenauer era, and had latterly been the Prime Minister of Schleswig-Holstein, belonged to the conservative wing of the CDU and stood for solid and cautious financial policy. Against the strong criticism of the SPD, and against the worker constituency of the Union itself, not to mention hundreds of special interest groups from all reaches of society, he pushed through a tax reform in 1988 that abolished numerous tax breaks and loopholes, but which also introduced a general lowering of the tax burden worth 30 billion DM to German taxpayers in the middle and higher tax brackets. By pursuing a policy of limiting government expenditure and benefits, chiefly in the area of social policy, he managed to put the government's finances in order and to curb the rate of increase in debt (in 1982, it had been 72.1 billion, in 1986 it fell to 38.4 billion, rising again to 52 billion in 1987). Nevertheless the debt mountain continued to rise, even if considerably more slowly than in the seventies. New social benefits, such as the introduction of educational grants (1986), and the adjustment of pensions to take account of years spent by women bringing up children (1986), were pushed through by the relevant ministries (primarily by that of Labour and Social Affairs under Norbert Blüm), and against the wishes of the Finance Minister.

MASS UNEMPLOYMENT IN A PERIOD
OF ECONOMIC RECOVERY

Overall living standards rose for the majority of the population during the 1980's. The economic cycle again turned positive, not least as a result of the fall in the price of oil from the middle of the decade. Exports boomed. The GNP, which had shrunk by 0.9% in 1982, began to grow again by 1.5% or more per year, and in 1984 and 1988 by as much as 3%. Inflation also receded rapidly (in 1982 it was 5.3%, in 1988 only 1.3%).

Nevertheless, the government remained powerless in the fight against unemployment. Although hundreds of thousands of new jobs were created between 1982 and 1990, over two million people remained unemployed each year up to 1989. The baby boom generation, the large number of immigrants, but above all the hurricane pace of rationalisation in the industrial sector were responsible for this situation. Attempts were made (by sending people to early pension or by shortening work hours) to prevent an even steeper rise in unemployment. It was, however, only after the reunification of Germany that unemployment sank temporarily under two million (by 1992), only to climb again steeply thereafter.

KOHL AS PARTY LEADER

The economic recovery of those years stabilised the electoral support of the coalition government in Bonn. Yet the Chancellor himself, by contrast with all his predecessors, was not a particularly popular politician in the Republic right up to the end of the 1980's. Lacking rhetorical flair and media-friendly attributes, he was for long unable to project himself effectively in the television age. His power base was and remained the CDU: this was his political home and the instrument by which he could realise his political aims. Early on he learned how to bind people to himself by directly communicating with, and promoting the careers of, individuals right down to the party's roots; also by distributing cash through official and unofficial channels, and finally by successfully neutralising internal party rivals.

In his early years as Party leader after 1973, Kohl nevertheless represented a renewal of the Union, successfully turning a party of fustian bigwigs into one with a more popular modern image, which appeared to have regained the confidence to win after the electoral defeat of 1972. In Kurt Biedenkopf he had a General Secretary of the party of intellectual breadth who turned the central office of the CDU in Bonn into a highly effective leadership tool. At the same time, he reoriented the CDU so that it was once again a centrist party for the common man, open to the varying streams of contemporary society; and he devised a political programme that was appropriate to this profile. This fresh wind blowing through the Party continued under Heiner Geissler, Kohl's Social Minister and colleague from his Mainz days, who succeeded Biedenkopf as General Secretary in 1977. The number of Party members doubled in a few years. The CDU again put issues on the agenda that became topics for public and political discussion ("new social questions", "equality of opportunity between men and women"), and also attracted media interest. Kohl benefited considerably from this, being viewed positively as the renewer of his party, despite, as leader of the opposition in the Bundestag from 1976, having to endure the handicap of standing in the shadow of the brilliant Helmut Schmidt, who spared him none of his ample reserves of mordant contempt. As soon as he became Chancellor, it became apparent that he also knew how to fashion his party into a highly effective electoral weapon to be used for the consolidation of his power. Less important to him was the role of his party as a forum for the discussion of the latest problems affecting society. Deficiency in this respect was the accusation levelled against him after the end of his Chancellorship in 1998 by formerly loyal political colleagues, who had nevertheless been content enough with his tight, power-oriented leadership of the Party when it was producing results. Only a few senior Christian Democratic politicians, such as the CDU General Secretary Heiner Geissler, who kept his post until 1989, actually criticised the leadership style of Kohl at the time, deploring also his minimal interest in the intellectual vitality of the CDU. Conflict between the two politicians therefore became inevitable.

THE GOVERNMENT IN A DUBIOUS LIGHT: THE SCANDAL OF PARTY CONTRIBUTIONS

Kohl managed to consolidate his chancellorship, despite the fact that in its early years it appeared more than once in a questionable light due to diplomatic clumsiness and political scandals. Respect for Kohl amongst the public was especially damaged by his joint effort with Genscher and Strauss in 1984 to push an amnesty law through the Bundestag, which would have made unlawful political contributions from the sixties and seventies retrospectively immune from prosecution. This was naked attempt to brush the scandal of the Flick affair under the carpet: the company's managing director, Eberhard von Bruchitsch had already admitted to "cultivating the political landscape" in Bonn by providing money for the CDU, CSU and FDP out of slush funds.

The Flick concern, with the agreement of the then Economics Minister, Friedrichs (FDP), had been able to sell shares to a value of 1.9 billion DM free of tax and then reinvest the proceeds. In connection with the deal, it was known that all sorts of favours had been offered both to parties and individual politicians. However, direct bribery was impossible to prove. These dealings fell into a grey area of the law concerning tax-free contributions and led, over a long period, to 1700 separate investigations, most of which ended with fines being levied. Kohl himself had also received money from industry and devised a way of covering up unlawful forms of party financing through so-called "citizens' unions". His close contact with Flick became known at the same time as his old rival, and at that time Parliamentary Speaker, Rainer Barzel, was forced to admit that, following the loss of the party leadership to Kohl, he had been on the payroll of Flick since 1973, albeit indirectly as a lawyer in a Frankfurt partnership. His yearly salary of a quarter of a million DM had been set off against tax by Flick as company expenses. Barzel was obliged to resign his parliamentary post.

The politician most deeply implicated in the affair was Graf Lambsdorff, the long-standing treasurer of the FDP in Nordrhein-Westfalen. With brass plate firms, indirect financing and money laundering through fake associations, he had bolstered the FDP, which had few members, with financial contributions from industry, especially from Flick. These contributions were then illegally offset against tax, besides remaining anonymous, which was also illegal. At the end of 1981 Chancellor Schmidt had already blocked an attempt by all the fractions represented in the Bundestag to have an amnesty law passed. Kohl's renewed attempt in the summer of 1984 to free both the contributors and organisers of this dubious type of financing from the legal consequences of their actions foundered on public outrage, as well as on the refusal of the FDP grass roots to go along with it. Lambsdorff resigned before his trial began in June 1984. Three years later he was convicted of tax evasion and fined.

The Lesson Not Learned

The scandals of illegal party financing created an impression among the public that politicians were up for sale. Widespread disillusion with both politics and politicians was the consequence. The Bundestag hastened to tighten up the laws regarding the financing of political parties and to make the avoidance of transparency in party contributions more difficult. However, as was demonstrated at the end of 1999 and the beginning of 2000, when illegal party financing for the CDU was again discovered, the people responsible for the original debacle had evidently learned nothing from it. In particular, Kohl continued to be an active fundraiser for his party, exhibiting a touching understanding for all contributors who wished to remain anonymous, although the law prescribed absolute transparency.

THE GENERAL ELECTION OF 1987:
THE UNION LOSES SUPPORT

At the eleventh election to the Bundestag in January 1987, the Union vote declined by 4.5%, achieving its worst result since 1953 with 44.3% of the vote. However, since the SPD with their chancellor candidate, Johannes Rau, slipped to 37%, the Union remained by far the strongest party, despite the unpopularity of the chancellor.

The chief gainers in this election were the Greens, who got 8.3% of the vote. It was clear that the Greens were taking votes away from the founding parties of the Republic, particularly from the SPD, for whose left wing, being an "anti-party", as they still saw themselves, they had begun to provide serious ideological competition. Many young voters and those disillusioned by conventional politics were attracted to the grass roots democracy of the Greens, as also to their ecological aims and their opposition to nuclear energy.

All in all, however, the government could draw comfort from the fact that the FDP raised its vote by 2.1% to 9.1%. Despite this, the coalition negotiations were drawn out over several weeks until agreement was reached between the Liberal and the Christian camps and Helmut Kohl could be elected Federal Chancellor on the 11th of March 1987, though with only four votes over the required absolute majority.

INTERNAL POWER STRUGGLES:
KOHL EMERGES VICTORIOUS

In spite of his still modest popularity ratings and several electoral defeats for the CDU at provincial level, as well as at the European elections in June 1989, Kohl managed to entrench his position as head of the government. The effective cooperation with his Liberal coalition partner was certainly a factor in this. In cabinet he was unchallenged, not least because a growing number of ministers owed their office entirely to him. Above all, he was successful in neutralising his opponents within the Party, people like the CDU General Secretary, Heiner Geissler, the Prime Minister of Baden-Württemberg, Lothar Späth, the Parliamentary Speaker, Rita Süssmuth, and a whole slew of other CDU politicians, who had plotted his downfall in 1988–89. These and other Christian Democrats accused Kohl of an authoritarian style of leadership, as well as a lack of political ideas and vision. But there were also differences on more basic areas of bread and butter politics, such as the policy on immigration. Kohl reacted to the growing criticism of his leadership with a cabinet reshuffle in April 1989. Two heavyweight politicians of the CDU/CSU supplied the ballast he wanted for his government by entering the cabinet: the CSU Party Chairman, Theo Waigel, became Finance Minister, and the able Minister in the Office of the Chancellery, Wolfgang Schäuble, became Minister of Home Affairs. However, the decisive factor was that Kohl received the support of the majority of the delegates at the CDU party congress in September 1989. In the light of the ever more dramatic developments in Eastern Europe since the summer of 1989, and also of the evident signs of crumbling power in the GDR, the delegates were taking no risks with a new Party Chairman. Kohl now installed Volker Rühe as the new CDU General Secretary. In the end, the rival candidate for Chairman of the Party, Lothar Späth, did not even stand against his leader, and the internal party plotters had to admit defeat. Kohl remained Chairman of the CDU until 1998.

CONTROVERSIAL REARMAMENT OF THE FEDERAL REPUBLIC

As far as foreign policy was concerned, the Kohl/Genscher government was determined that there should be no doubt whatsoever regarding the Federal Republic's commitment to the western alliance. Although Kohl, like Genscher, was by no means in agreement with every aspect of US President Ronald Reagan's policy of confrontation with the Soviet Union and tolerated no interference by America in German–Soviet direct trade, both men nevertheless demonstratively backed Washington on general policy.

After the collapse of the American–Soviet negotiations in Geneva over the removal of middle range rockets in Europe (this collapse itself followed eleven hours of ultimately fruitless talks between Genscher and the Soviet Foreign Minister Gromyko in Vienna a few days earlier), the governing coalition agreed to the deployment of American medium range rockets in the Federal Republic in November 1983, in line with the NATO double strategy decision of 1979. The SPD and the Greens voted against this in the Bundestag. Thereby Helmut Kohl put into effect, and in defiance of fierce protest amongst the public, the security plan worked out by his Social Democrat predecessor, while the SPD for its part now overwhelmingly rejected the plan.

The mood in certain quarters of the West German public was very tense. The initiators of the peace movement, which was partly manipulated and financed by the GDR, was able to bring hundreds of thousands of citizens onto the streets. Prominent writers like Heinrich Böll and Günter Grass, intellectuals, artists, high school teachers, as well as many ordinary citizens of all ages took part in sit-down actions to prevent deployment. The anti-armament groups seemed to be justified when the Kremlin immediately broke off disarmament talks with the Americans in Geneva and began their threatened counter-measures a few months later, namely the deployment in Central Europe (including the GDR) of middle range rockets with a limited capability. The policy of détente of the previous years thus received a serious setback and German–Soviet relations deteriorated dramatically.

JUDGEMENT WITH HINDSIGHT

At the time there was much talk in the press of a new ice age in East–West relations. In fact, the firmness of the NATO states, and above all that of the Federal Government and the US government under President Reagan, accelerated a rethink in security policy that was already beginning in the Soviet leadership, and that was subsequently to bear fruit after 1986 under General Secretary Mikhail Gorbachev. Years later, when the Soviet Union no longer existed, senior Soviet politicians and academics confirmed that the then extremely controversial and much criticised armaments policy of the Kohl/Genscher government, together with the consistent policy of deterrence of the Reagan administration, was a major factor in Moscow's momentous change of course in respect of foreign policy. The Politbüro gradually came to realise that the Soviet Union, due to its economic weakness, was simply unable to compete any more in the arms race with America.

AMERICAN POLICY OF SUPERIOR STRENGTH

The US President Reagan was unfazed by the financial burden required to confront the Soviet Union with a policy of strength through deterrence, but his uncompromising campaign against what he called the "centre of evil in the modern world" aroused little sympathy among the majority of West Germans. His pondering of the possibility of limiting nuclear war to Europe, and his plans for a "Star Wars" defence system in space to protect America from hostile rockets (Strategic Defence Initiative—SDI), was grist to the mill of widespread anti-Americanism and a gift to the pacifist groups. Both on the left and the right of the political spectrum, albeit for different reasons, there was now increasingly "a fear of our own friends". In the GDR, the propagandists of the SED exploited the new US security policy to terrify the population—and of course to justify the ever increasing Soviet military presence in their own land.

That Reagan expressly coupled his policy of military deterrence with an offer of dialogue was deliberately overlooked by his critics in the Federal Republic: "Deterrence is of supreme importance for the maintenance of peace and the protection of our way of life; but deterrence is not the beginning and the end of our policy towards the Soviet Union. We must, and we will, bind the Soviets into a dialogue which... will serve to promote peace, will serve to reduce overall the number of armaments and will bring about a constructive working relationship... the demonstration of strength goes hand in hand with dialogue." (US President Reagan in a televised address at the beginning of 1984.)

RELIABILITY AND LOYALTY TO THE ALLIANCE

As far as the Federal Republic was concerned, Kohl's policy of demonstrative solidarity with the western alliance, and West Germany's absolute reliability as a NATO partner, was later to pay dividends. He managed simultaneously to strengthen the German–American partnership for security without allowing his country to be dragged into an economic and political crusade against Moscow. The continued development of the European community in close collaboration with the France under President François Mitterand was the second pillar of the Kohl/Genscher government's foreign policy, since both the CDU leader and his FDP colleague were committed and discerning Europeans. At the same time, Chancellor Kohl signalled to the Soviet Union and the GDR his willingness to enter into talks to reduce tension. Right from the beginning, the new Bonn coalition left no doubt in people's minds that the upgrading of armaments considered necessary by its predecessors in government was also a priority for this coalition; at the same time, it aimed to pursue a policy on intra-German relations that was based on cooperation and dialogue.

POLICY ON INTRA-GERMAN RELATIONS:
CONTINUATION OF THE NORMALISATION PROCESS

In his public utterances Chancellor Kohl was harsher than the previous government had been in his condemnation of the illegal nature of the SED hegemony, regularly denouncing the wall, the barbed wire and the "shoot-to-kill" order of the GDR authorities, as also the expulsion of the opponents of the regime: in short, he called a spade a spade. On the other hand, he talked of reunification in extremely abstract terms, since nobody at that time reckoned with such an eventuality. His main concern was to emphasise the difference in kind between the free Federal Republic and the ideological system of Communism, and to do so in a rather more pointed way than his predecessors. At the same time he based his day-to-day approach on the actual existing situation and the realities of power. Kohl's general policy was therefore no different from that of Schmidt, insofar as he sought a further normalisation of intra-German relations on the basis of existing treaties and agreements. Cooperation was, as far as possible, to be extended into every area of policy. This perhaps came as a surprise to the population of the Federal Republic, which recalled the sharp rejection of the Groundwork Treaty (*Grundlagenvertrag*, 1972), and also of the Helsinki Agreement (CSCE Final Document, 1975) by the Union. However, for the SED it was no surprise at all, since a number of prominent spokesmen for the Union had nurtured (with Kohl's approval) confidential contacts in East Berlin and had intimated to these that a change of government in Bonn would not alter the West German approach to the question of intra-German relations.

KOHL AND HONECKER ESTABLISH CONTACT

Immediately after entering government, Kohl repeated Schmidt's existing invitation to Honecker to visit Bonn. In the course of numerous telephone conversations and letters the two politicians also began to develop a certain familiarity.

The first personal meeting between them occurred in February 1984 in Moscow on the occasion of the obsequies for the deceased Soviet leader, Yuri Andropov. In a relaxed atmosphere, Kohl and Honecker principally discussed the particular tasks facing both German states in the context of an improved climate of relations between the two super powers, and the two of them found themselves largely in agreement on this topic. In March 1985, there arose another opportunity to continue this graveyard diplomacy at the burial of Soviet Party chief Chernenko, which took place one day after the new General Secretary of the Soviet Communist Party, Mikhail Gorbachev, took office. In a joint declaration with his East Berlin interlocutor, Kohl confirmed their mutual view that the "sovereignty of all European states as presently constituted" was the "basic condition for peace". This was nothing new, and indeed was already stated in the Warsaw Treaty of 1970; moreover, Kohl had used the same formulation shortly before in his report to the Bundestag concerning the "situation of the nation in the context of a divided Germany". However, in Moscow he moved somewhat closer to Honecker's demand for equal status and recognition, a movement which led to a further improvement in relations between the two governments.

The "Coalition of Understanding"

In return for financial support and special economic privileges from Bonn, the GDR was to introduce more humanitarian concessions, especially in respect of travel. Further, the two leaders emphasised, both in their telephone conversations and correspondence, that there should never again be a war that originated with Germany; indeed they stressed their unique mutual responsibility to ensure that this would never happen. At a time when rockets were being deployed and when the nuclear arms race between East and West was still in full swing, Honecker and the Chancellor committed themselves to a "coalition of understanding" and spoke of the "community of responsibility" shared by the two German states. They demonstrated that they were at one on the need for more cooperation, whose ultimate aim was "damage limitation" in respect of Europe as a whole.

Without doubt the two lines of credit, each of one billion DM, which the Federal Republic provided for the GDR in 1983 and 1984, played an important role in this process of intra-German cooperation. The fact that the economically collapsing SED regime was stabilised by these loans was of course known to the Bonn government. However, nobody, neither in the opposition nor on the government side, saw any alternative at that time to a policy of pragmatic negotiation with the Communist rulers in East Germany. In the final analysis, this was because nobody in the West was in a position to force the SED regime to implement the desired humanitarian concessions for travel, for visiting and for the reuniting of families, and more generally for the improvement of intra-German relations. What counted was the overall result of this policy of financial support, and that was incontrovertibly positive: in the event of family emergencies, more and more GDR citizens under pensionable age could travel to the Federal Republic;

exit applications and permissions for members of split families to rejoin their kith and kin were more generously assessed; and the border controls were made a little more humane.

POLITICAL TOURISM TO EAST BERLIN

For the moment, the SED dictators had the whip hand and West German politicians accommodated themselves to reality. In the eighties, a kind of political tourism developed, whereby every significant Bonn politician, either from the government camp or the opposition, travelled regularly either to East Berlin or to Leipzig for the annual trade fair, and each of them laid particular stress on the need to remain on good terms with Honecker. Some of these politicians seemed to forget altogether that their interlocutor was the incarnation of a dictatorship. Others, for example the head of the SPD fraction in the Bundestag, Hans-Jochen Vogel, used their contacts to find solutions for cases of humanitarian need, without bringing into doubt their personal political convictions in regard to the incompatibility of democracy and dictatorship. In general it may be said that the stress on a somewhat ambiguous "security partnership" between the two countries, although understandable at the time, through the heavy involvement of prominent Social Democrats like Egon Bahr, Erhard Eppler or Oskar Lafontaine, tended to result in neglect of human rights abuses in the GDR; and to this extent it was a boon to the SED. Chancellor Kohl showed a profounder understanding of the problem, at least in his public statements in the Bundestag, when he criticised the threat to human rights posed by the use of coercion in the GDR (1984), or stressed that "for us there is no middle way between democracy and dictatorship" (1985). His chief coordinator for intra-German policy from 1984, Wolfgang Schäuble, was particularly blunt when he met his most important and most frequent negotiating partner of the SED, Schalck-Golodkowski, in East Berlin to explore confidential ways of cooperation. On the other hand, neither the SPD politicians nor those from the government side kept up much contact with the GDR opposition—indeed the only exceptions to this general rule of avoiding controversial contacts were provided by the Greens. Still, developing a network of contacts with the influential members of the Politbüro and the GDR government was certainly a necessity dictated by *realpolitik*, and it appears to have been the right course to pursue when looked at with the benefit of hindsight.

MOSCOW OBJECTS TO HONECKER'S VISIT TO BONN

What counted was not the intentions of the two German governments, but the general political climate in the world and the interests of the respective leaderships of the two great alliances. This became apparent when the visits of the SED boss to Bonn, planned first for April 1983, then for September 1984, had to be cancelled. The 1984 visit, minutely planned with East Berlin in the strictest confidence by Kohl's confidant and Minister in the Chancellor's Office, Jenninger, had to be abandoned when Moscow objected. Honecker and various high-ranking comrades were summoned to the Kremlin shortly before the visit was due to take place and were told that the Soviet leadership, under its new General Secretary, Konstantin Chernenko, disapproved strongly of the GDR's deals with Bonn on the basis of finance-for-humanitarian concessions. The "friends" saw this as leading to too many intra-German contacts and mutual involvement, which they feared would jeopardise the Soviets' own security. They also feared that the SED regime could become dependent on the Federal Republic. It was only when Mikhail Gorbachev took office, and began to seek a comprehensive accommodation with the US world power, that the Soviet veto fell away and the intra-German summit urgently wanted by Honecker could take place in Bonn in 1987.

THE INTRA-GERMAN SUMMIT

This major event in intra-German relations was prepared for months in advance by Wolfgang Schäuble in the Chancellor's Office (reporting to Kohl) and by the chief GDR negotiator Schalck-Golodkowski (reporting to Honecker), and no detail was left unattended. Chancellor Kohl welcomed the Communist head of state and party boss from East Berlin with all the honours laid down by protocol for receiving the head of state of a sovereign nation. Honecker interpreted this state visit, which the Bonn government characterised as a "working visit", as the unconditional recognition of his regime by the Federal Republic. Most West German citizens placed the same interpretation on it, especially when they watched Honecker's appearances in several *Länder* on television, and saw the friendliness displayed towards him on these occasions by prominent federal politicians in Bonn, Düsseldorf, Mainz, Trier, Neunkirchen and Munich.

Chancellor Kohl used the occasion of a banquet speech in Bad Godesberg on the 7th of September 1987 (which was also broadcast in the GDR), to recall the right of the Germans "to be free to choose to complete the unity and freedom of Germany". He went on to demand the lifting of the shoot-to-kill order on the border ("It is precisely the use of force against the defenceless that damages the peace"), as well as the removal of the wall. Honecker's answer to this was sobering, but hardly surprising, when he spoke of the unchangeable reality of two German states ("Socialism and capitalism can be no more reconciled than fire and water"), but nevertheless stressed the improvement in mutual cooperation.

SATISFACTION ON BOTH SIDES

Intra-German relations now seemed to have entered calm and predictable waters. Business as usual seemed to be the order of the day and both sides indicated their satisfaction with this. By the end of 1987, the Federal Government could point to a sharply rising number of visits by GDR citizens of pensionable age (from 1.6 millions to 3.8 millions) compared to the previous year, with more of them visiting the West German provinces (a rise to 1.2 million from 0.573 million). Likewise, more Federal citizens visited the GDR (a rise to 4 million from 3.6 million). The rulers in the East Berlin Politbüro felt strengthened in their power and judged the Honecker/Kohl meeting in Bonn to have been a major success: as Egon Krenz remarked a little later, "They [the West Germans] can no longer deny that the GDR exists."

CHRONOLOGY

1982

1 October 1982	The Bundestag passes a motion of no confidence in Chancellor Helmut Schmidt, with the CDU, CSU and FDP voting in favour. Helmut Kohl is elected the new Federal Chancellor with 256 votes over 235. There are four abstentions.
10 November 1982	The General Secretary of the Soviet Communist Party, Leonid Brezhnev, dies; his successor is the head of the KGB, Yuri Andropov. While attending the obsequies for Brezhnev in Moscow on the 14th of November, Federal President Karl Carstens holds talks with the Chairman of the State Council of the GDR, Erich Honecker.

1983

7 January 1983	Federal President Karl Carstens dissolves the Bundestag.
6 March 1983	The early elections for the 10th West German Bundestag result in a clear endorsement for the Christian–Liberal coalition. The

CDU/CSU Union wins 48.8% of the vote, the SPD 38.2%, the FDP 7%, the Greens 5.6% (thus entering parliament for the first time). The turnout is 89.1%.

13 March 1983   Honecker announces that he will visit the Federal Republic during 1983, but shortly thereafter cancels the visit, following critical press comment when a West German citizen dies in an incident on the internal German border.

23 March 1983   US President Ronald Reagan announces comprehensive research and development work in the USA in the field of missile defence (Strategic Defence Initiative—SDI).

29 March 1983   Helmut Kohl is elected Federal Chancellor.

12 May 1983   Six Federal MPs from the Greens demonstrate on East Berlin's Alexanderplatz in support of disarmament both by the East and the West; they are expelled to their homeland after interrogation by the GDR authorities.

29 June 1983   A Federal bond is issued for the one billion DM credit drawn on West German banks in favour of the GDR, which the Bavarian Prime Minister Strauss, ignoring criticism in his own ranks, had negotiated.

4–7 July 1983   Chancellor Kohl and Foreign Minister Genscher visit the Soviet Union. An attempt is made to set relations between West Germany and the Soviet Union on a better footing.

21 July 1983   Martial law is lifted in Poland.

24 July 1983   The Bavarian Prime Minister, Strauss, meets General Secretary Honecker in the GDR during a private visit.

1 September 1983   A rally of the GDR peace movement is broken up by the People's Police.

15 September 1983 The Mayor of West Berlin, Richard von Weizsäcker, meets Erich Honecker in East Berlin.

28 September 1983 The GDR begins dismantling the self-firing devices on the internal German border.

14 November 1983   Deployment of American cruise missiles begins in Great Britain.

18 November 1983   At a special party congress in Cologne, the SPD votes overwhelmingly against upgrading the armaments in the Federal

Republic. The Greens in Duisburg also demand that West Germany should leave NATO.

22 November 1983   The Bundestag votes to support NATO's double strategy, with the SPD and the Greens voting against.

23 November 1983   The Soviet Union breaks off the Geneva disarmament talks dealing with middle range missiles (INF).

10 December 1983   The deployment of middle range nuclear missiles begins in the Federal Republic and in Italy.

1984

20–22 January 1984   Six GDR citizens, who had sought political asylum in the US Embassy in East Berlin, are allowed to travel to West Berlin.

9 February 1984   The Soviet Communist chief, Andropov, dies. His successor is Konstantin Chernenko.

13 February 1984   First meeting between Kohl and Honecker during the obsequies for Andropov in Moscow.

13 March 1984   The GDR begins building a second wall in the immediate vicinity of the Brandenburg Gate.

6 April 1984   35 GDR citizens who had spent five weeks in the Federal Republic's Embassy in Prague, return to the GDR; they receive permission to leave in the near future. In October, 168 GDR citizens manage to leave their country using similar tactics.

15 May 1984   The Soviet Union begins deployment of further short range missiles as reaction to the NATO armaments upgrade.

23 May 1984   Richard von Weizsäcker (CDU) is elected Federal President.

5 July 1984   55 GDR citizens agree to leave the Federal Government's Permanent Representation in East Berlin after their permission to leave the country has been confirmed.

9 July 1984   Lufthansa and Interflug (GDR) agree to run regular flights to the trade fairs at Stuttgart, Düsseldorf, Hamburg and Leipzig.

25 July 1984   A second credit of one billion DM for the GDR is announced by the Head of the Office of the Federal Chancellor, Jenninger.

1 August 1984   The GDR eases travel restrictions for East German pensioners. In 1984, 40,900 GDR citizens are able to travel to the Federal Republic.

17 August 1984	The Moscow leadership expresses its disapproval of the planned visit of Honecker to the Federal Republic.
20 September 1984	A working party of the SED and SPD begins discussions on making Europe into a chemical weapon-free zone.
22 September 1984	Chancellor Kohl and President Mitterand visit the battlefields of Verdun together.

1985

20 January 1985	Ronald Reagan begins his second term of office as US President.
11 March 1985	Death of the Soviet leader, Konstantin Chernenko. The new General Secretary of the Soviet Communist Party is Mikhail Gorbachev. During the obsequies for Chernenko in Moscow, Kohl holds talks with Honecker and Gorbachev.
12 March 1985	The Soviet Union and the USA resume disarmament negotiations in Geneva.
2 April 1985	The two leading members of the "Red Army Fraction", Christian Klar and Brigitte Mohnhaupt, are convicted and sentenced to lifelong imprisonment at the Superior Court in Stuttgart for their part in various murders and attempted murders.
26 April 1985	The Warsaw Treaty is extended by 20 years.
2–4 May 1985	Eleventh world economics summit in Bonn.
5 May 1985	US President Reagan, accompanied by Chancellor Kohl, visits the military cemetery at Bitburg in the Eifel region. The visit arouses fierce criticism, since members of the Nazis' Waffen-SS are among those buried here.
8 May 1985	In a speech commemorating the 40th anniversary of the end of the war in Europe, Federal President Richard von Weizsäcker stresses that "the 8th of May was the day of liberation". Both at home and abroad the speech is received with great approbation.
12 June 1985	Spain and Portugal, after eight years of negotiation, sign the Treaty for joining the European Community in 1986.
14 June 1985	France, the Federal Republic and the Benelux States sign an agreement in Schengen to make cross border traffic easier.
28 June 1985	Against the votes of the SPD and the Greens, the governing coalition passes a law restricting the right to demonstrate (the "prohibition in disguise").

19 August 1985	Hans-Joachim Tiedge, an official in the Office for the Protection of the Constitution (*Bundesamt für Verfassungsschutz*) in Cologne, who has been responsible for counter-espionage against the GDR, defects to East Berlin.
29 August 1985	In the Bonn Regional Court the trial begins of the former Economics Minister, Otto Graf Lambsdorff (FDP) and of his colleague Friederichs (FDP), together with Flick Manager Eberhard von Brauchitsch. The charges concern illegal payments to political parties and tax evasion.
10 October 1985	SPD and the Greens form a coalition government in Hesse. Joschka Fischer becomes Minister for the Environment.
19–21 November 1985	American–Soviet summit in Geneva between President Reagan and the Soviet leader, Mikhail Gorbachev.

1986

19 February 1986	The President of the GDR's People's Assembly, Horst Sindermann, makes a four day visit to Bonn.
25 February 1986	The leader of the SPD parliamentary fraction, Hans-Jochen Vogel, rejects an attempt by the left wing of the SPD to have the requirement that every government should work for German reunification deleted from the Basic Law.
1 March 1986	Self-dialling telephone communication between the Federal Republic and the GDR is extended to 1106 local networks.
19 March 1986	German–American agreement over the participation of the Federal Republic in the Strategic Defence Initiative (SDI) of the USA.
5 April 1986	A bomb attack by a Libyan terror organisation on a Berlin discotheque kills two people and injures 200.
26 April 1986	The failure of an atomic reactor at Chernobyl in the Soviet Union, north of Kiev, causes mass anxiety in the Federal Republic.
17–19 May 1986	The first of several serious clashes between demonstrators and police near the planned nuclear reprocessing plant in Wackersdorf in the Oberpfalz. At Brokdorf on the Lower Elbe and at Gorleben there are also repeated violent clashes between police and anti-nuclear protesters.
6 June 1986	A Ministry for the Environment is created in Bonn. At its head is the former Mayor of Frankfurt, Walter Wallman.

9 July 1986	Karl Heinz Beckurt, a member of the board of Siemens, together with his driver, are victims of a bomb attack by the RAF. Three months later, the head of the political department of the Foreign Ministry, Gerold von Braunmühl, falls victim to assassination by the RAF.
18 September 1986	The GDR, on the urging of the Federal Republic, places restrictions on the transit of asylum seekers, who had hitherto been travelling in large numbers to West Germany via East Berlin.
10 October 1986	Saarlouis and Eisenhüttenstadt are the first example of town twinning between the two Germanies.
21 October 1986	At a press conference in Bonn the leading SPD politician, Egon Bahr, and the SED Politbüro member, Hermann Axen, put forward a joint proposal whereby both parties should work for a nuclear-free zone in Central Europe.
1 November 1986	The River Rhine is seriously polluted following a fire in the Basel factory of the Sandoz chemicals concern.

1987

4 January 1987	At the national congress of the CDU in Dortmund, Chancellor Kohl calls the GDR a regime that "keeps 2000 people imprisoned for political reasons in gaols and concentration camps". This formulation provokes a protest from the GDR's Permanent Representative in Bonn.
25 January 1987	Despite the Union's heavy losses at the polls, the Bundestag election leads to a continuation of the Christian–Liberal coalition under Chancellor Kohl. The CDU/CSU get 44.3% of the vote, the SPD 37%, the FDP 9.1% and the Greens 8.3%.
16 February 1987	The former Flick manager, von Brauchitsch, and the former Minister for Economics, Graf Lambsdorff, together with his colleague Friedrichs are heavily fined for tax evasion in connection with the Flick affair.
15 March 1987	The Bavarian Prime Minister, Franz Josef Strauss (CSU) meets with Erich Honecker in Leipzig.
23 March 1987	Willy Brandt resigns his post as Chairman of the SPD. He becomes honorary chairman for life. The new chairman is Hans-Jochen Vogel.
27 March 1987	Talks between the Head of the Chancellery Office, Wolfgang Schäuble, and Erich Honecker.

1 April 1987	Talks between Chancellor Kohl and the GDR Economics Minister, Politbüro member Günter Mittag.
1 May 1987	Meeting between the Bavarian Prime Minister, Franz Josef Strauss, and the head of the GDR body responsible for Commercial Coordination (KoKo), Stasi Colonel Alexander Schalck-Golodkowski.
15 May 1987	Meeting between the Chairman of the SPD parliamentary fraction, Hans-Jochen Vogel, with Erich Honecker in East Berlin.
9 June 1987	Around 3000 people, ignoring a huge police presence, gather on East Berlin's Unter den Linden and chant their demand for the demolition of the Wall and freedom. Shouts in support of Gorbachev can also be heard.
12 June 1987	US President Ronald Reagan visits West Berlin. He challenges the Soviet Head of State and Party Chief, Mikhail Gorbachev, to have the Wall demolished.
17 July 1987	The GDR abolishes the death penalty.
17 August 1987	Rudolf Hess, Hitler's former secretary and the last prisoner left in the Spandau gaol for war criminals, dies at the age of 93 in the British military hospital in Berlin.
27 August 1987	The joint paper of the SED and the SPD entitled "Ideological Disputes and Mutual Security" is published in East Berlin and Bonn. Both sides stress the ability of the respective systems to reform themselves and both advocate a climate of peaceful rivalry.
7–11 September 1987	"Working visit" to the Federal Republic of the GDR's Chairman of the State Council, Honecker.
23 November 1987	Talks are held between Wolfgang Schäuble and Alexander Schalck-Golodkowski in the Office of the Federal Chancellery.
25 November 1987	The GDR's State Security Service searches the premises of the Lutheran Church of Zion in East Berlin. Members of the peace and environmental movement of the GDR are arrested.
8–10 December 1987	US President Reagan and the Soviet leader, Gorbachev, sign the Treaty for the Destruction of Middle Range Missiles (INF) in Washington.

11. The Collapse of the SED Dictatorship and the Fall of the Wall in 1989

HONECKER'S CRITICISM OF THE REFORM COURSE OF THE SOVIET UNION

In many respects 1987 was a fateful year for the GDR. Having achieved the symbolic recognition of his regime through his visit to Bonn, Honecker believed that he had entrenched his power for the long term, and that he could thereby resist the pressure for reform coming from Moscow, pressure which was beginning to have an effect in the GDR itself. While he fully agreed with the Soviet leader, Mikhail Gorbachev, on security matters (disarmament in the East and the West, destruction of nuclear weapons), and even liked to pose as the instigator of the new policy of détente with the USA, Honecker completely rejected Gorbachev's other plans for the modernisation of Socialism. *Glasnost* (transparency) and *Perestroika* (economic and political reconstruction), the slogans with which the new leader in Moscow fascinated the Western world, and which were designed to get his people used to the major liberalisation and democratisation of state and society that was implied by his reformist aims, were seen by Honecker and his cronies in the East Berlin Politbüro as an attack on the very basis of their their power.

The initial harmony between Gorbachev and Honecker had been due to the fact that the former greatly esteemed the German politician's "antifascist" roots. When Honecker claimed in their first discussions that the GDR was an economically successful and politically stable country which could demonstrate significant achievements, and which was embarked on the right course for the future, Gorbachev did not contradict him. Nevertheless, conflict between the two Communist leaders was already brewing by the end of 1986. In numerous private discussions, Honecker began to realise that Gorbachev was not about to lend him his unqualified support in cementing the division of Germany. Since his Soviet ally now made it ever more plain that good relations with the great economic power of West Germany and the American superpower were more important than the special wishes of its "friends" in East Berlin, Honecker turned violently against Gorbachev's policy of total "rethink". Henceforth he saw himself (in his own words) as "a fighter on two fronts", struggling both against the capitalist Federal Republic and against the Socialist leadership in the East, whose reform policies endangered the very existence of the GDR. Honecker was firmly convinced of this danger, and for this reason a policy of conformity to Moscow was no longer an option.

The Loss of a Sense of Reality

As far as the situation within the GDR was concerned, its rulers' insulation from reality was truly remarkable. As emerged from his talks with the politicians from the Federal Republic who zealously courted him up to 1989, Honecker appeared to be convinced that "the policies of the SED were supported by every generation of GDR citizens". This was the way he put it to the Prime Minister of the Saarland, Oskar Lafontaine, in September 1987. However, Lafontaine's illusions were hardly less astonishing than those of Honecker; he apparently accepted this rosy picture at face value and even used it in his attack on Chancellor Schmidt for not having done enough to integrate the Federal Republic's young people.

Honecker either could not or would not see that his state visits to Bonn (1987), and one year later to Paris, which he believed crowned his life's work, were a matter of complete indifference to the majority of GDR citizens, because they were not interested in symbolic gestures and diplomatic subtleties, but in an improvement in their living conditions. However, it was not only Honecker, but also other members of the Politbüro who contributed their share to the dissatisfaction in the country, insofar as they openly boasted of their absolute opposition to reform. A not untypical example of this was provided by the 72-year-old Kurt Hager, the Politbüro member responsible for art and science; dismissing the reform of the GDR that so many urgently desired in an interview with *Stern* magazine in April 1987, he remarked that, just because one's neighbour changes his wall paper, one should not feel obliged "to redecorate one's own home". Everyone in the GDR could read this interview, reprinted in *Neues Deutschland*, and even the grass roots of the Party were outraged by its complacency.

Socialism in GDR Colours
Instead of Reform

After decades of total dependence on Moscow, and of unconditional subordination to the prevailing political line emanating from there, the SED rulers now for the first time began openly to oppose the course being signalled by the Kremlin. The greater room for manoeuvre in domestic politics that Gorbachev now allowed the East Bloc states was used by Honecker, not for liberalisation of the SED regime, but on the contrary, to obstruct internal reform.

The Party leadership believed that its non-acceptance of the changes taking place in Poland, Hungary and the Soviet Union could be made into a plausible policy under the slogan "Socialism in GDR colours". In talks with West German politicians, Honecker reiterated that he saw no need for reforms in economic or social policy, because in these areas the GDR was ahead of the other Socialist countries. "In economic and social policy we have great achievements" he proudly informed the Prime Minister of Nordrhein-Westfalen, Johannes Rau, in mid-March 1989. The fact that millions of GDR citizens felt themselves to be hostages in their own land did not seem to have occurred to him. Instead, he praised the "generosity" of his government in allowing travel to the Federal Republic in 1988 (out of 15 million inhabitants of the GDR, 5 million made the trip in that year). Assuming the airs typical of absolute rulers who have complete discretion in the treatment of their subjects, Honecker warned that "hitherto we have kept the reins loose", but that this situation could change "if everyone who jumped over the green border is celebrated as a hero in the Federal Republic".

THE SOVIET UNION IS NO LONGER THE MODEL TO FOLLOW

Honecker allowed no discussion concerning the democratisation of his regime, and nor did the West German visitors attempt to initiate such a discussion, since it was clear that it would bring nothing. They preferred to concentrate on the extension of partnerships (twinnings) between towns in the two Germanies. The dictator could be persuaded to approve these, so that he could affably proclaim them as examples of the praiseworthy good relations that the GDR had with most of the West German *Länder*. Even such minutiae as his gracious consent bestowed on the winegrowers association of the Saarland ("Of course wine will continue to be imported, as hitherto") was something he considered important. On the other hand, the pluralism in society and the open discussion that all of a sudden was being propagated by the Soviet leadership, and which it hoped would be a stimulus to productivity in a collapsing economy, was seen by the East Berlin dictators as a serious threat to their rule. The fact that the Polish and Hungarian Communists now saw their deliverance in the adoption of Western democratic standards was simply another indication for the East German Communists of the extreme danger posed by the course set by Moscow.

Honecker watched with suspicion as Gorbachev began to show ever more interest in a reappraisal of Soviet relations with the Federal Republic. By
the same token, Honecker could see no guarantee of the GDR's existence in
Gorbachev's political vision of a "common European house". The slogan
that had been propagated for decades in the GDR ("To learn from the Soviet Union means to be sure of victory") was no longer valid. Instead, the
SED leadership played for time, in the expectation that the reformist leader
in the Kremlin would run into trouble with his ambitious plans and would be
removed by the orthodox faction in the Soviet party leadership. Until that
happy day came, it was believed that the bacillus of freedom could be kept
away from GDR citizens by forbidding Soviet films and magazines ("*Sputnik*") and by extremely selective reporting of the speeches made by Soviet
politicians. In the censored media of the GDR, but also by the deliberate
spreading of false rumours, Gorbachev's course was presented as likely to lead to such everyday disasters as the disappearance of meat from butchers'
shops. The Berlin party boss of the time, Günter Schabowski, later revealed
how these tactics were employed. Yet all this was grist to the mill of the
opposition, who no longer subscribed to the stereotyped thought patterns
ordered by the state; moreover it was also ammunition for certain elements
in the SED itself who were keen to hitch their wagons to the Moscow star.

While Honecker believed himself to be at the summit of his power at the
end of the eighties, the foundation of that power was daily crumbling. The
economic plight of the GDR and the reform policies of Gorbachev were subsequently revealed as the driving forces behind the collapse of Communism
in East Germany, even though this was certainly not Gorbachev's original
intention. He wanted to bring about economic reforms, not start a revolution.

THE SOVIET EMPIRE IN DECLINE

The gigantic Soviet military sector had for years overstretched the economic capacities of the Soviet Union. In the 1980's, the living standard of the
population sank ever more precipitately. There were shortages of everything: even the supply of staple foods was not always guaranteed. The health
system was on its knees, the destruction of the environment was catastrophic and the technological backwardness of Russian industry compared to the
Western industrial states was increasing exponentially. It was therefore the
economic problems of the Soviet Union which stimulated Gorbachev, when
he came to power in 1985, not only to introduce political reforms in his own
country, but also to reform the relations between the Soviet Union and its

Communist allies in the Warsaw Pact. He certainly did not want to over-throw Socialism in Eastern Europe; instead he hoped to improve its performance, stem its years of under-achievement and modernise the Soviet economy in order not to miss the boat leaving for the 21st century. "Everything is rotten. There must be radical change" he is reported as saying to his long-standing friend, the Georgian party boss, Eduard Shevardnadze, when the latter visited him in the Crimea in 1984. All the same, he did not wish to abolish the monopoly of power held by the Communist Party.

Because the overstretched empire threatened to suffocate as a result of its "hermetic sealing", the new Party leader first set about removing the "foreign policy overload" (Klaus Hildebrand). The rejection of the Soviet Union's imperialistic claims that is linked to Gorbachev's name had in fact begun much earlier, as has recently been revealed from newly available Soviet sources. Contemporaries could not of course realise this was happening. For them, the change in relations with the outside world began with Gorbachev, which is true insofar as he put into action energetically what his predecessors had already been forced to contemplate.

THE BREZHNEV DOCTRINE LOSES ITS FORCE

There had been signs of the exhaustion of the Soviet Union's global strategy from the beginning of the 1980's, when it became apparent that the super-power was increasingly unable to finance the maintenance of its empire. From the economic and political points of view, the alliance with the East Bloc states was becoming ever more of a burden for the Moscow centre.

In 1968, the Soviet leadership had not hesitated to suppress the "Prague Spring" and to remove the reform Communists from power in Czechoslovakia. At that time, the doctrine that everybody knew dictated the reality of Soviet hegemony was given specific verbal expression: Moscow reserved the right to intervene with troops "if internal or external forces hostile to Socialism attempted to deflect the development of a Socialist land and to restore capitalist conditions". These words, known as the Brezhnev doctrine, made clear the limits on sovereignty and self-determination imposed on Socialist countries. For the SED, as also for the other Communist leaderships, it was a guarantee of their power. All the same, from the beginning of the 1980's they could no longer build on this power base. Indeed, when the question of possible military intervention in a Socialist country again arose in 1980–81, this time to suppress the Solidarity movement in Poland headed by the workers' chosen leader, Lech Wałęsa, the Moscow leadership under Brezhnev rejected the use of force and contented itself with threats. Out of anxiety for the consequences a successful Polish freedom movement might have for his own regime, Erich Honecker urged Gustav Husak (Czechoslovakia) and Todor Zhivkov (Bulgaria) to insist that the Moscow leadership should send Warsaw Pact troops into Poland. While the Soviet generals were keen to oblige, the Moscow Politbüro decided almost unanimously at the end of 1981 against a military intervention, even though the end of the Communist monopoly of power in Poland was visibly on the horizon.

An influential role in this decision was played by the KGB chief, Yuri Andropov, who succeeded Brezhnev one year later. The Moscow leadership had finally realised that Socialism could no longer be rescued by military means, and the man who first forced it to accept the implications of this insight was Andropov. A remark he made at the end of 1981 anticipates what Gorbachev, who was already a member of the Politbüro, would later translate into action: "We cannot risk such a step [i.e. intervention in Poland]...I don't know how events will turn out [there], but even if Poland falls under the control of Solidarity, then that's how it has to be... Our first priority is to attend to our own country... to the strengthening of the Soviet Union."

So began the retreat from the Brezhnev doctrine, which Gorbachev then publicly resiled from in the autumn of 1986 in a speech to Party leaders attending a meeting of the Council for Mutual Economic Assistance in Bucharest. Here he laid down the new Moscow line, the drift of which was that the assembled leaders were individually responsible for ensuring the consent of their own people; and he made it clear that they could no longer rely on the Soviet Union to keep them in power.

A decisive change of course in the Soviet policy towards its allies was again evident from Gorbachev's remarks during a state visit to Prague in April 1987, when he highlighted the "equal rights of determination of all Socialist lands" and emphasised the autonomy of every Communist party in regard to its ability to decide over "questions concerning the development of the country". Later, in July 1989, the Soviet reformer made similar remarks to the European Council in Strasbourg, emphasising the "sovereignty of all peoples" of Europe in deciding over their internal affairs. At this point, the leading clique around Honecker was forced to realise that the guarantee for their monopoly on power had gone once and for all. Despite this, the geriatric dictators were unable and unwilling to draw the obvious conclusions.

CHANGE OF COURSE IN SOVIET FOREIGN
AND SECURITY POLICY

The second revolutionary change of course engineered by Gorbachev from 1987 onwards was the ending of the confrontation between the world's two superpowers, something that was decisively to alter the political landscape in Europe and indeed in the world.

In order to head off the imminent economic collapse of his country, Gorbachev required economic assistance from the West and an extension of trade with the USA and the Federal Republic. At the same time, he realised that the Soviet Union's exorbitant expenditure on military forces and hardware had to be drastically reduced. Having formulated a new security concept, which envisaged for the first time real cuts in nuclear and conventional weapons, Gorbachev and his Foreign Minister, Eduard Shevardnadze, grasped the initiative. In November 1985, Gorbachev and US President Reagan agreed in Geneva on a five per cent reduction in nuclear weapons by the middle of the 1990's, whereby the Soviet side was naturally also concerned to try and forestall the American plan for a missile defence system in space (SDI).

A decisive breakthrough in Soviet–American disarmament negotiations was achieved finally during 1987, namely the removal of all middle-range missiles from Europe. This was agreed by the US President with the Soviet leader in Washington in 1987 at their third summit conference. Both countries began to retreat from nuclear deterrence as a policy weapon, a process that was complete by 1991.

THE NEW SOVIET MILITARY DOCTRINE: PUTTING AN
END TO THE STOCKPILING OF ARMAMENTS

Also in the course of 1987, the Soviet leadership declared itself ready to dismantle its huge military preponderance in conventional weapons in Europe. It was now deemed that a "defensive balance" between NATO and the Warsaw Pact was sufficient for security. This represented an absolutely revolutionary change in the longstanding security doctrine of Moscow, according to which the Soviet Union had to be armed massively in excess of any imaginable opponent. For the first time it was admitted that the Soviet military and defence establishment was costing the country a quarter of its GNP, which was three or four times as much as it cost the Americans to maintain their defence sector. Now it was decided to terminate this grotesque waste of economic resources. At a summit meeting in Moscow at the end of May and the beginning of June 1988, the members of the Warsaw Pact were informed of the details of the new military doctrine. At the end of the year, the Soviet leader announced before the United Nations in New York that the Soviet Union was undertaking a unilateral reduction of troops of half a million men over the coming two years, as well as other disarmament measures within the Warsaw Pact to take effect by 1990. In March 1989, negotiations between the two superpowers began in Vienna over the reduction of conventional weapons in Europe.

At his appearance in New York in December 1988, Gorbachev had finally renounced the use of force as an instrument of foreign policy and even spoke of the "freedom to choose" that should be valid for the capitalist, as for the socialist system. In view of the dramatic contemporary political changes taking place in Hungary and Poland, this remark amounted to a promise by the Soviet side that it would not intervene in favour of the Communist parties of those states. The Brezhnev Doctrine was finally laid to rest.

THE AMERICAN STRATEGY: FREEDOM FOR CENTRAL EUROPE

The American government under a newly elected President (from January 1989), George Bush, cautiously registered the signals from Gorbachev, without however taking at face value the fireworks of Soviet disarmament offers, initiatives and announcements. It was thought by no means certain that Gorbachev could hang onto power. The fact that influential politicians like the Moscow Party boss, Boris Yeltsin, and the Georgian Foreign Minister, Eduard Shevardnadze, stood on Gorbachev's side, did not yet mean that the conservative faction in the Politbüro would follow him through thick and thin. And indeed Gorbachev's position in his own country was steadily weakening, because it was impossible to reform the Soviet command economy so rapidly, and the novelty of free reporting (*Glasnost*) on ecological destruction, criminality and corruption unleashed a fear of chaos and anarchy in the population. In addition, the nationalities of the Soviet Union now began to rise against the Russian dominance of that union. The sense of crisis amongst the people grew, together with criticism of Gorbachev. By contrast, the latter enjoyed an ever higher reputation abroad, on account of his willingness to make foreign policy concessions.

The strategy adopted by the Americans under President Bush was that of subjecting Gorbachev's "new thinking" to a specific test. Such a test could most obviously be applied to the countries of East Central Europe. According to the US government, it was there that the Soviet leadership needed to show that it would turn its rhetoric into concrete action, if the USA was to be convinced. Moscow really did wish to pursue a completely new foreign policy. At a time when Gorbachev had risen in popular esteem in most Western European countries, and in particular in the Federal Republic, to the extent that he was one the most admired politicians on the world stage and many were gripped by a veritable "Gorbimania", Bush stood out against Moscow for the freedom and self-determination of the peoples of East Central Europe.

A free democratic East Central Europe was to be the pre-condition for a new East–West relationship, and not the consequence of it, as many politicians in Washington and even more in West Germany advocated. In numerous keynote speeches between April and May of 1989, both in the USA and in the Federal Republic, Bush developed this American position, which, as we now know, made a fundamental contribution to the ending of the division of Europe. The Soviet side were left in no doubt that words were not enough; economic assistance and disarmament would only be forthcoming when it allowed a democratic development in Europe. "The Soviet Union should understand that… a free, democratic East Central Europe, as we understand it, would be a threat to nobody and to no country. Such a development would lead to further improvement in East–West relations in every respect; it would contribute to disarmament, and strengthen political relations and trade in such a way that security and welfare in the whole of Europe would be promoted. There is no other way."(US President Bush on the 17th of April 1989 in Hamtrack, Michigan.) With these prerequisites fulfilled, America would welcome the Soviet Union into the community of nations: "The cold war began with the division of Europe. It can only end when Europe is no longer divided… As President I will continue to do everything within my power to help the closed societies of the East to open up. We are struggling for the self-determination of an undivided Germany and of the whole of East Central Europe." (Bush in Mainz on the 31st of May, 1989.)

POLAND AND HUNGARY AS TRAILBLAZERS FOR LIBERATION FROM THE COMMUNIST DICTATORSHIP

From the middle of 1989, there was no longer any doubt that the Soviet Union would keep its promise to its allies in the Warsaw Pact regarding the "freedom to choose". Poland and Hungary played the role of audacious trailblazers in the demolition of the hegemony of the Communist party in their countries.

In Poland, the writing had been on the wall since the breakthrough at the end of the 1970's when the independent trades union Solidarity (*Soli-darnośc*) was founded. With strikes that began in the Danzig shipyards, the workers' leader, Lech Wałęsa, and his co-fighters made the first breach in the Communist system of the East Bloc, and did so despite years of persecution by the authorities and even imprisonment. Solidarity survived the period of martial law in Poland by going underground. At the beginning of 1989, the Head of State, General Jaruzelski, removed the prohibition on the union. Talks concerning a peaceful transition followed, with the Communist Workers' Party sitting down to negotiate with representatives from Solidarity and other oppositional groupings, including the Catholic Church.

The ever louder calls for freedom and democracy among the Poles culminated in June 1989 with free elections for the Polish Parliament, at which the Communists suffered ignominious defeat. At this crucial moment, Gorbachev, against the wishes of some of his fellow leaders of the Warsaw Pact, intervened to persuade the foot-dragging Polish Communists to accept the result of the election. From these elections a coalition government emerged led by Wałęsa's adviser, the Catholic intellectual, Tadeusz Mazowiecki, who became Prime Minister. The Communists now held only the Ministries of the Interior, of Defence and of Transport. General Jaruzelski was elected President with the votes of the Solidarity MPs, after he had laid aside his office as Communist Party chief. After nearly half a century, the Polish people had opted for the market economy, the rule of law and freedom of conscience.

In Hungary, the most liberal of the East Bloc Communist regimes, the longstanding Communist leader, János Kádár, was obliged to resign under pressure from reformers in his own party. The new Hungarian party leadership under Károly Grósz likewise embraced economic and political reform and committed itself, with a new constitution, to the principles of parliamentary pluralism, the rule of law and the market economy. From the beginning of 1989, the Hungarian Communists accepted the founding of competing political parties. Hungary's turn to the West was linked by the rulers in Budapest to the promise to observe henceforth both the spirit and the letter of the UN Convention on Human Rights. From the beginning of May 1989, work began on the demolition of barbed wire and electronic security devices on the border with Austria, which was done without prior consultation with East Berlin. There the demolition was downplayed, although at least some of the members of the Politbüro realised that the Socialist camp was crumbling. The end of the Iron Curtain that had divided the continent since 1945 was clearly imminent.

WHAT WILL BECOME OF THE GDR?

The other East Bloc states showed a great deal less enthusiasm for reform. Above all, the GDR did its best, up to the autumn of 1989, to ignore the changed climate in world politics. The SED regime under Honecker cherished its image of "an island of orthodoxy in a sea of structural change involving the political, the economic and the ideological" (Manfred Görtemaker). That time had run out for it was not apparent to anybody in the middle of 1989, even if prominent western politicians and journalists later claimed that they already knew that the reunification of Germany would soon be on the agenda. In reality only a very few observers were able to interpret the crisis in Communist Germany correctly.

Symptomatic of the general myopia was the decision of the conservative broadsheet *Die Welt*, which for years had only printed the name of the GDR in inverted commas ("DDR"), to drop the relativising punctuation for the future. Reforms on the Soviet model in a continuingly Socialist GDR: anything more than this the imagination of western politicians was apparently unable to conceive. Even Helmut Kohl, who was to go down in history as the reunification chancellor, confessed that he could not have imagined in 1988 that Germany would be reunited in his lifetime. Only when the whole of the rest of Europe was united, according to the conventional wisdom, could the German problem also be solved. Until that time therefore, the task was to build bridges, make borders more porous, and encourage states to cooperate. This was the view of the Chancellor as set out in February 1989 at a celebration of the 40th anniversary of the founding of the Federal Republic of Germany.

Nevertheless, it would be wrong to use the benefit of hindsight, and in the knowledge of the happy outcome of this turbulent period of change, to claim that things had to turn out like this, simply because that is what actually happened; and it is unfair to accuse those who didn't see it coming as merely blind or prejudiced. In reality, nobody could precisely have foreseen whether the Soviet Union, notwithstanding its previously described public commitment to peace as enunciated by Gorbachev, would really give up the historic claims that it based on its victory over Hitler's Germany; and if it did give them up, nobody knew what price it might demand for doing so. Considerations of this nature were deemed at the time to be purely speculative, because the Honecker regime had so successfully managed to convey an aura of stability. The most that anyone could imagine in the summer of 1989, either in Bonn or among West Germans generally, was an injection of youth into the Politbüro, a modest reshuffle of important posts to promote so-called men of the future like Egon Krenz or Hans Modrow, all of them nevertheless long-serving politicians but supposedly flexible elements in the fossilised elite of the SED. Nor should one ignore the confidence of the Stasi leadership around Erich Mielke when judgements were being made about rising unrest among the East Germans. When the Secret Service chiefs asked him during a meeting at the end of August 1989 whether another "June 17th" was brewing, he gave them a reassuring answer. "It won't happen tomorrow, or ever; after all we're here to see that it doesn't."

SYMPTOMS OF CRISIS

The reality, however, was that the GDR had been in crisis for a long time. The SED, by sticking to its course of denying all reform, simply intensified the dissatisfaction in the population and drove even many SED members into a sort of resigned despair. Dissidents in their own ranks who permitted themselves critical questions were simply excluded, because they deviated from the Party line and apparently cast doubt on "the successes of our Socialist state" (in the words of the Control Commission of the SED in January 1989).

So that nobody in East Germany, seeing the events in Poland and Hungary, should have his hopes raised about the freedom to travel, Honecker also stated in January 1989 that the Wall would still be there in fifty or a hundred years, if the "reasons for it" had not been removed. The wall was essential "to protect our Republic from robbers".

With a parody of judicial procedure, and with constant threats, the authorities proceeded against all who articulated the public's vexation, or even demanded the right to leave the country. The Party leadership attempted to intimidate its critics in the opposition by applauding the bloody suppression of the student uprising in Peking by the Chinese leadership at the beginning of 1989. At the same time, they were at pains to demonstrate the entirely fictitious unanimity between Party and people by rigging the local elections in May 1989. Although the Party privately reckoned with a greater number of votes cast against the National Front than usual, the leadership announced that the results, which everybody for years had known in advance, showed an "overwhelming endorsement of the policies of the SED", this time with 98.84% of the vote in its favour on a supposed turnout of 98.77%. Naturally no one believed this. However, what was more significant was that this time courageous human rights supporters openly described the election as fraudulent, after comparing results that they had personally witnessed in individual constituencies with those officially announced for the same. By making objections and presenting information to the relevant authorities, they managed considerably to unsettle the regime. The secret service ordered that the objections should simply be ignored. Order and calm was to be restored. However, it was only the calm before the storm. The East German critics of the elections were given their say on western television and gathered regularly on Berlin's Alexanderplatz on each 7th of the month to protest the fraudulent elections. Although the Stasi intervened, new groups always appeared to prevent the authorities pretending that everything was normal and under control.

In vain the Party also tried to give the impression that youth was on its side by organising a "political Fata Morgana" (Günter Schabowski) in the form of a Whitsun rally of 750,000 members of the FDJ in East Berlin. Honecker acknowledged the ovations of the roaring crowd. Yet in the Party central office everyone knew that the people were totally unimpressed by such stage-managed shows of solidarity, and that the cynical youth put up with the "Hard pedalling for Hony" simply in order to get to Berlin.

From the SED leadership under Honecker, however, little more could be expected than such futile manoeuvrings. While millions of frustrated people inwardly rejected the GDR, the Party chief was boasting to West German politicians about the closeness of the SED to the population of East Germany. He claimed that the "problem of accommodation" had been "solved". He praised the GDR as the "tenth most productive country in the world", where, as the local elections had just demonstrated, Socialist democracy had been achieved, which meant "peace and security for the people". As late as the end of June 1989, the Party chief was enthusing over the stability of the GDR society, although he must surely have known better. Only weeks earlier Gerhard Schürer, the Head of the State Planning Commission, had revealed to the innermost circles of the SED leadership the dangerous level of debt, which threatened to sink the GDR, and had warned that drastic cuts in consumption would be required. However, only a few months before the 40th anniversary of the founding of the GDR, which was to be celebrated with much pomp, the Politbüro feared to do anything that would affect the living standard of the population. Honecker and his co-dictators were caught in a trap, but they refused to realise the gravity of the situation, because they were banking not only on financial assistance from the Federal Republic, but also on the downfall of Gorbachev.

BONN AND MOSCOW DRAW
CLOSER TOGETHER

During this period, politicians in the Federal Republic exercised restraint in their remarks about the East German rulers and were demonstrably uninterested in a destabilisation of the Honecker regime. A worst case scenario envisaged by politicians in Bonn was that the GDR rulers might embark on a "Chinese solution" to their problems, if provoked. For this reason the Federal Government concentrated on reconstituting German–Soviet relations, on the correct assumption that the internal German situation could only be markedly improved if the Soviet government gave its approval to change.

At first there seemed little likelihood of this. The Chancellor's first visit to Moscow took place only in October 1988, because a clumsy remark by Kohl comparing Communist propaganda to that of Goebbels had put difficulties in the way of contacts with the reformers in Moscow. Even when this matter had been resolved, the Soviet leader was for long unforthcoming and made every effort to ensure that the future of Germany was not up for grabs. It was only when Gorbachev visited the Federal Republic in June 1989, and was widely acclaimed everywhere that he appeared in the company of his wife, Raisa, did he and his Foreign Minister, Shevardnadze, intimate to Kohl and Genscher that they foresaw the end of the division of Germany. At any rate that was how both politicians saw matters in retrospect. This interpretation is leant weight by the joint communiqué they issued, by Soviet standards a sensational one, in which it was stated that all peoples and states had the right "to determine their fate freely". Relations on a personal level also improved considerably. Between the Chancellor and Gorbachev, as also between the two Foreign Ministers, a bond of mutual trust was established, which was to prove its value later in negotiations over the future of Germany. The partners in diplomacy found that they were all on the same wavelength. In confidential talks, Gorbachev indicated to Kohl that he was critical of Honecker and registered his satisfaction at Kohl's assurance that his government would do nothing to destabilise the GDR.

REFUGEES AND APPLICANTS
FOR EMIGRATION: THE PEOPLE VOTE WITH
THEIR FEET AGAINST THE SED

In the short term, however, it was not the rulers who were able to control developments in Germany, but the citizens themselves in East Germany, who took their fate in their hands by fleeing from the GDR, or used spectacular tactics to force the authorities to let them leave, and finally in ever greater numbers demonstrated in favour of reforms, and eventually even for the reunification of Germany. Bonn, like Moscow and Washington, reacted with caution, applying crisis management as and when the situation demanded (Karl-Rudolf Korte). Years later the Bonn Minister of Home Affairs at the time, Wolfgang Schäuble described the events of that time, which seemed too good to be believed: "We sat like children in front of the Christmas tree and could only run our eyes in wonder."

The feelings of claustrophobia and frustration caused by the Communist hegemony in East Germany, but also the evident economic ruin, made ever more GDR citizens determined to leave their country for good. Although the GDR was increasingly generous in issuing permits for travel to the Federal Republic, the number of applicants for "permanent departure" grew from a stream to an avalanche. Up to the end of June 1989, the Stasi had already registered 125,429 applicants, who ever more frequently overcame their fear and (as reported by the secret service) attempted to "blackmail" the organs of the State with "publicity seeking demonstrations".

HUNGARY OPENS HER BORDERS

Thus the avalanche of refugees from the summer of 1989 onwards was the real harbinger of the collapse of the GDR. This "voting with their feet" came to a head in May 1989 on the Hungarian–Austrian border and developed into a mass exodus in September 1989. During the holiday period, ever more GDR citizens, especially the young, took refuge in the Embassies of the Federal Republic in Budapest, Prague, Warsaw and East Berlin, in order to compel the authorities to let them leave. Because East Berlin, despite a request from the Hungarians, categorically refused to provide the Budapest refugees (now numbering several thousand) with exit permits, the Hungarian government decided to open the borders, partly out of humanitarian considerations, but with a political motive. Without economic assistance and credits from the West, in particular from the Federal Republic, the Hungarian Prime Minister Németh and the Foreign Minister, Horn, saw their country being sucked into a serious economic crisis. At the same time, they no longer saw any point in showing solidarity with the GDR. The Hungarian government's will to survive was stronger than their willingness to play the role of border guards for their nominal ally. At a top secret meeting with Chancellor Kohl and Foreign Minister Genscher near Bonn at the end of August, an agreement was reached over mutual cooperation: for Hungary that meant a rise in the Federal German credit standby of half a million DM.

On the 10th of September, Gyula Horn announced the historic decision to open the border; from midnight onwards over 6000 refugees left the Federal Republic's Budapest Embassy and travelled in Trabants, Wartburgs and buses over the border into Austria, and from there on to Bavaria. The pictures of joyful and shaken people went round the world. Thousands now began to follow them out of the GDR on a daily basis, since many feared that the government would somehow manage to close the Hungarian loophole. By the end of September, already 32,500 had gone.

EMBASSY REFUGEES

From the West German embassies in Prague and Warsaw another 14,000, mostly young, GDR citizens were able to leave for the West with their children at the end of September and beginning of October 1989, this time travelling in sealed trains of the Deutschen Reichsbahn and making a detour across GDR territory. The SED had made their consent to this form of departure dependent upon such a condition, which supposedly demonstrated the sovereignty of the GDR and its competence to decide over the refugees. As the train travelled through the GDR, there were constant attempts of would-be GDR refugees to get on it. At the Dresden railway station on the 4th of October, there were scenes reminiscent of civil war, when a huge detachment of security forces attacked the would-be refugees and other demonstrators. The GDR now experienced the greatest exit of its people since the building of the Wall in 1961. Honecker showed that he was completely out of touch: after an absence of several weeks through illness, he marked his return to his duties by adding his comment to a characteristically calumnious commentary in *Neues Deutschland*, remarking smugly that "one should weep no tears at the departure of the refugees".

THE CIVIL RIGHTS MOVEMENT IS FORMED

The mass exit of GDR citizens acted as a catalyst to the civil rights movement, which was now spreading all over the country. There were ever more frequent mass protests in East German cities, the most significant being the Monday demonstrations in Leipzig after the weekly prayers for peace in the Nikolaikirche. The possibility of flight or emigration now became a means to put pressure on and threaten the Party leadership, from which reforms were demanded. To the protests of the would-be refugees, shouting "We want out!" was added the defiant chant of "We're staying here!" Encouraged by these actions, the opposition (that had hitherto met only privately or under the protective cloak of the church) went public and founded new organisations such as *"das Neue Forum"*, *"Demokratie Jetzt"* (Democracy Now), and *"Demokratische Aufbruch"* (Democratic Awakening), as well as a Social Democratic Party (SDP), this last an unheard of event in a country where, for four decades, the ruling Party had violently suppressed any form of political pluralism. The various organisations mentioned above were committed to a democratic renewal of the GDR, while the Social Democrats wanted a parliamentary democracy. All of them demanded free elections, respect for human rights and the removal of the Communists' monopoly on power. Reunification was not one of their preoccupations. In vain the SED tried to muzzle the courageous spokesmen and spokeswomen of these groups, such as Bärbel Bohley, Jens Reich, Martin Gutzeit, Markus Meckel, Ulrike Poppe, Wolfgang Ullmann, Rainer Eppelmann, Friedrich Schorlemmer or Konrad Weiss, and many others, hoping to intimidate them, and to infiltrate the movements with Stasi spies (IMs) in order to manipulate their further development. However, all this was to no avail. These opposition groups became the pacemakers of the peaceful revolution in the GDR. Their supporters and speakers displayed unusual civil courage, since the dictators still held all the power of a police state in their hands.

In retrospect it should not be forgotten that the East German civil rights movement was actively supported by only relatively few women and men (a hard core of a few hundred with up to 3000 sympathisers), whose courage was of great benefit to many others and articulated the protests that many wanted to hear. That this minority was able to mobilise so many normal citizens was due to the strategic sophistication of the protagonists. They set store by moderation in their public demands, did not call for the overthrow of Socialism, but propagated theoretically unexceptionable slogans such as "We are the people" and sang the words of the Communist International that urged all to "...fight for human rights". The ruling powers thus found it extremely difficult to make a plausible case for their being simply criminals or counter-revolutionaries.

CELEBRATION OF THE STATE AND PERSECUTION OF DEMONSTRATORS

In this tense situation, that for many brought hope and fears in equal measure, with the question of how the dictatorship might react to its ever greater loss of authority increasingly on people's minds, the Communist Party celebrated the 40th anniversary of the founding of the GDR.

As it turned out, this was to be the last pompous show of self-praise by the Communist dictators in East Germany. In the days leading up to the celebrations, the People's Police and the security services brutally attacked demonstrators in many cities of the GDR and temporarily arrested several thousand of them. Then the geriatric professional revolutionaries of the Politbüro celebrated their police state on the 6th and 7th of October with mass torch-bearing parades, flag-waving and fanfares. The most prominent guest of honour at this grotesque show, Mikhail Gorbachev, could hardly fail to notice that his emphatic warning to set in motion reforms—"When we hang back, life punishes us immediately... If the Party does not react to life, it is condemned"—had fallen on deaf ears as far as the East German comrades, and particularly Honecker, were concerned. He also had no difficulty in interpreting the spontaneous shouts of East German demonstrators: "Gorbi, help us!" As soon as the TV cameras from abroad had finished their transmission, the security forces violently dispersed a demonstration of several thousand people in Berlin. In the following days police units brutally attacked demonstrators and arrested 3500 of them. Many subsequently had to endure chicanery and degrading treatment by the police.

MASS PROTEST AND THE VICTORY OF THE PEACEFUL REVOLUTION IN LEIPZIG

All these attempts by the regime to intimidate its opponents were no longer effective. Despite their fear, ever larger numbers of people took to the streets. They were fully aware that they thereby risked injury, perhaps even death. But the demonstrations did not cease and indeed developed into a nationwide mass protest.

The decisive breakthrough of the peaceful revolution in East Germany occurred on the 9th of October in Leipzig. The forces of the state capitulated in the face of 70,000 demonstrators, allowed the peaceful crowd to continue, and withdrew its highly armed units. That this was possible is owed to the prudent behaviour of negotiators on the spot, who urged everyone to avoid violence, and also to the political manoeuvring of Egon Krenz, who was already planning to depose Honecker. However, there was also a fortuitous element in all this, because the chain of command from the Politbüro to the security services no longer functioned perfectly. Following the happy outcome of this standoff between the regime and the citizens, there were of course many who were anxious to claim the credit for it in retrospect.

THE FALL OF HONECKER

Honecker remained uncomprehending until the bitter end and even wanted to send tanks against the demonstrators. However, he was no longer in control of events. The group around his crown prince, Krenz (Stasi boss Mielke, Prime Minister Stoph, the Berlin SED boss Schabowski and a few others) had already decided that he must go. Moscow raised no objection. Against the fierce resistance of Honecker, the Politbüro changed to a more conciliatory tone in a public declaration and for the first time spoke of necessary renewal, and of the fact that Socialism needed the support of all. The use of weapons during the upcoming Monday demonstration in Leipzig on the 16th of October was expressly forbidden. The demonstration went off peacefully. 150,000 demonstrators now promulgated the image of Leipzig as "a city of heroes" in the world at large. The people had lost their fear and over the next few weeks took to the streets in hundreds of thousands all over the GDR. On the 18th of October, Krenz and his co-conspirators compelled Honecker to resign in a palace revolution; in addition, the "dictator for economics", Günter Mittag, and the head of propaganda, Hermann, were obliged to take their hats. Egon Krenz took over from Honecker, his confirmation by the Central Committee being no more than a formality.

REACTION IN BONN: KRENZ IS
VIEWED AS A REFORMER

In Bonn the change at the top of the SED was viewed with a certain amount of relief. Perhaps there was still a chance for reform in the GDR. However, Chancellor Kohl, in contrast to prominent Social Democrats like the Mayor of Berlin, Walter Momper, had no illusions that even a somewhat modified GDR would earn a place among the free nations of Europe.

Although the new Party chief and President of the State Council, Krenz, attempted to set up direct contact with Kohl, it was soon apparent that he had made a total misappreciation of the situation. A man who was regarded in Bonn as a hardliner and ideologue of the kind typical of the dictatorship's functionaries was in truth not really committed to reform. He held strictly to the SED's claim of monopoly on leadership, while at the same time calculating that the Federal Republic would throw him a lifeline in the form of financial assistance. The "change" that he proclaimed merely implied a modernised Socialist GDR, which in reality held no attraction for ever larger numbers of citizens.

That Krenz also was not Gorbachev's man was something that Kohl inferred from a telephone conversation with the reformer in Moscow. The Federal Republic therefore now declared that it was only willing to provide economic assistance under certain conditions, namely that the SED set in hand genuine reforms. Mere declarations would not suffice. Thus Kohl demanded unequivocally, in his first telephone conversation with Krenz, a further easing of the right to travel, and an amnesty for political prisoners; he repeated that there would be no recognition by his government of a separate GDR citizenship. The Chancellor was not prepared to make any cosmetising agreement with a party that still maintained its claim on the monopoly of power. Kohl's influential negotiators, the Minister of Home Affairs, Schäuble and the Minister in the Chancellor's Office, Seiter, made this abundantly clear in a series of confidential talks with East Berlin's chief emissary, Alexander Schalck-Golodkowski. The latter indicated how desperate the economic situation of the GDR actually was and only a few days before the wall fell was angling for a credit of ten billion DM. Schäuble reacted to this by demanding as a precondition of any negotiations the legitimisation of the oppositional groups. In order to avoid national bankruptcy with the help of credits from Bonn, Krenz persuaded the Politbüro to legalise the *Neue Forum* on the 8th of November. He concealed from the comrades the fact that this was a demand of the Federal Republic and instead implied that this was the wish of Gorbachev.

KOHL'S TACTIC: AVOID POURING OIL ON FIRE

For his part, Kohl continued to pursue the policy he had followed for months of showing great verbal restraint, in order that the demonstrators in the GDR should not be provoked into any imprudent action against the Soviet troops in their country, and also to avoid stimulating the flood of refugees; but above all, not to awaken any mistrust in the West regarding the solidarity of the Federal Republic with the western alliance. While the Federal Republic, with good reason, adopted only the role of spectator as events unfolded in the GDR, she was certainly a catalyst for change in Poland and Hungary as they adopted reform, all the while continuing to reassure her western partners that she would remain reliable and predictable in terms of policy, and would continue to accelerate the integration of Western Europe. West Germany's response to the reforms in Eastern Europe, and to the prospect of the reunification of Germany now being openly discussed in the foreign press, remained her commitment to Europe, as Kohl reassured the French president Mitterand in Bonn at the beginning of November. Only in a united Europe was the reunification of Germany imaginable: on this both politicians were agreed. Kohl particularly stressed the necessity of not losing any more time in bringing about the economic and monetary union of Europe in the West, precisely in view of the ongoing turbulence in Eastern Europe

POWER LIES WITH THE PEOPLE IN THE STREETS

The inhabitants of the GDR showed themselves little impressed by the change of personnel in the SED leadership and Krenz's vague promises. They easily saw through the tactic of attempting to gain time, in order to bring the population to heel thereafter. The SED had lost its credibility and instinctively more and more GDR citizens felt they now had a chance to change the system itself. The Monday demonstrations in Leipzig regularly attracted hundreds of thousands of people onto the streets. On the 4th of November, almost a million people protested on Berlin's Alexanderplatz against the "SED bosses", against the Stasi, and in favour of the freedom to travel and democracy. Mielke's secret service in Berlin's Normannenstrasse was by now preparing for the worst, expecting even that the headquarters of the hated Stasi would be stormed or an attempt made to break through the border at the Brandenburg Gate. In case this should occur, a hot line was instituted to Moscow, as well as permanent direct ones to the Soviet army in Wünsdorf and to the KGB branch in Karlshorst. On that 4th of November, Krenz, Stoph, Mielke and Defence Minister Kessler sat in the office of the Minister of the Interior, Dickel, and tensely followed the events outside on Alexanderplatz over a TV monitor. However, everything passed off peacefully, as millions of TV viewers were able to witness. The demonstrators applauded speakers such as the writer Stefan Heym, when he said: "It is as if a window has been half opened, after all the years of stagnation, all the years of hollowness and fustiness, of empty phrase-making and bureaucratic caprice." At the same time they simply booed off the podium weather vanes like Günter Schabowski ("We are indefatigable in our capacity to learn") or representatives of the old regime like the ex-head of espionage, Markus Wolf.

MASS EXODUS AND POLITICAL RESIGNATIONS

The mass exodus from the GDR immediately continued as soon as the East German authorities re-opened the border with Czechoslovakia on the 1st of November. Almost 50,000 people left their country by this route in the first weeks of November. Under the double pressure of this exodus and of the protests, all the 44 ministers of the government resigned on the 7th of November, and one day later the whole Politbüro as well, a unique occurrence in the history of Communist parties. By choosing the longstanding Dresden Party chief, Hans Modrow, as his Prime Minister, a man deemed even by observers in the Federal Republic to be honest and a genuine reformer, Krenz hoped to plug the gaps in his own credibility. However, even before Modrow was officially elected by the *Volkskammer* (People's Assembly) on the 13th of November, the new government's options had already radically altered.

The people were no longer prepared to hear half-hearted promises of reform or be content with politicians' resignations, which now came also from the ranks of the so-called "block parties" loyal to the SED. The number of refugees continued to rise and the regime had clearly forfeited its credibility. People believed the SED to be capable of anything and everything, and feared that it would once again seal off the refugee route across Czechoslovakia. A bill for reform of the right to travel published on the 6th of November still breathed the spirit of the authoritarian and incompetent totalitarian state, and immediately hundreds of thousands openly campaigned against it.

The citizens, for so long treated as subjects, now demanded no less than their freedom to travel wherever and whenever and however often they wished. Appeals to remain in the country and to participate in the building of a "truly democratic society", which the writer Christa Wolf delivered on the 8th of November on GDR television in the name also of civil rights campaigners like Bärbel Bohley, no longer had any effect. The number of refugees continued to rise. On the 8th and 9th of November alone, 110,000 East Germans left for the West via Czechoslovakia. The Prague government demanded that East Berlin should immediately halt the refugee wave, or else it would close the border. The reason for this was that the Czech Communists feared that their own population would be infected by this stampede to freedom.

The Politbüro's Hand Is Forced:
A Decision Is Made on Freedom to Travel

In this situation, the Politbüro decided to bring forward the "permanent permission for travel" (without, therefore, the need for a detour via third counties) that it had anyway planned for December. In East Berlin it was calculated that the discontented and the agitators should rapidly be able to leave the country; then peace and calm would return amongst those who remained. Gorbachev was informed via the Soviet ambassador, Kotschenmassov, and on the morning of the 9th of November, Moscow signalled agreement.

In the Ministry of the Interior four experts, two of them Stasi officers, drafted an appropriate order allowing "private travel abroad without preconditions", whereby they actually exceeded their brief and made no distinction between visits abroad and permanent resettlement; all that was now required was a visa (available at short notice) and a passport. Only about four million citizens possessed a passport; all the rest, (and this was the calculation) would have to wait several weeks before they received one, so that not all GDR citizens would be able to cross the border at the same time. Krenz evidently did not realise that the hastily conceived measures went beyond what Moscow had approved, besides which it infringed the rights of the four victor powers in Berlin in the absence of their approval being sought.

At midday, Egon Krenz informed all the Politbüro members attending this meeting of the Central Committee of the new measure regarding travel rights, which was thereupon approved. Later he brought it before a plenary session of the Central Committee and subsequently planned to give Günter Schabowski, the press spokesman of the new Politbüro (who was not present at the plenary session), the two pages of text to be made public at press conference in the early evening. Krenz hoped that the situation in the GDR would immediately calm down, as soon as media had reported on the new measure, thus allowing freedom of movement to be introduced in an orderly manner.

MISTAKEN INFORMATION AND
ITS CONSEQUENCES

Schabowski did not know the precise contents of the order and also (on his own admission) failed to read it on his way into the International Press Centre. Above all he was unaware that the Ministerial Council had not as yet made any formal decision, and as a result the border guards had also not yet been informed. In fact it was only towards the end of his press conference towards 7 p.m. that he began almost casually to speak about the new order, whereby he made a mistake with fateful consequences. In answer to a journalist who inquired when the order would come into force, he appeared to show some irritation and after rapidly scanning the text, answered "At once, without delay." This was not actually in the text. But now there was a statement of a member of the Politbüro on the record concerning the "immediate" freedom to travel in the world, and the western media made sensational headlines out of it. At 8 p.m. the ARD led with the news that "the GDR is opening the border" and a little later the first few hundred of what were to be thousands of people streamed towards the border in East Berlin.

THE FALL OF THE WALL AND THE
OPENING OF THE BORDER

In Bonn, the Bundestag was debating a law on subventions for associations, involving such important questions as the tax free limit for directors of training, when the Minister from the Chancellor's Office, Seiters, made a short statement giving the sensational news. The MPs spontaneously broke into the third verse of the National Anthem, although at this point in time, the Wall was still closed in Berlin. The news flashes from the agencies were ahead of events. In the end, that was of no consequence. The avalanche had been set on its way and a slip of the tongue had had historic consequences: after a few hours it became clear that a plan devised only eight days earlier by Krenz in the strictest secrecy, and in collaboration with the top economists around Gerhard Schürer, was now so much waste paper. The plan had been that the West should supply massive credits to the GDR, which in return would open up the Wall. But now the "only remaining credible collateral of the GDR" (Rainer M. Leppard) had lost its value.

Since most of the top SED politicians were in continuous session in the Central Committee until late in the evening, the first they knew about all this was when it was realised that many of East Berlin's streets were jammed with Trabants on their way to the border. The Party, the government and the military were completely overwhelmed by events.

Under pressure from the sheer mass of people, the Stasi border guards, who had no clear orders and were thus left to cope alone, opened the border barriers. Shortly after midnight all the crossing points were opened, and all the control stations around Berlin and between the GDR and the Federal Republic could now be passed.

The Wall was brought down, but quite unspectacularly, even, one might say, inadvertently. In cars and on foot tens of thousands of people pressed across the border to West Berlin, still dazed with joy and disbelief: "It's crazy!" was the phrase on everybody's lips. In a mood of popular rejoicing, they celebrated this historic moment, together with many thousand West Berliners. Jubilant young people hopped on top of the wall at the Brandenburg Gate. They simply ignored the shouted commands of the border guards that they should come down. "Wall woodpeckers" worked on the "anti-Fascist protection barrier" with chisels and sledgehammers. Later, most people returned to East Berlin, as if their excursion had been the most normal thing in the world. Even today it is not absolutely clear whether the Party leadership considered taking military action over the next few days. At any rate, units of the National People's Army stationed near Berlin were put on the highest alert for two days, but were never deployed. The fall of the Wall was something that could not be reversed: in the first few weeks thereafter, nine million GDR Germans visited West Berlin and the Federal Republic.

CAUTION IN THE EAST AND THE WEST

After the fall of the Wall, two strands of development ran concurrently, but influencing each other politically: domestically the SED tried desperately to preserve its core position by signalling willingness to reform, while the civil rights movement fought for participation in power and for the democratisation of the GDR. On the intra-German level, the Federal Republic sought to gain influence over the reform process in the GDR and to set out the course for an eventual political and economic unification. At international level, the four former victorious powers embarked on a long process of consultation to fix their attitude to the new issues on the agenda regarding Germany. Eventually they came to an agreement with the Federal Republic and a now democratically legitimised GDR on a joint concept for reunification.

For those in government in the East and the West and their numerous advisers, the opening of the Berlin Wall was no less of a surprise than it was for the Germans themselves. Chancellor Kohl was on a state visit to Poland when he received the dramatic news from Bonn on the 9th of November. "That can't be so, that is incredible!" was his first comment, quickly followed by the decision to break his visit to Warsaw and, on the following day, to speak at two rallies in West Berlin. Willy Brandt too, the long-serving former Mayor of Berlin and architect of the policy of negotiation with the East (*Ostpolitik*) in the seventies, flew to Berlin on the 10th of November, to see events at first hand. He summed up his feelings in a succinct and subsequently much quoted observation: "Now what belongs together is growing together."

Kohl reached Berlin via a detour, because he was not allowed to overfly Berlin in a military aeroplane of the Federal Republic. In Hannover he climbed aboard an American machine, organised for him by the US Ambassador to Bonn, Walters, and eventually landed at the scene of events in the late afternoon. At a rally in front of the Schöneberg *Rathaus* (Town Hall), Kohl was careful to avoid nationalistic slogans. Having in mind the unpredictable consequences of possible attacks on Soviet symbols or on the troops of the Soviet army in the GDR, he exhorted the Berliners to remain cautious and to act prudently. This was also his public answer to a personal message that Gorbachev had sent both to him and the other western heads of government shortly before, in which he warned against action deliberately aimed at destabilising the GDR. Such action was indeed not contemplated either by the West German government or by the other allies, as Chancellor Kohl expressly assured the Soviet leader a little while later.

That the removal of the Wall, the symbol of the division of Germany and of the whole continent, was accomplished so peacefully was due to the restrained and coolly calculated reaction of Gorbachev, who pursued a policy of adaptation to events and did not allow himself to be diverted either by the hotheads in the Soviet leadership or those in the SED. On the 1st of November he had already made it clear to Krenz in Moscow that all measures to liberalise border passage to and from the GDR were to be discussed with him and were to be matched by corresponding concessions from the Federal Government. The events of the 9th of November in the GDR went far beyond that. In retrospect (1999), Gorbachev described the situation at the time as follows: "In the autumn of 1989 the situation in East Germany was really explosive. In a territory in the grip of unrest, where the largest units of Soviet military forces were stationed, the smallest provocation could have led to the spilling of blood and to uncontrollable consequences. And provocations were certainly on the cards: some influential representatives of certain circles in the USSR, as also in the GDR, demanded that order should be restored." Yet Gorbachev and his closest advisers decided to praise the courageous step taken by the SED leadership and thereby to accept that the wall was a thing of the past. However neither he, nor the other actors on the diplomatic stage, remotely conceived at the time that only one year later the GDR would no longer exist.

CHRONOLOGY

1988

7–9 January 1988   Honecker makes a state visit to France.

17 January 1988   During the official celebrations marking the 69th anniversary of Karl Liebknecht and Rosa Luxemburg's deaths, 120 civil rights activists are arrested; some of them are subsequently expelled to the Federal Republic, including the film director, Freya Klier, and the songwriter, Stephen Krawczyk; they had unrolled a banner bearing a quotation from Rosa Luxemburg: "Freedom is always the freedom of those who think differently."

29 January 1988   The Lutheran Church holds a service of intercession for arrested civil rights campaigners; over the following days, many services of solidarity with the activists are held in towns right across the GDR.

17 February 1988	Werner Jarowinsky, a member of the Politbüro, delivers an ultimatum to the Chairman of the Alliance of Lutheran Churches, Bishop Leich, whereby the church is to cease its support for opposition groups and for those demanding the right to leave the GDR.
15 May 1988	Soviet troops withdraw from Afghanistan.
18 May 1988	In the magazine *Literaturnaja Gazeta*, V. Daschitschev, an historian and adviser to the Foreign Minister, Eduard Shevardnadze, describes the Berlin Wall as a relic of the Cold War, which should be done away with. The GDR bans him from visiting the country thereafter.
29 May–2 June 1988	Fourth summit meeting between US President Reagan and the Soviet leader, Mikhail Gorbachev, in Moscow. Exchange of the ratification documents of the INF Treaty concerning the reduction of middle range missiles in Europe.
15 August 1988	The GDR and the European Community establish official diplomatic and political relations.
24–27 October 1988	Chancellor Kohl makes a state visit to Moscow. He and Gorbachev agree to end the "ice age" in German–Soviet relations.
8 November 1988	The Republican George Bush is elected 41st President of the USA. On the 20th January 1989 he is sworn in.
18 November 1988	The soviet magazine *Sputnik* is banned in the GDR.
7 December 1988	Gorbachev announces to the UN a plan for unilateral reduction in armaments by the Soviet Union.
31 December 1988	There are increasing signs of economic crisis and difficulties of supply in the GDR.

1989

15 January 1989	At the CSCE conference in Vienna, the Soviet Union votes with the Western states on human rights. Bulgaria, the GDR, Romania and Czechoslovakia vote against. Eduard Shevardnadze observes that "the Vienna meeting has smashed the Iron Curtain". The GDR commits itself, nevertheless, to guaranteeing the right of free travel. In Leipzig, several hundred demonstrators demand freedom of speech and freedom of assembly. 80 of them are arrested.

6 February 1989	Border guards of the GDR shoot 20-year-old Chris Gueffroy as he is attempting to flee to West Berlin. He is the last victim of the Wall. The guard who fired the fatal shot is later (1992) sentenced to three and a half years in prison. Another soldier will receive two years, suspended with probation.
6 March 1989	The cities of Bonn and Potsdam are twinned.
12 March 1989	600 people demonstrate in Leipzig for the freedom to leave the country.
3 April 1989	The shoot-to-kill order on the border is set aside.
5 April 1989	After tough negotiations, a "Round Table" is established in Poland, by means of which the Communist rulers can meet and negotiate with representatives of the opposition. Solidarity, the long banned trades union led by Lech Wałęsa, is once more permitted. It is announced that free elections are to be held in June.
13 April 1989	Cabinet reshuffle in Bonn. The new Finance Minister is Theo Waigel (CSU), and the new Minister of Home Affairs is Wolfgang Schäuble (CDU).
2 May 1989	Hungarian soldiers begin to dismantle the barbed wire on the border with Austria.
7 May 1989	Civil rights activists in the GDR denounce the massive electoral fraud by the government in the local elections.
23 May 1989	President von Weizsäcker is re-elected to a second term by the two houses of parliament (the *Bundesversammlung*—Federal Assembly).
31 May 1989	For the first time since 1982, the number of unemployed in the Federal Republic falls below two million.
4 June 1989	The movement for democracy in Peking is brutally suppressed. Several thousand are either killed or arrested. The People's Assembly of the GDR unanimously declares its support for the action of the Chinese authorities.
12–15 June 1989	On a state visit to Bonn, Mikhail Gorbachev is jubilantly received by the crowds. The two governments sign a joint declaration in which they recognise the right of self-determination for all peoples and their freedom to choose their political and social systems.

From July 1989	A growing wave of refugees from the GDR travels to Hungary, with the aim of reaching the West from there. Many would-be refugees gather in the embassies of the Federal Republic in East Berlin, Budapest and Prague.
7 July 1989	At a summit of the Warsaw Pact, Gorbachev rescinds the Brezhnev Doctrine limiting the sovereignty of Socialist states.
24 July 1989	A group named the Social Democratic Party of the GDR calls for the setting up of an ecologically oriented Social Democracy. In addition, church activists set up an oppositional body called Democratic Awakening (*Demokratischer Aufbruch*).
19 August 1989	Some 660 GDR vacationers seize the opportunity of a public festival at Sopron (Ödenburg—on the Hungarian–Austrian border) to flee to the West.
25 August 1989	A secret meeting takes place in Bonn between Hungarian Prime Minister Németh, (Hungarian) Foreign Minister Horn, Chancellor Kohl and (West German) Foreign Minister Genscher.
4 September 1989	Over 1000 people demonstrate in Leipzig in front of the Nikolaikirche, chanting the slogan: "We want to leave!"
10 September 1989	Civil rights activists in East Berlin found the *Neue Forum,* whose leading lights include Bärbel Bohley, Katja Havemann, Jens Reich. This is the first nationwide opposition group not operating under the protective mantle of the church. The GDR Ministry of the Interior refuses their application, delivered on the 19th of September, to be recognised as a citizens' association. The Ministry pronounces the movement to be hostile to the state. In the following weeks, thousands sign an appeal for dialogue within society at large concerning the crisis in the GDR.
11 September 1989	Hungary opens its border with Austria to let through all the waiting East German refugees, thereby breaking a 1969 agreement with the GDR. Within three days, 15,000 GDR citizens travel across Hungary and Austria to the Federal Republic. By the end of October, 50,000 have left. Their first accommodation is in tents and gymnasiums.
12 September 1989	The civil rights movement Democracy Now (*Demokratie Jetzt*) is founded in Berlin.
25 September 1989	For the first time since 1953, a large demonstration is held in Leipzig. Around 5,000 people demand democratic reforms and

chant the slogan "We're staying here!" Ever more people join the subsequent Monday demonstrations. On the 2nd of October there are more than 20,000. Many arrests are made.

30 September 1989   Foreign Minister Genscher and Chancellery Office Minister Seiters announce in the Prague embassy of the Federal Republic that the refugees occupying the embassy will be allowed to leave the GDR. About 6,000 refugees are transported in special sealed trains of the Reichsbahn to the Federal Republic. Honecker remarks: "We should shed no tears at their departure."

4 October 1989   Almost 10,000 more refugees leave Prague in special trains and travel through the GDR to the Federal Republic. In Dresden, around 3000 people attempt to storm the railway station in an attempt to get on the trains. There are violent clashes with the police.

7 October 1989   The 40th anniversary of the founding of the GDR is celebrated by the dictators. Guest of honour Mikhail Gorbachev tells the GDR leadership that it must institute reforms ("Those who arrive too late are punished by life"). In East Berlin and in other cities of the GDR, the police and the Stasi attack demonstrators. There are mass arrests. The Social Democratic Party of the GDR (for the time being simply referred to as SDP) is founded in the rectory at Schwante bei Oranienburg.

9 October 1989   Mass demonstration of around 70,000 people in Leipzig in favour of democratic reforms. Their slogan is "We are the people". For the first time the security services do not intervene. In Dresden, the first "Round Table" is formed in the GDR, by means of which opposition representatives negotiate with the SED.

10 October 1989   The Communist Party in Hungary is dissolved. Ten days later, the Hungarian constitution of 1949 is altered to encompass the requirements of a pluralistic democracy and the rule of law. Private ownership is now generally permitted. On the 23rd of October, the Republic of Hungary is proclaimed.

11 October 1989   The SED Politbüro announces that it is willing to engage in dialogue with the people.

18 October 1989   Erich Honecker is compelled to resign by the Politbüro. Egon Krenz becomes the new General Secretary of the SED.

23 October 1989   300,000 demonstrate in Leipzig. There are further demonstrations in Berlin, Dresden, Eisenach, Greiz, Halle, Magdeburg, Schwerin, Stralsund and Zwickau.

| 28 October 1989 | Mass demonstration for freedom and democracy in Prague. |

1 November 1989 — The GDR again allows travel to Czechoslovakia without passports or visas. Thousands of GDR citizens again seek refuge in the Prague embassy of the Federal Republic.

4 November 1989 — Nearly one million people demonstrate on East Berlin's Alexanderplatz demanding political reform. The GDR allows citizens to leave for the Federal Republic via Czechoslovakia. Within a week, 62,000 people avail themselves of this possibility.

6 November 1989 — A draft law concerning the right to travel proposed by the GDR government, is criticised by the public as insufficient. In Bonn, Alexander Schalck-Golodkowski, on behalf of Egon Krenz, presents a request for credit lines worth billions of DM.

7 November 1989 — All members of the Stoph government resign.

8 November 1989 — All members of the Politbüro resign.

9 November 1989 — The Berlin Wall and other border crossings to the Federal Republic are opened. In the following days and weeks, millions of GDR citizens visit West Berlin and the Federal Republic.

13 November 1989 — Hans Modrow, longstanding First Secretary of the SED District Administration in Dresden, is elected by the People's Assembly to be (as it turns out) the last Prime Minister appointed by the SED in the GDR. In his government proclamation on the 17th of November, he puts forward a proposal for a treaty-based community of the two German states.

12. The Unanticipated Reunification: The New Course for Germany and International Reaction to It, 1989–90

SCEPTICISM AND UNEASE IN PARIS AND LONDON

In the immediate aftermath of the opening of the Wall, the responsible politicians in the capitals of the West reacted with extreme reservation to this symbol-laden event. In London and Paris, but also in The Hague, Rome and elsewhere, the dominant preoccupation of the politicians and diplomats was that debates over border changes, or even over German reunification, could lead to a dangerous destabilisation of the European order, as well as hindering the democratisation process in East Central Europe and under-mining Gorbachev's authority. In particular the British Prime Minister, Margaret Thatcher, was not at all happy with the prospect that Germany might be reunited within the foreseeable future. She urgently warned the American President against giving the nod to reunification, and emphasised that the West must respect Gorbachev's wishes that the borders of the Warsaw Pact should be preserved. At the beginning of December, she even demanded that German reunification should be put on the back burner for ten to fifteen years. The French President, Mitterand, also indicated his unease at the prospect of a united Germany, which only seemed to him acceptable, though hardly desirable, in the context of a still closer European alliance. In any other event he thought that Germany would automatically become the dominant power in Europe.

All of a sudden, the old fears of the large and small nations of Europe that Germany could become too strong were again aroused. All neighbouring states had tacitly believed that the division of Germany had been a factor for stability in Europe for decades. The security structure that had existed hith-erto seemed to be put in question by the events in the GDR, at least in the event that the Federal Republic should give priority to German reunifi-cation, so that this goal should take precedence over its commitment to the alliance. In Paris and London it was hoped that, with the support of the American government, it would be possible to keep further developments in Germany under control by adhering to a halfway house formula, name-ly: "self-determination for the Germans, yes; reunification of the two states, perhaps later."

THE GERMANS AND AMERICANS WORK IN TANDEM

By contrast, President Bush and Foreign Minister Baker in the USA showed that they viewed the peaceful revolution in the GDR positively. However, they also emphasised the need for an orderly and gradual process of change in Germany. Above all, Bush and his advisers wanted to avoid pouring oil on fire by making demands or giving advice to Moscow in public, which might supply ammunition for the hard-line opposition to Gorbachev. On the other hand, the US President had accepted the principle of German reunification right from the beginning and was unimpressed by the anxious warnings emanating from West European governments. "Let the people in Germany decide this matter" was how Bush summed up his attitude in an interview with a foreign journalist at the end of November 1989.

The American strategy was to promote the end of Communist domination in East Central Europe in cooperation with Gorbachev, not by working against him, and without deliberately taking measures to speed up the process. Kohl too reassured the Soviet leader that his government would do everything necessary to prevent the GDR from dissolving into chaos; it would support political and economic reform, but with the proviso that free elections should be held in East Germany. Like Bush, he decisively rejected any limitation on the rights of all Germans to self-determination. In order to calm the French President, he repeatedly stressed the necessity of integrating the German issue into that of Europe as a whole. The Federal Republic would heed the interests of its neighbours and provide a motor for the intensification of European integration, inclusive of Germany. Notwithstanding these assurances, Mitterand unexpectedly announced at the end of November two hastily arranged meetings, one with Gorbachev in Kiev, and another with Modrow, to take place in the GDR in December.

INEFFECTIVE PROMISES OF REFORM

In November and December, however, things began to move with a momentum of their own in a way that neither the Western Foreign Ministers nor Bonn had foreseen. The inhabitants of the GDR wanted freedom and prosperity. Fewer and fewer people believed in an improved and democratic version of Socialism, of the type that Egon Krenz purported to promise them. Scaremongering by artists and writers long privileged by the regime (e.g. the rallying cry *"For our country"* raised on the 26th of November), in which the autonomy of a radically transformed GDR was proclaimed and the possible sell-out of [the country's] material and moral substance was conjured as the likely consequence of reunification, left most of the population unimpressed. The dream of Socialism had become a nightmare for millions who had experienced "real existing Socialism". Günter Kunert, a writer and former GDR citizen who had lived in the Federal Republic since 1979, expressed what many felt about such appeals: "The present demands for a renewal of the system by the zealous architects of the ruin [that the GDR had become] are seen by most people as a joke at the wrong time and the wrong place."

The vague proclamations of reform made by the new Prime Minister, Hans Modrow, and his suggestion of a treaty-based community to be formed out of the two German states, were also hardly likely to arouse the enthusiasm of the population for a renewed version of the GDR.

The people's mistrust was well founded. The dissolution of the hated Ministry of State Security proceeded at a snail's pace. At the same time, files were being destroyed and preparations made for a possible continuation of the fight against the enemy under a new aegis, the so-called Office for National Security. Thus, the first secret order of Mielke's successor, General Wolfgang Schwanitz, concerned the provisional continuation of all the hitherto valid instructions of the MfS (Ministry for State Security). The citizens of the GDR had no idea at that time that half of the new Modrow government anyway consisted of Unofficial Assistants (IMs) of the Stasi. Out of eleven members of the cabinet who came from the ranks of the block parties (the LDPD, the CDU, the NDPD and the Peasant Party, known popularly as *Blockflöten*, or recorders, i.e. those who piped the regime's tunes) seven had been or still were Stasi collaborators. Possibly in ignorance of the candidate's CV, Modrow appointed a State Secretary to the Ministerial Council (the central government body) who turned out to be a high-ranking officer in the special unit of the Secret Service (OibE).

THE SED HEGEMONY IN DECLINE:
MODROW AS ADMINISTRATOR IN BANKRUPTCY

No stabilisation of the situation in the GDR took place. The population was in upheaval and 2000 people were leaving the country daily. In November and December 176,650 people turned their backs on the GDR. At mass demonstrations in Leipzig, Halle, Chemnitz, Schwerin, East Berlin, Dresden, Cottbus and in smaller towns there were ever more frequent calls of *"We are one people"*.

Almost every day there were new reports of the abuse of power, of corruption, and of the secret luxury which the leading comrades of the state and the Party had enjoyed, arousing fury among the people and accelerating the crumbling of Party membership, which lost hundreds of thousands of members in just a few weeks. In numerous districts and regions the once all-powerful Party's First Secretaries were compelled to resign. The leaders of mass organisations like the FDGB (trades unions) and the FDJ (youth movement) lost their jobs. From the beginning of December, civil rights activists occupied the offices of the Stasi in Erfurt, Dresden, Leipzig and other regional centres, sealing their archives and founding committees to oversee the dissolution of the Secret Service, whose functionaries were nevertheless usually able to cover their traces to a remarkable degree. In the middle of January 1990, thousands of demonstrators stormed the Stasi headquarters in Berlin's Normannenstrasse; however, they were unable to penetrate many of the most important parts of the building, where the Stasi had stored the most explosive material. Even today it is unclear whether the Secret Service itself was still active here, manoeuvring to distract the attention of the furious crowds while functionaries went ahead with their plan to shred documents.

That the GDR's economy lay in ruins, and that the state was practically bankrupt was now known to virtually everybody. This problem was a constant topic of public discussion at the Round Tables that had been set up on the Polish model. Here the new political forces in the country, such as the *Neue Forum* and the East-SPD, together with other reformers and representatives of the SED and the block parties, negotiated under the chairmanship of church representatives, the aim being to prevent anarchy and violence. For the first time, the Communists sought to negotiate with an opposition that they had anathematised for decades. Now they were prepared to make concessions, if only for the sake of hanging on to power. However, their strategy did not work out as they had hoped. The new Prime Minister, who enjoyed the reputation of a reformer and had a hot line to Moscow, increasingly found himself in the role of the administrator of a once mighty concern that had lost its monopoly position and was facing bankruptcy.

At the beginning of December 1989, the People's Assembly removed the clause from the constitution that enshrined the leading role of the SED. In the same way, the militia (*Betriebskampfgruppen*) of the working classes, 400,000 men who were at the service of the SED, were dissolved; likewise the Politbüro and the Central Committee of the SED. Their Chairman, Egon Krenz, ended his brief tenure of office, losing all his functions as (SED) General Secretary, Chairman of the State Council and Chairman of the National Security Council. Hans Modrow's appointees took over his posts. Manfred Gerlach, the longstanding Chairman of the East German LDPD, who had never in his life uttered a single word of criticism of the SED dictatorship, became Chairman of the State Council and thus nominally the GDR's Head of State. In the middle of December, the once all-powerful monopoly party of state renamed itself SED-PDS (Party of Democratic Socialism). This name change was intended to indicate a willingness to reform and to demonstrate a break with the Stalinist past. However, the new party was not prepared to disgorge the SED's huge accumulation of property. Its Chairman was the lawyer, Gregor Gysi, who had earlier defended prominent civil rights activists, while simultaneously nurturing close relations with the Stasi.

Under pressure from mass protest, mass exodus to the Federal Republic and the imminent economic collapse of the GDR, Modrow and the SED-PDS declared themselves willing to accept the demands made at the Central Round Table in East Berlin and to bring forward the first free elections to the People's Assembly to the 18th of March 1990 (previously they had been planned for the 6th of May). At the beginning of February 1990, seven representatives of the civil rights movement entered Modrow's government as Ministers without Portfolio in an administration that Modrow characterised as a government of national responsibility. The representatives included Pastor Rainer Eppelmann, a long-time target of the Stasi. At this point, the spokesmen for civil society and the old parties still assumed that the GDR would last for a considerable length of time, albeit as a democratised state.

In reality, however, the course towards reunification had already long since been set. The vast majority in the GDR wanted that and the governments in Bonn, London, Paris, Washington and Moscow had prepared the way for it in a negotiating marathon that lasted over several months, and which ensured that the necessary conditions were achieved and agreements reached.

KOHL'S GRADUALIST PLAN TO
ACHIEVE REUNIFICATION

Chancellor Kohl grasped the initiative on the 28th of November 1989 with a ten-point programme for overcoming the division of Germany and Europe. This initiative was designed to prevent the burgeoning chaos in the GDR from getting further out of hand, and to win over the doubters in the ongoing international debate on the German question. In view of the contradictory signals coming out of Moscow, Paris and London, he thought it best to offer concrete suggestions, rather than simply react to events. A foreign policy adviser to President Bush later characterised this step as "policy made at the edge of the abyss" (Robert L. Hutchings), and praised the Chancellor's foresight, since Kohl thus prevented the British, French and Soviets from making tactical agreements to block reunification.

The plan, chiefly devised by Kohl's closest foreign policy adviser, Horst Teltschik, but with points of emphasis that were Kohl's own, was based on the assumption that the Federal Republic should cooperate with a democratically legitimised GDR under the rule of law in a treaty-based community of states. From this point onwards, an ever more closely integrated network of confederative structures should be developed between the two Germanies, with the aim of creating a federal order for the whole of territory. Kohl expressly integrated this gradualist plan for reunification, which he expounded before the Bundestag, into the pan-European process of coming together to strengthen European integration. ("The future architecture of Germany must fit into the future architecture of Europe as a whole.")

With this draft plan for a double strategy with regard to Germany's future, the inhabitants of the GDR should be given an encouraging perspective and Germany's neighbours should be calmed. In terms of domestic politics, Kohl wanted to secure some aces in the debate over the future of Germany, which had now become the central theme of the upcoming election campaign for the Bundestag in 1990. Deliberately he did not set a timetable. Kohl privately envisaged a time-scale of between five and ten years for the plan to be fulfilled.

REACTIONS AND APPRAISAL

Only the American President was to be informed of this plan in advance. Other governments privately criticised this move by Kohl, which had not been discussed with them; but they had no alternative recipe on offer that added anything to the widely perceived requirement that the process of uniting the two Germanies should not be rushed into.

Mitterand emphasised in talks with US President Bush that the German unification process and European development should run harmoniously. "It should proceed like horses in harness: if one horse moves at a different pace from the others, an accident occurs." Gorbachev in particular displayed irritation at Kohl's initiative, which he described as a great political nonsense. He deliberately laid stress on the continuing sovereign existence of the GDR as a member of the Warsaw Pact. ("There are two German states. History has so determined.") On the 9th of December, 1989, he declared to the Central Committee of the Communist Party of the Soviet Union: "We will not abandon the GDR"; on the other hand, he was simultaneously signalling to the Americans that Moscow would not intervene.

Nevertheless, disturbing reports from the GDR began to reach Washington, which suggested that a confrontation between the people and the military could not absolutely be ruled out. It was known that in Gera the Stasi officers had incited their units to armed resistance. The Soviet troops in the GDR were on full alert and the Soviets themselves warned the Americans that these units might be compelled to use force if the security situation ran out of control. After his resignation in 1991, Eduard Schevardnadze revealed that the opponents of himself and Gorbachev in the leadership had demanded that the tanks be sent in. At this moment the situation was certainly dangerous.

What was decisive for the German side was the positive reaction of the American government. At the beginning of December 1989, while attending the summit in Brussels of the 16 member states of NATO, Bush linked the German reunification process to the firm anchoring of Germany in NATO and the European Union, and also to the recognition of the Oder–Neisse border. As long these guarantees were forthcoming, he promised Kohl the full support of the USA.

December 1989 saw hectic diplomatic activity at international level. This included the Soviet–American summit at Malta, the NATO summit in Brussels, the European Community's summit in Strasbourg, the meeting of the ambassadors of the four victorious powers at the Control Council's headquarters in Berlin, Mitterand's trips to the Soviet Union and the GDR, Genscher's meeting with Gorbachev in Moscow, Thatcher's trip to see Bush at Camp David, and US Secretary Baker's visit to London, Berlin and Potsdam. The deliberations and negotiations ended up with practically all actors on the world stage recognising that the era of a divided Germany was coming to an end. However, it remained open when and how its demise should be finally sealed without disturbing the balance of power in Europe.

CALLS FOR UNIFICATION BECOME LOUDER

At first, the responsible politicians hoped to be able to steer developments in a cautious direction. However, both the Bonn and East Berlin governments, as well as the governments of the victorious powers, were soon forced to bow before the evident determination of a large majority of the East Germans, who wanted a united Germany as soon as possible.

The GDR was no longer capable of surviving economically. And by contrast to the pioneers of the peaceful revolution, a large part of the population were no longer to be satisfied simply with the offer of reforms. *"Germany! Germany!"* was the shouted slogan of hundreds of thousands at demonstrations in the streets of Leipzig and elsewhere. It was the same scene in Dresden when Chancellor Kohl arrived there on the 19th of December 1989 for his first talks with Prime Minister Modrow. Kohl was later to describe this visit to Dresden as being the "key experience on the road to unity", as far as he was concerned.

Modrow's candour regarding the desolate economic situation of the country, and the enthusiasm with which Kohl was received by tens of thousands of GDR citizens at a rally in front of the ruins of the Frauenkirche, made him realise that the regime in East Germany had no more mileage in it. Modrow asked for an immediate aid of 15 billion DM from the Federal Government, in order to stabilise the East German economy. Only when Bonn had made available such an "equalisation of financial burdens for 1990–91", did he see any possibility of introducing the market-oriented reforms that were demanded by the Federal Republic. The Federal Government's standpoint, however, was exactly the opposite of Modrow's: it wished to make the provision of comprehensive assistance dependent on irreversible economic and political reforms. Kohl showed that he had no interest in stabilising the Modrow government, since he did not believe it was really committed to reforms. To Modrow's irritation therefore, the Federal Government withdrew at the beginning of January 1990 from the originally planned negotiations over the details of a treaty-based community of states. Only after the elections to a new People's Assembly was Kohl prepared to enter into the appropriate agreements with a now democratically legitimised representation of the GDR. With this new strategy, Kohl deliberately accelerated the inner developments of the GDR, which could only lead to the final demolition of the lingering SED hegemony; and he saw himself as acting in accord with what the majority of the East Germans actually wanted.

THE STATE AND ECONOMY OF THE GDR
ON THE VERGE OF COLLAPSE

The fears of the population that the SED could recover its power led to a further wave of emigration in January and February 1990: some 50,000 mostly young and well qualified people went to the West. Modrow's government had no support amongst the population at large, and also no longer had any effective authority in the bureaucracy and in the factories. The state infrastructure began to crumble. Mayors and entire districts declared themselves independent of the central government and took decisions on their own account. Several firms began trading with each other exclusively in D-Marks. The municipal authorities of East Berlin requested the Senate of West Berlin to take over all the city's communal services, such as hospitals, transport, the police and rubbish collection. In a few cases, officers of the National People's Army applied to be commissioned in the *Bundeswehr* (Federal Armed Forces).

Modrow himself painted a grim picture of the internal situation of the GDR at the end of January 1990, both to the Chancellery Minister Seiters, and to the People's Assembly a little later. In view of the rapid crumbling of the state's authority, and also of constant strikes and the ever-present danger of clashes between police and citizens, he again applied for economic and financial assistance from the Federal Government to ward off the total collapse of the GDR. However, the Bonn government remained unforthcoming; it was clear that time had finally run out for Modrow.

THE SIGNALS FROM MOSCOW

Modrow made one last throw with an initiative that provided for the gradual establishment of German unity. At a meeting on the 30th January 1990, he obtained Gorbachev's approval for this. In principle, the Soviet leadership had reconciled itself to the fact that the reunification of Germany could no longer be avoided. By the end of January 1990, Gorbachev was already beginning to reckon with the withdrawal of Soviet troops from the GDR. However, Gorbachev's circle of advisers on the German question continued to disagree on a time-frame for events; above all they were divided on the issue as to which alliance Germany would belong to in future. Gorbachev himself seemed as yet undecided. He was still reluctant to let the GDR go its own way and be completely absorbed into the Federal Republic. On the other hand, there were repeated comments from him and other Soviet leaders at this time which made Bonn prick up its ears. Thus, shortly before his talks with Modrow in Moscow, Gorbachev declared to foreign journalists that "the unification of the Germans had in principle never been in doubt".

MODROW'S REUNIFICATION PLAN

Gorbachev raised no objection to Modrow's initiative, but privately thought it illusory. "What should the Federal Republic wish to have closer relations with?" was how he put it later. For Modrow had presented an unvarnished picture of the ineluctable decline of the GDR and himself had admitted that the majority of the population of the GDR wanted something different from what was on offer. On the other hand, he suggested to the Soviet leader that this rapid decline could be slowed by applying the rights vested in the four victorious powers in a way that would stabilise the situation. As Gorbachev later wrote (1999), it was not clear to him what the GDR Prime Minister actually meant by this, and he could not exclude the possibility that Modrow was hoping that, in the last resort, the Soviet Union would be ready, by means of armed intervention, to stop the powerful mass movement demanding reunification. For his Soviet interlocutor, these were all further indications that he could no longer bank on Modrow.

However, by the beginning of February 1990, having adopted the new slogan of *"Germany, one fatherland"*, Modrow appeared to have come round to Kohl's plan of November 1989, and now propagated the notion of a gradual unification of the two German states over several years, albeit only on the basis of neutrality for the new Germany.

Both government and opposition in Bonn immediately rejected the idea of neutrality, which would have meant giving up the Federal Republic's place in NATO. All the same, as soon became evident, long-standing differences between Kohl and his Foreign Minister Genscher kept cropping up on important details concerning a united Germany's membership of NATO. Genscher, for instance, considered that it would be possible not to integrate East Germany into NATO after reunification, but to give it a special status that would encourage the Soviets to approve unification. On another occasion he suggested the reconstitution of NATO into a pan-European system of collective security. These solutions no more appealed to Kohl than the concept of a neutral Germany. A little later Modrow weakened his neutrality proposal, not least because the imminent economic collapse of the GDR now had priority over all other considerations.

KOHL SEIZES THE INITIATIVE FOR A RAPID REUNIFICATION

More significant for the Federal Government than Modrow's last attempt to influence the further course of events in the German question were the surprisingly positive signals emanating from Moscow. Kohl now considered it possible that "the unification could indeed come about even more quickly than we had assumed up till now", as he put it to his cabinet on the 31st of January 1990. Three days later, he was confirmed in this conviction, and in his view of the dramatic situation in the GDR, after talking to Modrow at the annual international meeting of influential academics and politicians at Davos. Modrow again raised the question of 15 billion DM in credits, which the Federal Republic should make available, as well as food and textiles, so that his government should be able to muddle through from March to May, and in the absence of which anything could happen. Modrow even thought it possible that the DM could be made the currency of the GDR: in such a case lower wages and salaries would be payable in the GDR, to reflect its low productivity. Time pressed, as both heads of government were well aware. However, the Chancellor held the whip hand.

Kohl saw his chance for a new initiative in the reunification question. It seemed to him that there was now a window of opportunity in favour of the unification process, but how long it would remain open was anyone's guess. There were now enough auguries for success, however. The US government under George Bush and James Baker let it be known that they considered there was no alternative to the rapid reunification of Germany and indeed had come to the conclusion that the sooner this was achieved, the better. No less important was the appearance on the horizon of a change of course in Moscow on the reunification issue. In the meanwhile Gorbachev had invited Kohl to Moscow for the 10th of February 1990. The situation in the GDR was becoming ever more dangerous. The first free elections for the People's Assembly were imminent on the 18th March 1990, from which it was already widely assumed that the Social Democratic Party would emerge victorious. Kohl was now faced with a dual challenge, both in his capacity as the head of the government and in that of electoral campaigner: as an experienced politician with an exceptional instinct for power, he did not hesitate to act.

Kohl's Proposal for an Economic and Currency Union with the GDR

On the 6th of February 1990, and to the surprise of many, Kohl declared to the CDU/CSU parliamentary fraction his intention to enter immediately into negotiations with the GDR for an economic and currency union. The Deutschmark should be introduced into the GDR in tandem with the social market economy, and that as quickly as possible. Few MPs were prepared for the government's change of course, and indeed only a few ministers had been informed of it. The Economy Minister Haussmann (FDP) came out a day later with a strong case for a gradual adaptation of the GDR to the Federal Republic over the period of a year. However, Kohl had already secured the agreement for his initiative from the fraction heads of the governing parties. The cabinet passed a resolution the following day, stating that an offer of negotiations should be made to the Modrow government. The President of the German National Bank, Karl-Otto Pöhl, despite serious misgivings, withdrew his fundamental reservations regarding the rapid introduction of the Deutschmark in East Germany. Kohl had not even informed him in advance, let alone consulted with him. Pöhl felt that he had been logrolled and was to resign one year later. Nevertheless he loyally put into operation the decision of the government.

In the SPD opposition, a minority led by Oskar Lafontaine, the chancellor candidate for the upcoming Bundestag elections at the end of the year, opposed the government's course, pointing to the burden that a rapid reunification would lay upon the West Germans, and arguing instead for an intensification of European integration, which should take precedence over German unity. The majority of the SPD however, including the Party Chairman Hans-Jochen Vogel, saw no alternative to the government's policy, especially in view of the fact that prominent Social Democratic politicians with an interest in finance and the economy had gone public with a similar suggestion only shortly before. The small opposition party of the Greens, on the other hand, decisively rejected the Waigel/Kohl plan.

How Shall the Currency Union Be Brought About? Planning, Misgivings, Problems

Later on, critics were often to speak of Kohl's decision as a panic reaction in the face of the tidal wave of emigration coming out of the GDR. However, this is not borne out by the facts. The idea of a currency union with the GDR, or more precisely, the extension of the D-Mark's area of circulation to include the GDR, had been in the air since the fall of the Berlin Wall. As early as the middle of December 1989, the Minister of Home Affairs, Wolfgang Schäubel, had raised the proposal in the course of a discussion at the Office of the Chancellery. However, at this point in time, Kohl and his advisers considered the idea to be too audacious and anyway impossible to pursue because of foreign policy considerations. This was soon to change.

Unnoticed by the public at large, the Bonn Ministry of Finance under the leadership of Minister Theo Waigel had been working out the technicalities of an economic and currency union since the beginning of 1990.

Waigel's financial experts drew up a realistic picture of the complex problems involved in the transformation of a command economy into a market economy. For example, it was known that the economic value of exchange between the wealth of GDR citizens and that of the holders of Deutschmarks was at least a ratio of one to five, and therefore politically impossible to negotiate. How this question was to be solved remained at first open. The official rate of exchange between the DM and the GDR Mark was one to three, and on the free market, one to nine. For trading between the GDR and the Federal Republic, a rate of one to 4.4 was used. These, however, rep-

resented purely economic measurements, which could not be made politically acceptable to the East Germans. Although the majority was aware that
such real currency values represented the consequences of low productivity,
itself caused by forty years of a command economy, they would still have felt
themselves massively dispossessed. The experts in the Bonn Ministry of
Finance also worked out what proved to be a pretty realistic scenario regarding the insufficient competitiveness of the GDR economy. As a consequence
of introducing market discipline to the GDR's industry, they calculated with
1.4 million unemployed in the industrial sector, or some 40% of those cur-
rently employed. The yearly costs for supporting the unemployed was estimated to be 10 billion DM.

It was clear that the step by step concept, the gradual introduction of the
Federal German market economy with the introduction of the DM as the
crowning element in the process, conformed better to what the textbooks
said than did a "sudden death" solution, that is, the introduction of the market economy and the DM into the GDR on a specific day. For this reason,
the economic experts outside government circles were against a hasty implementation of economic and currency union and instead favoured a process
that would allow several years for adaptation.

In view of the danger of uncontrollable mass emigration of qualified
workers from the GDR to the Federal Republic—up to the summer of 1990
another 240,000 were recorded—Waigel and his advisers rejected all plans
for a gradual implementation and argued for an immediate dissolution of the
GDR Mark, to be replaced by the much coveted and respected currency of
West Germany.

A more gradual transformation to the market economy, one controlled by
the state, could only succeed if a customs barrier were to be erected between
East and West with comprehensive controls. Yet a new intra-German border
was politically unacceptable. This view was also shared by Kohl's advisers in
the Chancellery Office, who recommended that the Chancellor adopt the
alternative ("sudden death") solution, which was certainly risky, but from
the political point of view, the only realistic one. In any case, there was no
time to lose: because of its acute balance of payments crisis, the GDR was on
the verge of bankruptcy. The citizens of the GDR were no longer to be con-
soled. They finally wanted "proper money" and were ready to embrace with
fervour the D-Mark, the symbol of West German prosperity. *"If the D-Mark
comes, we stay; if it doesn't come, we will go to it!"* was now the slogan of
many would-be emigrants at demonstrations in the GDR. In order to stop
the mass exodus, which was now also arousing criticism and discontent
among the population of the Federal Republic, and to hinder the implosion
of the GDR, Chancellor Kohl finally decided (against the advice of many

economists, who of course did not have to bear the political responsibility) for an immediate economic, currency and social union between the two Germanies. Thereby all the previous gradualist plans were so much waste paper. With the introduction of the D-Mark into East Germany the political reunification would automatically follow.

The population of East Germany was jubilant when Bonn's decision was made public. The Modrow government, however, was principally concerned about the risk of high unemployment that would inevitably be bound up with this process, as well as the destruction of the population's entire savings; for this reason it felt that a gradual unification lasting until 1992 would be a better way of achieving the currency union. Once again Modrow, this time at his meeting with Kohl in Bonn on the 13th of February 1990, repeated his request for a solidarity contribution from the Federal Republic of 15 billion DM to stabilise the situation in the GDR, which he felt would otherwise be unable to meet its financial obligations. The East Berlin Prime Minister was in this respect in agreement with the non-Communist members of his government who accompanied him to the meeting. However, it was too late for such measures. The Federal Government had made a policy decision to await the results of the upcoming elections to the People's Assembly. In addition, the Soviet leader now also gave his consent to the Chancellor's leap into the unknown.

Success for the CDU in the First Free Elections to the People's Assembly

The surprising success of the East CDU under Lothar de Maizière at the first free elections to the People's Assembly in the GDR on the 18th of March 1990, almost exactly 58 years (November 1932) since the last free elections in East Germany, removed any further hesitations regarding Chancellor Kohl's course towards economic and political unity. His appearance at rallies in the GDR became major events. Hundreds of thousands of delighted citizens applauded him ecstatically.

The Alliance for Germany (*Allianz für Deutschland*) consisting of the East CDU, the Democratic Awakening (*Demokratischer Aufbruch*—DA) and the German Social Union (*Deutsche Soziale Union*—DSU), with massive support both from the Western CDU and Kohl personally, stood for the rapid reunification of Germany, winning 48.1% of the vote with this programme. Indeed it was only eight mandates short of an absolute majority. The SPD, which argued for a gradual unification, and which was identified with the conspicuously sceptical remarks of its senior colleagues in West Germany who stressed the costs of unification, suffered a bitter defeat, achieving only 21.8% of the vote. The successor party to the SED, now called the PDS, won 16.3% of the vote, while the Liberals and civil rights group (*Bündnis 90*, Alliance 90) won only 5.3% and 2.9% of the vote respectively, the Greens getting 2%.

With a record turnout of 93%, the results were clear enough: the GDR should be united with the Federal Republic as soon as possible. "The workers had voted for the CDU", was Kohl's proud boast to the American President Bush, when the latter rang to congratulate him. In five years, Kohl added, one could make a flourishing land out of the territory of the GDR. His optimism was grounded in part on prognoses put out by the Federal Economics Institute, which expected a generally high rate of growth of nearly 4% in the coming years. In this scenario, the state would rapidly dispose of enough financial means for the modernisation of East Germany, and for the amelioration of social costs incurred as a consequence of restructuring.

THE GRAND COALITION UNDER PRIME MINISTER LOTHAR DE MAIZIÈRE (CDU)

In East Berlin, the Alliance for Germany rapidly agreed with the SPD and the (liberal) Alliance of Free Democrats (*Bund Freier Demokraten*) to form a grand coalition with Lothar de Maizière as Prime Minister. The governing parties also agreed that, in accordance with Article 23 of the Basic Law (*Grundgesetz*), at a time yet to be specified, the GDR should unite with the Federal Republic. The alternative way, founded on Article 146 of the Basic Law, foresaw a new joint constitution for a reunited Germany, and was supported only by civil rights campaigners and many Social Democrats. As against this, well over 80% of the population wanted to adopt the Basic Law as the constitution for the whole of Germany, and that without any fundamental changes.

In his announcement of the government programme on the 19th of April 1990, the first democratically elected leader of the GDR proclaimed as his most important aim the unification of Germany as quickly as possible, but also as circumspectly as would be required. However, he alluded only very generally to the problematic economic and financial state of the GDR, although Kohl's chief negotiator for the currency union, Hans Tietmeyer, had urged him to be more specific. Tietmeyer, an experienced financial expert and long-standing State Secretary in the Bonn Finance Ministry, had been on the board of the German Federal Bank since 1990, and later became its President. Reminiscing in the year 2000, Tietmeyer pondered whether de Maizière "under pressure from his coalition partners, held back from telling it like it was, or whether he himself decided that the need to walk 'with head held high', which he had demanded of GDR citizens, did not permit him to be more candid. But one thing seems to me clear: a realistic description of the economic situation would have made many things a great deal easier later on."

INTRA-GERMAN NEGOTIATIONS ON ECONOMIC, CURRENCY AND SOCIAL UNION

A joint commission of experts consisting of representatives of the Federal Government under the leadership of Hans Tietmeyer, and of the GDR government under the leadership of Günter Krause, who was Parliamentary State Secretary to Prime Minister de Maizière and the Chairman of the CDU fraction in the People's Assembly, took only three weeks to work out the details of the State Treaty encompassing currency, economic and social union. In fulfilling this task, the commission was able to base itself on comprehensive preliminary work carried out by the Federal Ministry of Finance, the German Federal Bank and other bodies.

The negotiations were complicated, since the material being dealt with was itself intractable, but above all because of the differing views of the negotiating partners. Particularly contentious was the rate at which the East Mark should be converted to the West Mark. At first, the negotiators from the GDR demanded a direct conversion at 1:1, to be accompanied by a simultaneous write-off of all the domestic debts of business concerns. This proposal, however, met with fierce resistance from the West German side, which warned of the exceptional danger this might pose to the competitiveness of the GDR economy, of the excessive wage costs it would create with concomitant unemployment, and of the likelihood of stoking inflation through excess liquidity. However, Kohl and other West German politicians had aroused expectations among the GDR population during the election campaign, and these could hardly now be reneged on, even if they were highly questionable in terms of economics. For this reason a compromise was agreed, as follows: salaries, wages, pensions and rents were converted at 1:1, bank savings and credits were generally converted at 2:1, while some age-limited free allowances with credit balances of between 2000 and 6000 Marks were to be converted at 1:1.

Hardly less difficult was the question of property ownership, where it was agreed that the expropriations carried out under Soviet occupation between 1945 and 1949 should not be reversed, while in the case of the later expropriations ordered under the GDR, the basic principle of restitution rather than compensation should apply. The extremely controversial details were, however, only dealt with later in the context of the Unification Treaty of August 1990. As regards welfare, notwithstanding the fears that were expressed that the health system of West Germany could be overwhelmed, no transitional arrangements were accepted, but instead the entire rights vested in the social security system of the GDR were transferred into the West German one. In addition, the Federal Government and the eleven West German *Länder* created the material basis for the reconstruction of East Germany with a jointly financed "Fund for German Unity", which it was anticipated would require 115 billion DM for the period up to 1994.

On the 18th of May 1990, the two German Finance Ministers, Theo Waigel (CSU) and Walter Romberg (SPD), signed the historic treaty for the introduction of the social market economy in the GDR and the substitution of the GDR currency by DM, to take place on the 1st of July, 1990. With the agreement of the new government in East Berlin, Kohl had fixed this date so that the GDR citizens should have the D-Mark already at their disposal before the beginning of the summer holidays. In addition, the GDR adopted the West German social security system, while the Federal Republic reciprocally guaranteed the deficits of the GDR budget for a transitional period and overtook the financing of East German social security. With these agreements, the GDR gave up its sovereignty in all financial areas once and for all.

FROM EUPHORIA TO DISILLUSION: THE D-MARK AND THE SOCIAL MARKET ECONOMY IN THE GDR

The vital step towards a single currency, the single most important milestone on the way to the reconstitution of German unity, had now been taken. From the 1st of July 1990, the citizens of East Germany could exchange their East Marks for the long coveted D-Mark. From the technical and organisational points of view, the implementation of this currency substitution can be seen as a bravura performance by the German Federal Bank, which organised the largest transport of money of all time: 28 billion DM were taken to 10,000 distribution points in East Germany. In all, 300 billion East Marks owned by private individuals in the GDR were exchanged for 182 billion D-Marks.

The transformation of a bombed out and largely uncompetitive command economy, with its extremely low level of productivity (30% that of the West Germans), into an internationally competitive social market economy, brought with it severe problems for millions of people, as they sought to adapt their lives. However, this downside to reunification only became clear later.

Both in West and East Germany people had largely false expectations. The inherited burden of a forty-year-long planned economy could not be cleared away in a few years, as had widely been assumed. With a knowing wink, prominent players on the scene later observed that, once you are obliged to fight campaigns in free elections, it is rash to set about unravelling a planned economy too quickly. However, the real ground for this mistaken forecast of the time that would be required for an economic cure, and for the misconceived initial optimism which led to so much disillusion among East Germans in the 1990's and produced electoral gains for PDS, was that the actual economic state of East Germany was at first very hard to assess. The GDR was by no means the tenth strongest industrial power of the world, as the faked SED statistics would have had people believe. No less illusory proved to be the estimates of the book value of the GDR's assets. In the GDR statistical yearbook of 1989, a value of 1.74 billion GDR Marks was put on these assets. At the beginning of 1990, Prime Minister Modrow was using a figure of 1.6 billion GDR Marks, while at the end of the year Detlef Carsten Rohwedder, the first head of the Trust Commission (*Treuhand-anstalt*) that had been formed to administer the assets after reunification, still estimated a value of 600 billion DM. A few years later, by the time all the combines and factories of the GDR (over 15,000) had been sold and priva-tised, or in many cases dissolved (3700), and restructuring measures had been widely carried out, the Trust Commission (still the one set up by the Modrow government) presented a negative closing balance of 205 billion DM. Instead of asset value, the GDR left only huge negative balances for the Federal Republic to deal with.

However, no one knew all this in the summer of 1990. The free market simply swept the East German economy away, and GDR citizens felt that they could never have enough of it. Often they only bought western prod-ucts. Consumer temples and shopping malls sprouted everywhere in the newly created trading areas. The now free trades unions managed to push through wage rises of 50% or more, and the employers gave in to them. Soon, an ever increasing number of large-scale GDR concerns faced bankruptcy: in the West they were not competitive and in the East their mar-kets had collapsed. Mass unemployment was the result. At the same time, half the country seemed to have become a building site. Streets, autobahns, railways and houses were renewed, the most modern telecommunications systems were installed, light engineering and hi-tech firms were established. Demolition and construction went hand in hand, and most GDR citizens had to adapt their mode of living and working to a degree that Federal citizens could hardly imagine.

In retrospect it can be seen that the economic and currency union provided the indispensable basis for the political union of Germany that occurred a few months later. The latter was like a high wire act, albeit with a certain safety net, since the economically strong Federal Republic supplied over 1500 billion DM in massive investment and social transfer payments over the period from 1990 to 1999. In addition, some 160 billion DM were made available to cover the immediate political and diplomatic costs of reunification, much of it being applied to assist in the political and financial stabilisation of the successor states of the Soviet Union and in the reformed states of Eastern Europe.

GORBACHEV GIVES THE GREEN LIGHT FOR THE RECONSTITUTION OF GERMAN UNITY

By the middle of February 1990, the necessary dispositions for the ending of Germany's division had in practice been made, whatever other impression may have been given from time to time. After his meeting with Modrow at the end of January (*see above*), Gorbachev finally realised that Chancellor Kohl and US President Bush would be his two most important partners in the process of managing reunification. Later, he explained how he came to accept that he needed to come to an understanding with them "if [he] wished to achieve a just solution that was more or less satisfactory for all interested parties". Soviet self-interest also required that he accommodate the economically strong Federal Republic. The fact that both Bonn and Washington emphatically rejected any idea that Germany should leave NATO, and had already confirmed that a united Germany would be a NATO member, was well known to the Soviet leader. Notwithstanding this, Gorbachev and his Foreign Minister Shevardnadze attempted over several months to take soundings as to whether Soviet assent to reunification might yet be coupled with the creation of a special status for Germany. This was because they knew that the Russian public was extremely ambivalent at the prospect of a reunited Germany that would also be a NATO member. Furthermore, this unease also supplied a useful issue for exploitation by the opponents of Gorbachev in the military and the bureaucracy, which they didn't hesitate to use in pumping up the general level of hostility to the unpopular reformer.

On the 9th of February, 1990, the Soviet leaders agreed with the American Foreign Minister, James Baker, that all questions concerning the external impact of reunification should be dealt with in the context of the "Two-plus-Four Talks" (proposed by the Americans and welcomed by the West German Foreign Minister, Genscher), involving the Federal Republic, the GDR, the USA, the Soviet Union, Great Britain and France. In this way, matters would be decided in partnership with Germany and not over the heads of the Germans themselves. The internal issues of reunification were to be solved by the two German states on their own, without intervention from abroad. It was unanimously agreed that in these negotiations the security interests of all European states must be taken into consideration, which implied the recognition of the Oder–Neisse border by the German government. The question of Germany's NATO membership remained a matter for dispute.

The next day Chancellor Kohl, Foreign Minister Genscher and several of their senior staff arrived in Moscow. Baker had previously informed the Germans of the outcome of his talks with Gorbachev. The result of the German–Soviet talks on the 10th of February 1990 was to elicit a clear statement from Gorbachev that the composition of a German state was a matter for the Germans, who of course would be expected to take into account the interests of their European neighbours in coming to any decision. The still open question of their choice of alliance was to be clarified in the upcoming "Two-plus-Four" discussions. As Gorbachev remarked to Kohl: "Nothing can be done without you!" With this political sensation in their luggage Kohl and Genscher returned to Bonn.

THE "TWO-PLUS-FOUR" NEGOTIATIONS ON THE EXTERNAL ASPECTS OF GERMAN REUNIFICATION

In the middle of February 1990, the Foreign Ministers of NATO and the Warsaw Pact agreed in Ottawa that the external aspects of German reunification, including the question of the security of Germany's neighbours, should be dealt with as the Americans wished, namely by negotiations between the four victorious powers and the two German governments. East Berlin and Bonn were to be responsible for all internal aspects of reunification, for example the economic and constitutional merger of the two states. This outcome was not as easy to achieve as it appeared, since at that time there was a slew of other negotiations under way, from which different governments hoped to achieve a better settlement of their individual interests in respect of Germany. For this reason the Italians, the Dutch, the Spaniards and others also wanted to sit at the negotiating table of the "Two-plus-Four". However, Genscher's bruising reply to his Italian opposite number, who complained that Italy had not been included in the negotiations, became public knowledge. He said simply: "You are not part of the game!" The Polish government also repeatedly demanded to participate in the talks and found a sympathiser in the French President, François Mitterand.

The US government rejected all these demands, however, just as firmly as it had rejected the earlier proposals emanating from East and West, from Moscow, Warsaw, Paris and London, urging a purely four-power conference of the former victorious powers, or a peace conference of all the previous enemies of Germany, or a conference of the 35 CSCE members. The position of the Americans never wavered; moreover they had the power to impose it. Further, their view corresponded to that of Bonn, namely that the six powers of the "Two-plus-Four" forum should agree as rapidly as possible on the reconstitution of a united German state and the unconditional abolition of the Four Powers' legal rights, as well as an acceptable method of binding reunited Germany into Europe and NATO. This last was to be achieved with the express approval of the Soviet Union, and in a manner whereby the Soviet state should not be made to feel that it had been defeated.

On the 5th of May 1990, the "Two-plus-Four" negotiations began at a foreign minister level in Bonn. They continued in Berlin in June, in Paris in July and were concluded in Moscow in September. At the Paris negotiations the Polish Foreign Minister also participated, since these discussions concerned the question of the Oder–Neisse border.

These negotiations over several months were successful because they were accompanied by a large number of meetings between the politicians of the Allied organisations, together with other bilateral discussions. At these meetings the heads of government and their Foreign Ministers could hammer out a common negotiating line in personal talks and overcome such differences as cropped up from time to time. The senior civil servants from the central governments and foreign ministries involved also played an important role, defending the interests of their governments with subtlety and using their diplomatic drafting skills where necessary, yet also constantly seeking compromise. Likewise in the early spring and summer of this eventful year, there was a series of meetings between western statesmen with the Soviet leadership, in the course of which the remaining open questions concerning German reunification were dealt with. The most controversial points, which dominated talks and negotiations for months, concerned a united Germany's membership of NATO, the strength of the German army, the security guarantees for Germany's neighbours, the final demarcation of Poland's western border and the withdrawal of Allied forces from German territory.

THE CENTRAL CONTROVERSY: GERMANY'S
MEMBERSHIP OF NATO

Initially, Gorbachev and Shevardnadze attempted to prevent a united Germany from remaining a member of NATO. However, they found no support for this position in Western Europe, and none either among the members of the Warsaw Pact, including Poland. All the governments of both Eastern and Western Europe were agreed that the security of their countries would be best guaranteed if a reunited Germany was not left to itself. Without Germany, NATO would sooner or later begin to crumble, which would then call into question the maintenance of American forces in Europe.

In two meetings in May 1990, one with the US Foreign Minister, Baker, and the other with the French President, Mitterand, Gorbachev was forced to realise that his stance on the NATO question was not sustainable. Both the Americans and the French insisted that Germany must be integrated into solid European and transatlantic structures.

Baker, however, offered the Soviet side a series of security guarantees in a nine point programme, which the US government had agreed in advance with Kohl, and which was designed to make it easier for Moscow to swallow the pill of Germany's membership of NATO. Amongst other points, it was guaranteed that, for a transitional period, no NATO troops would be stationed on former GDR territory. Also to reassure Moscow, it was stated that NATO strategy would be revised to incorporate an undertaking not to engage in pre-emptive military action, while at the same time there was to be a drastic reduction of nuclear and conventional forces in Europe. In addition, Baker stated that Germany would renew its undertaking not to develop nuclear, biological and chemical weapons. Finally, the economic interests of the Soviet Union would be taken into consideration when reunification occurred, with compensation being paid where necessary.

A few days later, Mitterand likewise advised Gorbachev to resign himself to the inevitability of Germany's incorporation into NATO in the way that the US Foreign Minister had formulated. France herself had meanwhile been reconciled to this: "There is no sense in spitting in the wind," said Mitterand in Moscow; "I have not the slightest doubt about the determination of the Federal Republic and its supporter, the USA, in respect of the NATO question. What possibilities do we have? The USA stands foursquare on the side of the Federal Republic. Great Britain has taken up a somewhat reserved stance. I think that she is actually against the idea of the reunification of Germany. On the other hand, the British are adamant about Germany's membership of NATO. So we have very little possibility of preventing the Germans from doing what they so strongly want to do."

Since the elections to the People's Assembly, which had gone so well for the CDU, French foreign policy had accommodated itself to the realities of the situation. Mitterand was now anxious to portray himself once more as a reliable partner of the Germans and to assist in integrating a united Germany into the European Community, which itself was shortly to become a currency union with a single currency for all member states.

GORBACHEV NEEDS THE ASSISTANCE
OF THE GERMAN ECONOMY

Gorbachev knew that he stood alone with his obstructive attitude; at the same time he was largely dependent on urgently needed financial assistance from the West, which in the nature of things meant from West Germany. He could see the advantages that might accrue if Germany could become "a reliable and powerful partner" (Gorbachev); in particular, he was prepared to admit that the question of Germany's NATO membership was more of a psychological than a real issue, and now had little military significance. After all, the Cold War was over.

In May 1990, he had already signalled to Bonn his urgent need for credits. The sums mooted were from 15 to 20 billion DM for seven to eight years, as well as a short-term unconditional credit of 1.5 to 2 billion DM "for the resolution of current difficulties". In order to accelerate the transition to a market economy in the Soviet Union, he needed credits for the purchase of food, for the modernisation of light industry and for the supply of consumer durables, so that the population should be able to see that "something was changing for the better". At this moment what the Soviet Union needed was "oxygen" to survive. Such assistance was not to be expected from the Americans. Gorbachev could not have made it more clear to the Federal Government how much his political survival at the upcoming Congress of the Soviet Communist Party depended on bankable guarantees from Bonn. What was at stake was his re-election, and thereby the entire future of the Soviet reform policy.

The German Chancellor lost no time in reacting. Having held immediate discussions with leading representatives of the German banks, on the 22nd of May 1990 he offered Gorbachev an unconditional credit of up to five billion DM and expressed the basic willingness of the Federal Government to "support your country in overcoming the next difficult phase of economic adaptation and in the new configuration of your international financial relations".

He linked a proposal for comprehensive cooperation between the two countries to his offer, something he had already discussed in Bonn in March and April of 1990 with the Soviet Ambassador in Bonn, Yuri Kwizinski. The latter had reacted "almost euphorically", as Kohl's closest adviser in the Chancellor's Office, Undersecretary Horst Teltschik, remarked at the time. In early 1990, the Federal Government had already given evidence of its willingness to support reform in the Soviet Union by generously delivering food worth a hundred million DM. Later it continued this policy, specifically by taking over the GDR's supply obligations in respect of the Soviet Union. All these were preliminary gestures of support for Moscow which were to pay off handsomely a few months later.

The Turning Point: America and the Soviet Union Reach Agreement on the Question of NATO

There was no longer any doubt that good economic relations with an enlarged Germany was more important for a Soviet Union teetering on the verge of economic meltdown than the obstruction of united Germany's membership of NATO. Largely in order to save face with his opponents in the Soviet leadership, Gorbachev tried a final bluff in the question of German membership of NATO at a summit with Bush in Washington and Camp David at the end of May 1990. Unsurprisingly, the American President stood by his position. Finally, both statesmen agreed to leave it to the Germans themselves to decide which alliance they wanted to join. In effect this was the diplomatically formulated acquiescence of Gorbachev to the German–American demand that united Germany should join NATO. The Soviet–American summit of 30th of May 1990 thus marked a turning point in European history. As a *quid pro quo*, Bush confirmed the security guarantees for the Soviet Union which Baker had already outlined.

The West Supports Gorbachev

All this attracted vehement criticism from the conservative faction in the Party leadership in Moscow. In its view, Gorbachev's policy involved a sellout of Soviet interests, and Foreign Minister Shevardnadze should be disqualified from office for evidently seeing himself as "the most influential agent of the Americans" (Valentin Falin). Western governments anxiously awaited the outcome of the power struggle in Moscow, as the Party Congress of the Soviet Communist Party began in the 1st of July 1990. An end to the Gorbachev era could not be ruled out.

In a coordinated action with the Americans, Kohl hastened to confirm his offer of credit made earlier in June, which was gratefully acknowledged by

Moscow. Only four weeks later the Soviet Union drew down on the offered credit of five million DM.

As far as the recognition of the Polish western border was concerned, the Federal Chancellor prevaricated for a while with one eye on the votes of the Germans expelled from Poland, a tactic that earned him fierce criticism from Poland itself; yet he was simultaneously letting it be known through diplomatic channels that Germany accepted the existing Oder–Neisse line without reservation and would sign an appropriate border treaty with the Mazowiecki government after reunification. On the 22nd of June 1990, the Bundestag and the East German People's Assembly publicly confirmed this in a joint resolution, even if this still did not constitute a final acceptance in terms of international law.

At the beginning of July 1990, the Western Alliance definitively demonstrated to Moscow its willingness (at a NATO summit in London and at the world economic summit in Houston) to embark on comprehensive disarmament, as well as to provide economic assistance to the Soviet Union and its former satellites. In the London Declaration by heads of state and government, issued on the 6th of July 1990, the time of hostility between NATO and the Warsaw Pact was formally pronounced to be at an end: "The Atlantic community turns towards the lands of Central and Eastern Europe, which were our opponents during the Cold War, and stretches out its hand in friendship."

All these offers and signals from the West came at an opportune moment. Above all, the London Declaration helped to keep Gorbachev afloat, as one of his closest associates later confirmed. Gorbachev's critics were driven onto the defensive at the Moscow Party Congress. In open confrontations that lasted over entire days, his opponents tried to portray Gorbachev's foreign policy as one of surrender, in vain as it finally turned out. In Shevardnadze he had a shrewd defender of his strategy towards Germany. The reformers were in the majority and on the 10th of July 1990, Gorbachev was confirmed in his office as head of the Party and Head of State. He had ridden the tiger successfully and was more powerful than ever, at least for the time being.

CORDIAL GERMAN AND SOVIET MEETINGS IN MOSCOW AND THE CAUCASUS

All the necessary preconditions now existed for the success of the planned second meeting between the Chancellor (who was accompanied by Foreign Minister Genscher, Finance Minister Waigel and his most important advisers and associates) with Gorbachev on the 15th and 16th of July 1990 in Moscow and in Archys in the Stavropol district of the Caucasus. Nevertheless it was impossible on the Western side to be absolutely sure of success. The unpredictability of power relationships in Moscow could always provide unpleasant surprises. The results of the meeting therefore came as all the more of a surprise for even the best informed politicians and diplomats in Washington. The negotiations between Kohl and Gorbachev, and those conducted at the same time between the Foreign and Finance Ministers and their entourages of advisers, were conducted in a relaxed and friendly atmosphere. The agreement reached on the 16th of July 1990 marked a historic moment in German–Soviet relations and was no less than sensational: Gorbachev agreed to the unconditional reconstitution of Germany as a sovereign state within the borders of the Federal Republic, the GDR and Berlin, and accepted that it should become a member of NATO. Both sides agreed on the mechanics of a transitional phase leading up to the withdrawal of Russian troops from the GDR. Furthermore, the Soviet side accepted the German–American insistence that a united Germany should not require any special status within NATO. At the same time, these agreements were couched in a manner that allowed the Russians to save face.

According to the German–Soviet accord, until the final withdrawal of Soviet troops from East Germany within three to four years, NATO structures should not be extended to the area, although the units of the Bundeswehr that were not yet integrated into NATO could nevertheless be stationed there. NATO's security guarantee, a fiercely contested point over several months, was valid right from the beginning and was unconditional for the whole of Germany. After the withdrawal of the Soviet troops, German NATO contingents could also be stationed in the former GDR, but no foreign troops and no nuclear weapons could be deployed there.

Chancellor Kohl declared the willingness of the Federal Republic to reduce the strength of its armed forces to 370,000 men and to abstain from the manufacture, possession of, and access to, nuclear, biological and chemical weapons. Further, a two-page treaty was agreed concerning all issues arising from the withdrawal of Soviet troops and the future cooperation of the two states in all related areas. Important in this respect was the willingness of the Federal Government to finance a programme of house-building to accommodate the Soviet soldiers returning to their homeland, a project which was expected to cost at least a billion DM.

In Washington, President Bush's closest advisers in the National Security Council baptised the 16th of July 1990 "Victory Day", a date that would stand, said Robert L. Hutchings, for the belated liberation of the continent almost two generations after the victory of the Allies in Europe in 1945. Gorbachev and Shevardnadze had opted for a realistic policy, against the will of the conservative, and of course much weakened, traditionalist elements in the apparatus of the Soviet Communist Party and state: "We are not in a position to prevent the reunification of Germany, except by the use of force. Yet the use of force would have catastrophic consequences" was how Foreign Minister Shevardnadze later summed up the situation. In Gorbachev's view, German reunification was "not an isolated phenomenon, but part of a general reorientation towards a new Europe". The two Soviet politicians who had the most say at that time in shaping the destiny of their country spoke of the advantages, in terms of economic and financial assistance and security, that would flow to the Soviet Union from a policy of standing shoulder to shoulder with a united and NATO- Allied Germany. The Soviet Union could not in fact be reformed without Western assistance. "NATO was the devil they knew; a neutral Germany was the devil they didn't know and could not assess."(Angela Stent)

THE TWO-PLUS-FOUR TREATY: UNITED GERMANY BECOMES A SOVEREIGN STATE

The meeting in the Caucasus was intended to symbolise the beginning of the German–Soviet partnership, a partnership which was not directed against anyone, because it merely gave expression to what had already been gradually worked out through a process of international diplomacy lasting months. To this extent, the conclusion of the "Two-plus-Four" negotiations was really only a formality. At last the legally binding and definitive recognition of the Oder–Neisse boundary was no longer a possible bone of contention, and the issue was sealed with a German–Polish treaty a short while later. Also confirmed was Germany's freedom to choose an alliance, so that nothing now stood in the way of NATO membership. Even so, there were last minute diplomatic skirmishes. A few hours before the signing of the treaty in Moscow, the British (with the Americans totally in the dark) suddenly demanded a change in the text, so that NATO manoeuvres should later also be allowed in East Germany. It was only with great difficulty that Genscher, Baker and Dumas were able to persuade their British counterpart, Hurd, to drop this demand. Finally the Foreign Ministers of the six states concerned agreed a document on the 12th of September 1990, which was headed "Treaty on the Concluding Arrangements concerning Germany" (Two-plus-Four Treaty), which fixed in international law the reunification of Germany on the basis of the agreements reached between East and West. The treaty ended the rights of the four victorious, and subsequently occupying, powers that had been operative for 45 years in Berlin and in Germany as a whole.

Germany once more became an unconditionally sovereign country, with the agreement of all its neighbours in the East and the West. As Chancellor Kohl pointed out with evident satisfaction at a cabinet meeting held on the same day, this was the first unification of a country in modern history that had been carried through without war, suffering or confrontation.

BILATERAL AGREEMENTS: HORSE TRADING UP TO THE LAST MINUTE

In the preceding weeks, the Federal Government and the Soviet Union had agreed on the basic features of the planned bilateral partnership treaty. There was also unity on the regulation of the GDR's economic obligations to the Soviet Union, which had absorbed 40% of all East German exports (principally machines, military equipment and chemical products); and on the financial assistance to be provided by the Federal Republic in respect of the maintenance (*Stationierungsvertrag*) and withdrawal (*Überleitungsvertrag*) of Soviet troops by the end of 1994.

In the last minute, the Soviets attempted to squeeze considerably more money out of the Federal Government than had been informally agreed. Bonn had originally reckoned with subventions of 4.25 billion DM to cover the four year withdrawal period of the troops, but now the Soviet Finance Minister demanded 17.5 billion DM for the Soviet installations in the GDR alone, and even came up with a possible grand total of 36 billion DM. In his first telephoned reaction to Gorbachev, Kohl, while he realised the Soviet leader was under strong domestic political pressure, hoped to get the latter to agree an offer of somewhat over 8 billion DM. However, Gorbachev reacted negatively, and with surprising harshness ("I have the impression I have fallen into a trap") and hinted that without an improved offer everything would have to be renegotiated ab ovo. The poker game only ended when Kohl, after intensive discussions with Finance Minister Waigel and Economics Minister Haussmann, on the 10th of September 1990 offered Gorbachev an improved deal, whereby the total sum was topped up to 12 billion DM, of which 7.8 billion was to be allocated for building homes for the returning Soviet soldiers and their families. In addition, there would be an interest-free credit of 3 billion DM. That was perhaps the most expensive telephone call of all time, yet it was logical that the German side applied the advantage they had, and what Gorbachev above all needed: namely economic and financial strength.

The German–Soviet telephone diplomacy worked, and in two treaties dated the 9th and the 12th of October 1990 both the financial arrangements and the logistics of the maintenance and withdrawal from Germany of a 380,000 strong Soviet army were settled. On the first anniversary of the fall of the Berlin Wall, that is, on the 9th of October 1990, the German–Soviet Treaty on Partnership and Cooperation, as well as a comprehensive Economic Treaty, were ceremonially signed in Bonn during a visit of Gorbachev to the Federal Republic. The German–Polish Border Treaty of the 14th of November 1990, followed hard on its heels, signed in Warsaw by Foreign Minister Genscher and his Polish counterpart, Skubiszewski. The two states declared in this treaty that the existing border between them "was inviolable now and in the future". A special German–Polish cooperation treaty followed on the 17th of June 1991 and sealed the new spirit which was henceforth to inform relations between the two countries.

THE UNIFICATION TREATY: NEGOTIATIONS BETWEEN THE TWO GERMAN GOVERNMENTS

Simultaneously to the bilateral and multilateral negotiations on the external political aspects of the German reunification, intra-German talks continued on the outstanding questions regarding a rapid legal and institutional union of the Federal Republic with the GDR.

On the basis of a second state treaty, soon to be called the "Unification Treaty", the two German governments regulated the inclusion of the GDR into the Federal Republic, and thereby into the Basic Law in accordance with Article 23 (old) GG. In April 1990, the People's Assembly had already rejected the creation of a new constitution, as favoured in particular by civil rights activists and Social Democrats. On the 23rd of August 1990, the same body decided by a large majority to approve the merger with the Federal Republic, which was to be completed on the 3rd of October 1990. As early as July, the reconstitution of *Länder* dissolved in 1952 (Mecklenburg-Vorpommern, Brandenburg, Sachsen-Anhalt, Sachsen and Thüringen) was decided, to take effect from the 14th of October, 1990.

From the end of July 1990 until the end of August, the two government delegations under the leadership of Home Affairs Minister Schäuble and State Secretary Krause negotiated on the transfer of Federal Law and administration to the East German territory, including a time-limited provision for exceptional cases. Inter alia the negotiations settled such tricky questions as the procedure for dealing with Stasi files, the regulation of property and ownership, the administration of the assets of the East German political parties and the required financial adjustments for the *Länder*. The details of the transition were extremely complex and naturally not uncontroversial in respect of many individual points where political beliefs played a role; indeed there was no precedent for taking a democratic legal system that had grown up over four decades and imposing it wholesale on (in this case) East German society, the only near-exception being the merging of the Saar region with the Federal Republic in 1957.

There were many possible causes of conflict, not only between East and West, but also within the delegations themselves, which tended to split along party lines, as between the Union and the SPD. In August, the Social Democrats left the de Maizière government, after the Prime Minister dismissed his Finance Minister, Romberg (SPD), who wanted to retain all the East German tax income, an idea rejected by de Maizière, who feared losing the possibility of substantial subventions from the joint tax kitty of a united Germany. Another matter for dispute was the five per cent clause: the CDU wanted this applied separately in the East and West for the first all-Germany elections, a proposal which favoured the smaller parties, but not the SPD.

In all core questions, the view of the West Germans tended to dominate. Only in a few contentious points could de Maizière manage to make his case successfully. For example, the right to abortion of the GDR was to remain in force for a few years in East Germany. In addition, against the wish of the West German negotiators, the Stasi files were not to be transported to the Federal Archives and consequently closed for 30 years, but made available to the public (and above all to the victims of the Secret Service) under the aegis of an independent authority (the later *"Gauck-Behörde"*) that would act on the basis of a special law (*Stasiuntelagengesetz*—1991). Finally, the East German representatives also managed to modify the West's principle of "return without compensation" for houses and land expropriated since 1949 with an "investment limitation", so that such land and buildings need not be returned to their owners in the case that they were required for investment that would benefit the economy as a whole. In that case, only compensation should be paid.

Despite all the matters that had to be cleared up, the negotiations proceeded at a cracking pace and involved whole armies of experts attached to ministers or politicians from both Germanies; meanwhile, the citizens in the East and the West were, in the final resort and understandably, only really interested in what would come out at the end of them. On the 31st of August 1990, Wolfgang Schäuble and Günther Krause signed the treaty in East Berlin. In 45 Articles and around 1000 typed pages, it laid down all that was thought to be necessary to carry through the union of the two states.

The subsequent parliamentary debates in Bonn and East Berlin were held in the shadow of the upcoming election campaign for the first elections of a united Germany. However, although the Social Democratic chancellor candidate, Oskar Lafontaine, criticised the over-hasty merger between the GDR and the Federal Republic, and the PDS denounced the agreement in the People's Assembly as an "annexation treaty", the Unification Treaty was passed by both parliaments on the 20th of September 1990 with overwhelming majorities. In the Bundestag, 442 voted for, 47 against (the Greens and 13 MPs from the Union), with three abstentions; in the People's Assembly 229 voted for and 80 against (PDS, Bündnis 90, the Greens), with one abstention.

THE GDR ADOPTS THE BASIC LAW

The end of the GDR's history as a separate state had been reached. The sister political parties of East and West now merged. After the Liberals set the ball rolling in August, the SPD followed suit at the end of September and the CDU on the 1st of October 1990. The FDP and CDU, by merging with their eastern counterparts, acquired a strong voter base and assets, these advantages being however compromised by their former collaboration with the SED; on the other hand, the East German SPD had only its 35,000 registered members, built up over just one year, and no assets.

The National People's Army of the GDR was integrated into the Bundeswehr on the 2nd of October 1990. The People's Assembly now held its last session. In the evening, at a government ceremony to mark the event, Prime Minister de Maizière bade the GDR a "farewell without tears": "What for most people was still only a dream is now reality, namely that what obviously belongs together can once again function as one." In a televised address, Chancellor Kohl emphasised Germany's commitment to neighbourliness and friendship with the peoples of Europe. "The young generation in Germany, like hardly any other generation before it, now has every chance to live out its life in peace and freedom... Germany is our fatherland, a united Europe is our future."

At midnight (Wednesday, the 3rd of October, 1990, 0 hours) the GDR was "transferred to the territory where the Basic Law applied", as the process was described in abstract juridical terms. A black and gold flag of 60 square metres, carried by fourteen boys and girls from Berlin, was hoisted on the Reichstag building watched by jubilant crowds. The division of Germany into two states was history. In festive mood, but without nationalist excess, hundreds of thousands of people celebrated on the Platz der Republik close to the Brandenburg Gate an event that, only a year before, most Germans would not have reckoned with. In other German cities too, the reunification was celebrated with fireworks and street parties.

On the next day, the entire Bundestag, now swelled by 144 East German members, and making 663 in all, entered the Reichstag in Berlin together for the first time. Five new Ministers without Portfolio from East Germany belonged to the newly elected all-German government: Sabine Bergmann-Pohl, Günther Krause, Lothar de Maizière (all CDU), Rainer Ortleb (FDP), Hans-Joachim Walther (DSU). The voters, for their part, had had two opportunities in this eventful year to have their say on the political decisions that had led to the unexpectedly rapid reunification of Germany.

ELECTIONS TO THE LANDTAGE AND BUNDESTAG ELECTIONS IN A REUNITED GERMANY

The Christian Democrats emerged as the clear victors in the elections to the *Landtage* in East Germany on the 14th of October 1990, and formed the government in all nine *Länder* with the exception of Brandenburg (where the SPD came to power). The first Bundestag election in reunited Germany on the 2nd of December 1990 was really more of a plebiscite on the reunification policy of the Federal Government. For the first time in his political career, Helmut Kohl registered as more popular than his challenger. The Chancellor candidate of the SPD, Oskar Lafontaine, hoped to defeat the "Reunification Chancellor" by attacking his high-handedness and arrogance, by warning of the concealed social and financial costs of unification, and by predicting that taxes would rise. In the new *Länder,* however, his warnings fell on deaf ears. The majority of the inhabitants, both of the East and the West, were more taken with the optimistic prognoses of the governing parties. "Together we can make it" or "Yes to Germany—Yes to the future!" was the message of the Union, in whose campaign Kohl played a key role. The governing coalition also won the Bundestag election with aa clear majority (CDU/CSU: 43.8% of the vote, FDP: 11% of the vote) over the SPD opposition (33.5%), who posted their worst result since 1957. Nearly one million voters who had supported the SPD in 1987 went over to the coalition; even in the East, the party only achieved 23.6% of the vote. The Liberals could thank their dream result (10.6% in the West, 12% in the East) primarily to the popularity of Foreign Minister Genscher, a man of East German origin who hailed from Halle. Thanks to a few excess mandates, the Union came quite close to an absolute majority in the Bundestag with 319 seats out of 662. The most outspoken critics of reunification, the PDS and the Greens, were also among the losers at the polls, together with the SPD. Because (exceptionally) the East and West were counted as separate electoral territories for this election only, the PDS, despite achieving only 2.4% of the overall vote in Germany, entered the Bundestag with 17 MPs, since it managed to get 11.3% of the vote in its (East German) electoral area. Likewise the Greens, whose overall vote was only 3.8%, and who failed to surmount the 5% hurdle in the West with only 4.8% of the vote, nevertheless entered Parliament with 8 members due to the performance of the *Bündnis 90/Grüne* (Alliance 90/Greens) in the East, where it got 6% of the vote.

On the 17th of January 1991, Helmut Kohl was elected Chancellor with 378 votes against 257. His coalition government of CDU/CSU and FDP included three ministers from East Germany: Angela Merkel (CDU) as Minister for Women and Youth, Günther Krause (CDU) as Transport Minister, and Rainer Ortleb (FDP) as Education Minister. Hans-Dietrich Genscher remained Foreign Minister and Vice-Chancellor.

Continuation of the Policies of Integration

Thus, by the end of 1990, a year of great political happenings culminating in the reunification of Germany, the German voters had, by a large majority, legitimised the policy that had paved the way for this epoch-making event. The CSCE's 34 heads of government and heads of state also expressly confirmed in the "Paris Charter for a New Europe", issued on the 21st of November 1990, that the "German people had achieved reunification in the context of complete harmony with their neighbours", and described the event as an "important contribution to a lasting and just dispensation of peace in a united, democratic Europe, a Europe that [is] sensitive to its responsibilities for maintaining stability, peace and cooperation." These friendly diplomatic words were also a diplomatically phrased reminder to the German government to abide by the proven policies of European integration coupled with firm transatlantic ties.

Few citizens of a Federal Republic that had just been enlarged by one quarter in terms of population, and by one half in terms of territory, can have realised at that moment that their country had just been transformed into "a continental great power with worldwide influence" (Gregor Schölgen). The political leadership in Bonn, and above all the two architects of the reunification, Kohl and Genscher, realised this very well, however. They therefore repeatedly declared that united Germany would continue the basic foreign policy direction and traditions of the old Federal Republic. This implied full membership of NATO for a united Germany and an active participation in the deepening of the European integration process, which was not only an important concern of France, but was also seen by all Germany's neighbours as a test of their large Central European partner's willingness to exercise political restraint. With its agreement to the creation of a common European currency at the Maastricht Treaty of 1991, and its definitive relinquishing of the D-Mark, favourite mascot of the German people though it was, the Federal Government demonstrated that even a newly empowered Germany would hold to its trusted course in Europe. In this way, the largely unanticipated reunification of Germany actually accelerated the integration process very considerably. In 1993, Europe went on to create a common internal market, then moved to an economic and currency union in 1999, in which the Euro became the common currency of an association of states that was progressing steadily towards a closer union of the peoples of Europe.

CHRONOLOGY

1989

10 November 1989	At 11.30 a.m., the General Secretary of the SED, Egon Krenz, puts the two units of the National People's Army stationed in Potsdam on "high alert".
11–12 November 1989	On the first weekend after the opening of the border, three million GDR citizens visit West Berlin and the Federal Republic. In addition, up 250 people daily are leaving the GDR for good.
13 November 1989	The GDR lifts the exclusion zone along the internal German border. Hundreds of thousands take part in the Monday demonstrations in Leipzig and Dresden, tens of thousands in Cottbus, Halle, Magdeburg and Chemnitz (at that time Karl-Marx-Stadt) in favour of free elections, freedom to travel, and against the "leading role" of the SED. Erich Mielke, the Minister for State Security, reports in the People's Assembly on the work of his authorities: "Dear Comrades, dear Members, we have an extraordinarily close contact with all working people" (*merriment*) "...I indeed love all people..." (*laughter*).
16 November 1989	Hungary applies to join the European Council.
20 November 1989	Mass demonstrations in Leipzig and in other cities of the GDR. The main slogan shouted is "Germany—one fatherland", a quotation from the first verse of the GDR national anthem.
24 November 1989	Reports appear in the GDR media concerning the privileged lifestyle of the political leadership of the SED (including exclusive access to hunting reserves, ownership of holiday homes and accumulation of western consumer goods).

28 November 1989	Chancellor Kohl explains to the Bundestag his "Ten Point Programme for Resolving the Division of Germany and Europe". *Neues Deutschland* publishes an appeal "For our country" signed by prominent GDR artists and members of the oppositional groups. The appeal demands that there should be an independent GDR as a "socialist alternative to the Federal Republic".
29 November– 1 December 1989	General Secretary Gorbachev visits Italy. He assures Pope John Paul II that in future religion may be practised without hindrance in the Soviet Union.
30 November 1989	The spokesman for the board of the Deutsche Bank, Alfred Herrhausen, is murdered by members of the "Red Army Fraction".
1 December 1989	The People's Assembly removes the "leading role" of the SED from the constitution.
2 December 1989	Summit meeting between US President Bush and the Soviet leader, Mikhail Gorbachev, on a warship off Malta.
3 December 1989	The Politbüro, with Egon Krenz at its head, and the Central Committee of the SED resign under pressure from their own membership base and in view of the continuing demonstrations. Honecker and other senior politicians are expelled from the SED. GDR citizens form a human chain across the country as part of a demonstration for democratic renewal. In Czechoslovakia, a new government is formed with the participation of independent groups.
4 December 1989	The end of the rule of the Stasi is heralded by the occupation of the local offices of the MfS in Erfurt, Suhl and Leipzig. The NATO Council meets in Brussels. President Bush sets out the conditions and framework for the solution of the German issue (including Germany's full membership of NATO). The Warsaw Pact meets in Moscow. The invasion of Czechoslovakia in 1968 is retrospectively condemned.
6 December 1989	Egon Krenz resigns as Chairman of the State Council and of the National Defence Council.
7 December 1989	The first session of the central "Round Table" is held in East Berlin with the participation of representatives of the SED, the Block Parties, the mass organisations and opposition groups. The Round Table is seen as a mechanism for auditing the govern-

ment. It decides that free elections should be held for the People's Assembly on the 6th of May, 1990 (later brought forward to the 18th of March). In addition, the successor organisation to the State Security Service is to be dissolved and a new constitution drawn up.

8–9 December 1989   The European Council meets in Strasbourg and confirms the right of Germany to be reunited in the context of the continuing European process of integration.

10 December 1989   The Communist President of Czechoslovakia, Husak, resigns in Prague; the Czech Communists lose their majority in a newly formed cabinet under Prime Minister Calfa.

14–15 December 1989 The NATO Foreign Ministers, meeting in Brussels, reconfirm the declaration of the European Council concerning German reunification.

16–17 December 1989 The SED gives itself a new name, the SED-PDS, and announces its commitment to radical reform of both state and society in the GDR; just prior to this declaration, the lawyer Gregor Gysi is elected Chairman of the new party; the motion for the complete dissolution of the Party, however, does not receive the necessary majority.

19 December 1989   Chancellor Kohl delivers an address to the Hungarian Parliament in Budapest.

20 December 1989   On his first visit to Prime Minister Modrow in Dresden, Chancellor Kohl is jubilantly received by the people. The two heads of government agree to hold negotiations concerning a treaty-based community comprising the two Germanies.
Around 50,000 East Berliners demonstrate in favour of a "sovereign GDR", and "against reunification and the sellout of our country". There are similar demonstrations in Rostock and Cottbus.
The Soviet Foreign Minister, Eduard Shevardnadze, becomes the first Foreign Minister of a Warsaw Pact country to visit NATO headquarters in Brussels.

20–22 December 1989 The French President, Mitterand, visits East Berlin and Leipzig, this being the first visit to the GDR of a head of state of one of the three Western Allied powers.

22 December 1989   Opening of the Brandenburg Gate.
                    The Romanian Communist dictator, Nicolae Ceauşescu, is over-
                    thrown after violent mass demonstrations.

23 December 1989   Symbolic removal of border defences on the Czech–German bor-
                    der at Waidhaus with the participation of the Federal German
                    Foreign Minister, Hans-Dietrich Genscher, and the Czech For-
                    eign Minister, Jiří Dienstbier.

24 December 1989   The GDR removes the visa obligation and compulsory currency
                    exchange for travellers from the Federal Republic and West
                    Berlin.

25 December 1989   Spring" of 1968, is elected President of the Czech Parliament.
                    Nicolae Ceauşescu and his wife, Elena, are put before a Roma-
                    nian military court, condemned to death and subsequently exe-
                    cuted.

29 December 1989   Václav Havel, a writer and longstanding dissident, is elected the
                    first non-Communist President of Czechoslovakia since 1948.

30 December 1989   Proclamation of the Republic of Poland.

31 December 1989   343,854 emigrants have left the GDR for resettlement in the
                    Federal Republic during the year.

1990

3 January 1990   On the initiative of the SED-PDS, 250,000 people demonstrate in
                    front of the Soviet War Memorial in East Berlin against Neo-
                    Fascism and "anti-Sovietism".

15 January 1990   The Stasi headquarters in East Berlin are stormed.

19 January 1990   Ingrid Matthäus-Maier, the SPD spokesperson for political fi-
                    nance, suggests a currency union between the two German states.

28 January 1990   The SPD, led by Prime Minister Oskar Lafontaine, wins 54% of
                    the vote at the *Landtag* election in the Saarland. Lafontaine
                    becomes the Chancellor candidate of the SPD for the upcoming
                    elections to the *Bundestag* in December 1990 (he is officially
                    nominated on 19th of March).

30 January 1990   Gorbachev supports the Modrow plan for a step-by-step creation
                    of a united, neutral Germany ("Germany, a united fatherland").
                    Poland applies to join the European Council (and is followed by
                    Yugoslavia, Bulgaria, Romania and Czechoslovakia).

5 February 1990   A "government of national responsibility" is formed in East Ber-
                        lin under Prime Minister Modrow and includes eight Ministers
                        without Portfolio drawn from the opposition.
                        With CDU Chairman and Federal Chancellor Kohl in atten-
                        dance, the "Alliance for Germany" is formed, an electoral alli-
                        ance to fight the upcoming elections to the People's Assembly.
                        It consists of the CDU, the German Social Union (*Deutsche
                        Soziale Union*—DSU) and the Democratic Awakening (*Demok-
                        ratischer Aufbruch*—DA).

5–8 February 1990   Talks with the Polish Foreign Minister, Skubiszewski, are held in
                        Bonn. He stresses the necessity of guarantees for the Polish wes-
                        tern border and that the process of reunification shall be carried
                        out within the wider context of European integration.

6 February 1990   Chancellor Kohl proposes to the GDR that negotiations should
                        be held leading to a "currency union with economic reform".

7 February 1990   A cabinet committee for dealing with the question of "German
                        unification" is formed in Bonn.
                        New Forum (*Neues Forum*), Democracy Now (*Demokratie Jetzt*)
                        and the Initiative for Peace and Human Rights (*Initiative für
                        Frieden und Menschenrechte*) come together to form "Alliance
                        90" (*Bündnis 90*).

7–10 February 1990   The US Foreign Minister visits Moscow. The Soviet leadership
                        accepts the "Two-plus-Four" conference mechanism for settling
                        the external aspects of the reunification of Germany.

10 February 1990   Chancellor Kohl and Foreign Minister Genscher visit Moscow.
                        Gorbachev consents to the reunification of Germany.

12–14 February 1990   During the conference of the 23 NATO and Warsaw Pact states
                        in Ottawa, the decisions of the "Two-plus-Four" mechanism (i.e.
                        both German states and the Four Powers) are made binding for
                        settling the external aspects of German reunification.

13–14 February 1990   GDR Prime Minister, Hans Modrow, arrives for a working visit
                        in Bonn with a government delegation. Kohl refuses an immedi-
                        ate solidarity payment to the GDR of several billion DM,
                        requested by Modrow.

21 February 1990   The People's Assembly passes a law enabling immediate free,
                        general and direct elections to be held. One year's civilian servi-
                        ce is introduced as an alternative to military service (national ser-
                        vice).

8 March 1990	The Bundestag delivers a guarantee on the Polish western border.
9 March 1990	The French President, Mitterand, assures the Polish President, Jaruzelski, and Prime Minister Mazowiecki of his support for Polish security interests. The Poles are to be involved in the "Two-plus-Four" negotiations and a border treaty is to be concluded before the reunification of Germany is completed.
14 March 1990	Wolfgang Schnur, Chairman and co-founder of the GDR's "Democratic Awakening" party, is revealed to have been a long-standing Stasi agent and has to resign.
15 March 1990	Gorbachev becomes the first President of the Soviet Union.
18 March 1990	The first free elections are held for the People's Assembly in the GDR: the conservative "Alliance for Germany" gets 48.1% of the vote (CDU: 40.9%, DSU: 6.3%, DA: 0.9%). The SPD gets only 21.8% of the vote, the PDS 16.3%, the Liberals (BFD) 5.3%, Bündnis 90 2.9% and the Green Party 2%.
12 April 1990	The GDR People's Assembly elects Lothar de Maizière (CDU) Prime Minister. A grand coalition is formed.
19 April 1990	Lothar de Maizière announces his government's programme: "Unification must come as soon as possible, but the conditions for it must be as good, as sensible and as potentially enduring as is required."
25 April 1990	The SPD Chancellor candidate and Prime Minister of the Saarland, Oskar Lafontaine, is the victim of an assassination attempt in Cologne by a mentally unstable assailant, and is seriously injured.
27 April 1990	Negotiations begin on the intra-German state treaty to bring about a currency, economic and social union of the two states.
28 April 1990	The European Council, meeting in Dublin, welcomes German reunification as a "positive factor" for the European integration process.
5 May 1990	First meeting in Bonn of Foreign Ministers to kick off the "Two-plus-Four" negotiations (between the Federal Republic of Germany, the GDR, France, Great Britain, the Soviet Union, and the USA). The central topic is the alliance to which a reunited Germany may or should belong. The Soviet Foreign Minister, Shevardnadze, states that a united Germany cannot be a member of NATO.

6 May 1990	The first free local elections are held in the GDR. The CDU wins 34.4% of the vote, the SPD 21.3%, the PDS 14.6%, the Liberals (BFD) 6.7%, and Bündnis 90, 2.4%.
10 May 1990	Rallies and warning strikes are held to draw attention to worries about social security in the context of a united Germany. Demands are made for a protected internal market in the GDR and for higher wages.
16 May 1990	Passports are no longer obligatory for those passing the internal German border. A fund is set up to finance German unification (estimated requirement: 115 billion DM up to 1994).
18 May 1990	The two Finance Ministers, Waigel and Romberg, sign the first intra-German state treaty covering currency, economic and social union. US Foreign Minister Baker holds talks in Moscow. He presents Gorbachev with a "Nine Point Plan" incorporating security guarantees for the Soviet Union, to make it easier for the latter to accept German reunification.
30 May–3 June 1990	Summit between Bush and Gorbachev in the USA. Agreement is reached that the choice of alliance of a united Germany shall be a matter for the Germans themselves to choose. Disarmament measures are also agreed.
5–8 June 1990	Kohl holds talks with Bush.
6 June 1990	The cumulative arrests of an end-total of nine RAF terrorists, who had lived clandestinely in the GDR with the help of the Stasi, begin with the detention of Susanne Albrecht.
7 June 1990	In Moscow, the Warsaw Pact states declare that the ideological confrontation between the East and the West is over.
7–8 June 1990	NATO Foreign Ministers meet at Turnberry in Great Britain. NATO "stretches its hand out in friendship" to the Warsaw Pact states.
9 June 1990	Wolfgang Thierse is elected to be the new Chairman of the SPD in the GDR at a special party congress. His predecessor, Ibrahim Böhme, has had to resign after his longstanding activity as a Stasi informer (IM) became known.
13 June 1990	The demolition of the Wall begins in Berlin.

21 June 1990 — With large majorities, the *Bundestag* and *Volkskammer* pass the State Treaty implementing the currency, economic and social union of the two Germanies; on the next day the *Bundesrat* also passes it, with only the *Länder* of Niedersachsen and Saarland voting against.
The two German parliaments pass a resolution declaring the irrevocability of the Polish western border.

22 June 1990 — Second session of the "Two-plus-Four" talks in Berlin.

23–26 June 1990 — The European Council in Dublin produces a plan for economic support of the Soviet Union. It is agreed to hold a governmental conference in December 1990 to discuss European economic and currency union.

1 July 1990 — The D-Mark becomes the only legal tender in the GDR. The social market economy is introduced at the same time. Chancellor Kohl declares: "No one will be worse off than before, and for many things will be better."

1–13 July 1990 — At the 23rd Communist Party Congress in Moscow, the Soviet Communist Party abandons its claim to monopoly power. There are vehement confrontations between reformers and opponents of Gorbachev, the former, however, winning the day. It is agreed that there should be a more intense cooperation with the USA, with the states of Western Europe and most especially with Germany after reunification. Gorbachev is confirmed as General Secretary of the Party.

5–6 July 1990 — The NATO summit in London draws a symbolic line under the Cold War. NATO heads of state and government make a public declaration to members of the Warsaw Pact, stating that they "no longer regard them as antagonists".

14–16 July 1990 — Chancellor Kohl, Foreign Minister Genscher and Finance Minister Waigel travel to the Soviet Union. Gorbachev gives his approval for a reunited Germany with full national sovereignty, that may also be a NATO member. Both sides agree on the withdrawal of Soviet troops from the GDR and the reduction of German military forces to 370,000 men by the end of 1994; in addition, a comprehensive treaty covering Soviet–German relations is to be drawn up.

17 July 1990 — The third round of the "Two-plus-Four" negotiations in Paris, which is attended by the Polish Foreign Minister, confirms the Oder–Neisse line as the western Polish border.

22 July 1990	The People's Assembly passes a law restoring the *Länder* status of Mecklenburg-Vorpommern, Brandenburg, Sachsen, Sachsen-Anhalt and Thüringen, all of which had been dissolved in 1952. The law is to take effect from the 14th of October, 1990.
2 August 1990	Iraq occupies Kuwait and one week later declares its annexation.
20 August 1990	The SPD leaves the GDR government coalition led by Prime Minister de Maizière. The latter takes over the Foreign Ministry.
23 August 1990	The People's Assembly fixes the date of the 3rd of October, 1990 for the merger of the GDR with the Federal Republic of Germany.
24 August 1990	The People's Assembly passes a law concerning the safe-keeping and evaluation of the files of the GDR's State Security Service.
31 August 1990	The second intra-German State Treaty (Unification Treaty) is signed in Berlin by the Federal Minister for Home Affairs, Wolfgang Schäuble, and GDR State Secretary, Günther Krause. This treaty regulates the details of the merger of the GDR with the Federal Republic.
4 September 1990	For several weeks, civil rights activists have been occupying the former Stasi headquarters in Berlin in support of their demand that the Stasi files should remain in the former GDR and be made available to the victims of Stasi activities. An agreement is now reached with the Federal Government. On the 20th of December 1991, the Bundestag will pass the law based on this agreement, whereby an individual authority ("Gauck Authority") will administer the files, with its central office in Berlin and other offices in the East German *Länder*.
12 September 1990	Conclusion of the "Two-plus-Four" negotiations in Moscow with the "Treaty Covering the Final Regulations concerning Germany".
13 September 1990	The Federal Foreign Minister, Genscher, and the Soviet Foreign Minister, Shevardnadze, sign a treaty in Moscow covering "Good Neighbourliness, Partnership and Cooperation".
1 October 1990	Even before the ratification of the "Two-plus-Four" Treaty, the four victorious powers of World War II issue a declaration in New York confirming the abolition of their priority rights in Germany.

3 October 1990	The day of German reunification. The GDR is incorporated into the legal territory of the Federal Republic, whose Basic Law henceforth applies.
4 October 1990	First plenary session in the Berlin Reichstag of the all-German Parliament of 663 MPs, including 144 from the People's Assembly of the former GDR territory.
12 October 1990	Soviet–German agreement on the maintenance and withdrawal of the Soviet troops in Germany. On a visit to the hustings, Wolfgang Schäuble is the victim of an assassination attempt by a mentally unstable assailant.
14 October 1990	The first free *Landtag* elections since 1945 are held in the five new *Länder*. In four of these, the CDU emerges as the strongest party, while the SPD is victorious in Brandenburg.
9–10 November 1990	The Soviet President, Gorbachev, visits Bonn. Several Soviet–German cooperation treaties are signed.
14 November 1990	The German–Polish border treaty is signed in Warsaw. On the 17th of June, there follows a German–Polish treaty on good neighbourliness.
19–21 November 1990	Summit of the 34 CSCE states in Paris. The "Paris Charter for a New Europe" is issued and the division of Europe is declared to be at an end. A comprehensive disarmament treaty concerning the reduction of conventional forces in Europe is signed.
1 December 1990	An arrest warrant is issued against Erich Honecker, whose "shoot-to-kill" order had resulted in numerous deaths on the intra-German border.
2 December 1990	The first elections for united Germany are held. The governing coalition (CDU/CSU and FDP) emerges as victorious. The CDU/CSU Union wins 43.8% of the vote, the FDP 11%, the SPD 33.5%, the PDS 2.4%, Bündnis 90/Greens (in the new *Länder*) 5.1%. The PDS and Bündnis 90 are deemed to have overcome the 5% exclusion clause because, for this election, their totals are counted separately in the territory of the former GDR.
30 December 1990	Opinion polls (*Allenbach*) show that 57% of the citizens in the old, and 50% in the new *Länder* enter the New Year with "feelings of optimism".

13. In Retrospect

IRONIES OF HISTORY

With hindsight it certainly seems apt to speak of the irony of history. At a time when the GDR, in the late 1980's, had finally become accepted by a majority of the citizens of the Federal Republic as a second sovereign state in Germany, when senior SPD and SED politicians had just published a joint paper on "The Clash of Ideology and Mutual Security", when Head of State Honecker was being received by Chancellor Kohl with all the honours demanded by protocol, and finally when a leading German newspaper decided to change a policy of decades by dropping the depreciatory inverted commas round the name "DDR" and henceforth unequivocally accepting the name its rulers had chosen, at this very moment the SED regime actually stood on the verge of economic collapse. The end was near, but there was no one who would have bet on it.

The GDR had lived beyond its means. The Communist rulers in the East Berlin Politbüro believed they could legitimise their unelected hegemony by building a socialist welfare state. Under Honecker, the regime at first showed signs of being more widely accepted, because it heeded the needs of its citizens for comprehensive social security. However, this did not lead to any lasting stabilisation of its rule because the SED distributed welfare which overburdened the budget and could not be financed by the unproductive planned economy. Foreign debt owed to western countries accumulated alarmingly and financial dependence on the Federal Republic was ever greater, although of course only a few top functionaries of the regime actually knew about this. Egon Krenz complacently remarked after the apparent success of Honecker's visit to Bonn that "they [i.e. the West Germans] can no longer deny our existence". Two years later he found himself acting as a sort of political "administrator in bankruptcy" for the SED regime, though of course still believing that he could stave off the unthinkable at the eleventh hour, the unthinkable being that the Communists should lose power.

All this is now history, just as the reunification of a country that had been divided for decades is also now an objective fact of history. Many have already forgotten that the much cited "window of history" opened at time when no one expected it to, least of all those contemporaries who have been consistently critical of the results so far of the adaptation of the Eastern *Bundesländer* to the Federal Republic.

A TURNING POINT IN WORLD HISTORY:
BASIC CONDITIONS AND THE EVERYDAY STRUGGLE

It is very understandable that the economic and social problems of transition took up so much of the energies of so many people in the East, to an extent that the most positive event of all, namely the end of the SED dictatorship, was soon no longer as appreciated as it deserved to be. In addition, the vast majority of West Germans were quite unable to grasp the extent of the adaptation required by the new Federal citizens of East Germany. What had happened in 1998–90 soon began to seem to them like a foregone conclusion. On the other hand, the inconvenience of the practical requirements of reunification began to loom large in public opinion during the 1990's. Above all, the oppressively high level of unemployment overshadowed in public perception the undisputed major successes of reconstruction in the East.

If the whole process is placed in an historical perspective, however, it will be seen that the collapse of Soviet Communism, which was what made reunification possible, indeed marked a major historical turning point. The merging of the GDR with the Federal Republic set aside the borders drawn up in the wake of the Second World War, while the opening of the "Iron Curtain" marked the end of the Cold War in Europe. The opening of the Berlin Wall on the 9th of November 1989 meant that an anachronistic internal European border that had remained perilous right up to the last minute of its existence was now consigned to the dustbin of history.

The reunification of Germany finally occurred under the sort of conditions that had actually been anticipated by Kurt Schumacher and Konrad Adenauer, those two astonishingly foresighted and realistic statesmen who were the founding fathers of the Federal Republic. As early as 1947, Schumacher had identified social and economic achievement as fundamental; it was the prosperity of West Germany that should act as "an economic magnet" for the East. "From the German point of view, and viewing the matter in terms of *Realpolitik*, there is no other way in which German unity can be achieved than by West Germany acting as a magnet, so that it exerts so powerful an attraction on the East, that in the long term simply possessing the required apparatus of power [in the East German dictatorship] will be no guarantee of being able to hang on to that power. Certainly, this is a difficult and long road to embark on." Konrad Adenauer chose to emphasise the foreign policy dimension, which he saw in terms of the Federal Republic's close identification with the western alliance. "One can only negotiate with Soviet Russia when one is equal to it in power... My policy is concerned to build Germany into the Western dispensation, thus avoiding the danger of being neutralised; to strengthen the West; and to achieve a position from which to influence any negotiations with Russia that might one day become possible, and indeed to influence them in the interests of Germany." (1952) Nor is it now disputed that Willy Brandt's concept of a new "*Ostpolitik*" in the early seventies, with its aim of "change through drawing closer together", was an appropriate answer to the German problem at the time, in view of the division of the world into Eastern and Western spheres of influence with gigantic nuclear powers of destruction on both sides. Naturally, however, it is a matter for dispute among historians as to the causal connections that may lie between these three political concepts and the collapse of the SED dictatorship.

Whatever historical research may reveal of the aims, concepts and visions in respect of reunification that existed from Konrad Adenauer to Willy Brandt, one fact remains surprising and requires explanation, now that we have substantial testimony from all the major political actors dealing with reunification since the 1950's. This is that there were never any concrete plans drawn up to explore the ways and means by which a command economy might be transformed into a market economy, and a Socialist order of society into a democratic one. This lacuna would also explain why, in 1990, practically all the politicians and economic experts deceived themselves about the extent of the difficulties involved in the transition. On the other hand, one could equally well object that it is not every day that a state simply falls apart, and such an outcome was hardly to be expected. That the economic textbooks were unable to supply the sort of advice that was applicable to this unique situation was scarcely surprising. Absence of the relevant knowledge and experience resulted in seriously mistaken assessments, the root causes of which lay partly in the euphoria of the unexpected opening of the border, partly in the specific conditions that were shaped by a year of election campaigns, and last but not least in the widely held mood of wish fulfilment.

Mistaken Assessments and Their Consequences

The mistaken assessments of the government regarding the speed with which economic and social problems could be dealt with, and which represented the consensus that obtained at the beginning of 1990, led to serious consequences in East Germany: false hopes were aroused, then dashed, in a manner that was to have long-lasting repercussions.

A few months after the epoch-making breakthrough of 1989, when the Wall fell and the SED state collapsed, many in the East and the West were united in the hope that the two Germanies would soon find their way to an harmonious union. Bringing the living standards of the East up to those of the

West seemed to be something that could be achieved in only a few years. Many influential politicians believed that the necessary investments could be made, as it were, "from the petty cash". On the other hand, those who argued for a slower adaptation process, so that the economy of the East could be gradually assimilated to western free market conditions, were unable to produce any realistic concept of their own as to how this was to be managed; moreover they failed to address the fact that the obvious wish of the majority of the East Germans was to merge their country quickly with the Federal Republic and likewise to introduce the Deutschmark to the East immediately.

Disillusioned by years of restriction in the planned economy and hungry for consumption, the new Federal citizens in the East were only too willing to believe the promises of their new rulers that a "flourishing landscape" would, in only a few years, replace the drab greyness of the "real existing Socialism" of the collapsed GDR. However, as early as 1991, it could no longer be overlooked that the union of the two states in reality represented only a first step in a fundamentally more complicated economic and social process of unification. The mass unemployment provoked by necessary measures of reconstruction and renewal applied to the East German economy, an economy that was no longer remotely competitive internationally once the D-Mark had been introduced, rapidly emerged as the most serious burden of reunification.

Discontent and impatience were soon widespread. The optimism of 1990 quickly turned to feelings of defeat and existential angst amongst many of the new Federal citizens. In the area of former West Germany, many citizens reacted with incomprehension to the critical distance that a growing number of East Germans exhibited from the middle of the 1990's towards the market economy and democracy. Likewise, they showed little or no understanding of the social impact of the drastic changes being imposed on the former GDR territory. Many expressed disappointment, or even anger, that around 20% of the voters in the East regularly opted for the PDS (the successor to the SED) at election time, something which was often viewed in the old Federal Republic as demonstrating rank ingratitude. Soon people were talking about a "reunification crisis".

AN ECONOMIC AND SOCIAL TOUR DE FORCE
AND THE MOOD AMONG CITIZENS

In reality, all this was a crisis that arose from false expectations. For a start, as opinion polls regularly demonstrated, most of the population in the new Federal states were well aware that many jobs would be lost through the restructuring of the East German economy. On the other hand, lacking any experience of these conditions, hardly any realised what this would mean in practice for their life-styles, nor were they aware that the problems of change would be so long-lasting.

The material success of unification was accepted unequivocally by most of the East German population. What hit the people hardest was the loss of security and predictability in their daily life. This explains the nostalgia for the social security that existed under the GDR, a nostalgia shared by many East Germans. Two feelings thus ran parallel: on the one hand, nostalgia for stable social conditions (an assured job and living quarters), even if this had been on a relatively low level; and on the other, recognition that living conditions had improved since 1990, as 50% of the East German population stated at the end of the 1990's (28 per cent said there had been no change, and 22 per cent said things had got worse for them). Almost a decade after reunification, 65% of the East Germans (73% of West Germans) were content with their living standard. The majority of the East Germans still felt positively about reunification (1990: 64%, 1997: 55%), while the number of sceptics remained relatively stable between 1990 and 1997 (1990: 20%, 1997: 25%), and since then has noticeably decreased (2000: 16%). In West Germany, the corresponding opinion polls were more negative: in 1997 for the first time more citizens said they were sceptical about reunification (1990: 25%, 1997: 40%); the optimists registered 58% in 1990 and sank to 37% in 1997. However, since 1998, the citizens who are happy with reunification (in 2000, exactly 50%) again have the upper hand over the sceptics (in 2000, about 25%).

These and many other data from opinion polls give a snapshot of opinion at any given moment, but over a period of years they reveal a hardly surprising trend: the huge effort required for reunification between two so fundamentally different forms of state, economy and society has left the Germans both in the East and the West somewhat disillusioned. The East Germans especially, ten years on from unification, are fundamentally more critical of the social market economy and democracy under the Basic Law than they were at the beginning of the 1990's. At that time, the Allensbacher Institute for Opinion Research found only 5% of East Germans had a poor opinion of the economic system of the Federal Republic, while 77% were positive about it. In the year 2000, the figure for negative opinions had risen to 33%, while 31 % remained positive. However, since then the trough of dissatisfaction seems to have been passed, when one considers that, at the end of 1995, there were still 45% with a negative view and only 26% with a positive one. Satisfaction with the political system of the Federal Republic has overall been in decline, and especially among the younger generation of East Germans, as current opinion research demonstrates. On the other hand, in 2000, 61% of the East Germans were of the opinion that democracy had proved its worth, as against 49% in 1994. Only 8% argued for an authoritarian form of government with a "strong man" at its head, while in 1994 there were still 20% who were in favour of this. The positive trend in respect of the entrenchment of a free and democratic basis for the new *Bundesländer* was somewhat overshadowed in the 1990's by the increasing incidence of brutal attacks against foreigners and other acts of violence by right-wing extremists. The revival of extreme right politics is, however, a feature of Germany as a whole in the 1990's, generally expressed in the western part of the country through political agitation, and in the East more often in terms of acts of violence.

INTERNAL UNITY AS OBLIGATION
AND ONGOING PROCESS

All relevant research tends to reinforce the impression that, subject to an improvement in the economic situation in the new *Bundesländer*, and particularly if there is a decrease in the huge level of unemployment (17.7% in the East in 2001, as against 9.5% in the West), sympathy for the democratic model of society, and specifically for the social market economy, will rise. The same pattern was observable in the old Federal Republic in the 1950's. And only when there is sustained economic improvement in the new *Bundesländer* will it be possible to halt the emigration trend (most notably among young people) from the East to the West. In the year 2000 alone, 50,000 more people left the new *Bundesländer* than settled in them. Since 1991, the figure has been around half a million. Between now and 2020, a further million people could leave, according to demographic trends, unless new job opportunities with long term perspectives can be created. At least every third adult aged between 18 and 29, replying to surveys made in 2001, said that they wished to move to the old *Bundesländer* because of the lack of career opportunities in the East.

After a decade of German unity, the sobering reality is that both the East and the West must reconcile themselves to a considerably longer period of transition before the equalisation of living standards, that politicians and experts originally thought would come quite quickly, actually comes to pass. The latest prognoses are for a period of adjustment lasting from 15 to 20 years. Every year, 6% of Germany's GNP has hitherto been taken from the public purse for the economic and social restructuring of East Germany. After deducting the tax income flowing from the new *Länder*, the net transfer payment from West to East up to the end of the 1990's was more than

1500 billion DM. However, one quarter of this enormous sum was used for investment, while the lion's share was applied to the consumer sector, and especially to social security needs. It also needs to be borne in mind, however, that social benefits are not special services for the East, but spring from the general legal requirements that cover the whole of Germany. These payments are the price that all citizens are obliged to pay for German unification. The real incomes of the inhabitants of East Germany now show near-parity with those in the West: since the middle of the 1990's they have reached 90% of the Western level, and continue to grow. However, most economists believe that this rapid equalisation of wages and salaries is a mistake and partly hold it responsible for the stubbornly persisting high level of unemployment in East Germany. The economic capacity of East Germany, as measured by GDP per capita, has risen from around one third to over 60% of the West German level (1998), which is indisputably a remarkable success. On the other hand, economic dynamism has markedly slowed since 1995, with the result that the economic catching up process is now expected to last correspondingly longer. That being the case, realism and endurance are still required, as well as an awareness of the historical background to the current situation in the new *Bundesländer*, as has been described above. In such a climate of realism, even the most comforting of legends would soon lose their appeal.

CHRONOLOGY

1991

2 January 1991	New number plates for automobiles are introduced in the new *Bundesländer*.
17 January 28–February 1991	The Gulf War. For the first time the Federal Republic is involved (indirectly) in war, by supporting the military action with finance.
8 March 1991	The Federal cabinet decides on a solidarity supplement of 7.5% to be levied on income tax for financing the economic reconstruction of East Germany.
1 April 1991	RAF ("Red Army Fraction") terrorists assassinate the head of the Trust Commission, Detlev Carsten Rohwedder. Birgit Breuel is the new Chairperson of the Trust which, by 1994, will have privatised 14,000 former "people's" factories of the GDR.
30 April 1991	The last Trabant rolls off the production line in Zwickau.

30 May 1991	The former head of the Stasi, Erich Mielke, is arrested. In October 1993, he is sentenced to six years in prison for the murder of two Berlin policemen in 1931, but released on the grounds of age in August 1995. Because of his poor health, he is never tried for his Stasi crimes and the "shoot-to-kill" policy he had ordered to be carried out on the internal German border. He dies on the 21st of May 2000, aged 93.

20 June 1991   The German Bundestag, voting 338 to 320 in favour, decides to move the seat of parliament and government to Berlin. Eight years later, parliament and administration finally move to the capital.

2 September 1991   The first trial relating to shootings on the Berlin Wall commences against four GDR border guards. Over 100 prosecutions follow in the period up to the year 2000.

11 September 1991   Lothar de Maizière resigns his parliamentary seat following accusations of collaboration with the Stasi (which he continues to deny up to the present time). He has already resigned his offices in the CDU.

20 September 1991   In Hoyerswerda in Saxony rightwing extremists attack a home for asylum seekers. 30 people are injured. In Mölln (November 1991), Rostock (August 1992), Solingen (May 1993) and Lübeck (January 1996) the wave of violence against Vietnamese, and sometimes Turks, continues. Up to the present, there have been repeated incidences of rightwing and racist violence against foreigners both in the East and West of Germany, at the cost of numerous lives.

9–10 December 1991   The European Council meeting in Maastricht decides on the founding of the European Union, to incorporate economic and currency union. The treaty is signed on the 7th of February 1992 and comes into force on the 1st of November, 1993.

20 December 1991   The Bundestag passes the law regulating the Stasi archive.

1992

2 January 1992   Erich Honecker returns from exile in Moscow to Berlin, where he is placed in detention. In November, a trial opens against him and other members of the Politbüro relating to victims of the "shoot-to-kill" policy on the Berlin Wall. Two months later, he is released as unfit to plead on the grounds of illness. Together with his wife, Margot, who was formerly Education Minister of the GDR, he is allowed to go into exile in Chile, where he dies aged 81 on the 29th of May 1994.

Stasi victims are allowed to see their own files under the aegis of the so-called "Gauck Authority". The former priest and civil rights activist, Joachim Gauck, presides as administrator (until October 2000) of the office of the "Federal Commissioner for the Documentation of the State Security Service of the Former GDR" (*Bundesbeauftragter für die Unterlagen des Staatssicherheitsdienstes der ehemaligen DDR*) with its seat in Berlin. Eventually this office employs up to 3000 people.

8 October 1992   The former Federal Chancellor Willy Brandt died at the age of 78.

1993

1 January 1993   The European Internal Market comes into force, instituting virtually free movement of persons, goods, services and capital between member states.

17 January 1993   The East German civil movement, Bündnis 90, and the West German Greens merge to form a single party.

13 March 1993   Government, opposition and *Länder* agree on a further solidarity pact to finance German unification.

26 May 1993   The Bundestag alters Article 16 of the Basic Law, with 551 votes in favour and 132 against. The controversial new formulation of the right to asylum sharply reduces the numbers of refugees arriving in Germany.

29 October 1993   The European Community's heads of state and government decide that the Maastricht Treaty should come into force on the 1st of November. Simultaneously, the European Community (EC) becomes the European Union (EU). The European Central Bank, which is to be set up to administer the single European currency, is to have its seat in Frankfurt am Main.

6 December 1993   The provincial Supreme Court (*Oberlandesgericht*) in Düsseldorf condemns the former head of GDR espionage, Markus Wolf, to a six year suspended sentence for treachery and bribery.

1994

23 May 1994   In Berlin, the President of the Constitutional Court, Roman Herzog, is elected Federal President by the *Bundesversammlung* (Federal Assembly of both houses).

31 August 1994   Completion of Russian troop withdrawal after 49 years during which Soviet troops were stationed in Germany. The Federal Republic finances a housing programme costing 1 billion DM for the 546,000 soldiers and their families returning to Russia.

8 September 1994   A great military tattoo at the Brandenburg Gate marks the official leave-taking of the troops of the Western Allies.

16 October 1994   Elections are held for the Bundestag. The ruling coalition of the CDU/CSU and FDP wins by a small margin: CDU/CSU win 41.5% of the vote, SPD 36.4%, FDP 6.9%, Bündnis 90/Greens, 7.3% and the PDS, 4.4%. Helmut Kohl remains Federal Chancellor.

31 December 1994   The Berlin Trust Commission (*Berliner Treuhandanstalt*) concludes its activities after four and a half years. It has privatised around 15,000 state enterprises of the former GDR. Of the four million formerly employed in GDR state concerns, three million have lost their jobs. The businesses leave a heritage of 275 billion DM in debt, which cannot be recovered through the proceeds of privatisation. Until the end of 2000, the Federal Commission for Special Duties Relating to Unification (*Bundesanstalt für vereinigungsbedingte Sonderaufgaben*—BfS) continues the work of the *Treuhandanstalt*.

1995

26 March 1995   The Schengen Agreement comes into force. Except for Britain and Ireland, all EU states remove border controls for those passing between countries of the EU.

15–16 December 1995   EU heads of state and government agree in Madrid that the Euro shall be the common European currency. From the 1st of January 1999, it will be available for non-monetary transactions; three years later it will come into circulation as the sole EU currency.

1996

18 April 1996   The Federal Constitutional Court decides that the expropriations of real estate carried out under the Soviet occupation zone between 1945 and 1949 cannot be reversed, and thus confirms the rule incorporated into the Unification Treaty of 1990.

5 May 1996   The proposed merger between the *Land* of Brandenburg and the City of Berlin fails. In a plebiscite, 53.4% vote in favour, but 62.7% of the Brandenburger vote against.

30 June 1996   With the first "Golden Goal" in football history, the German national team defeats that of the Czech Republic at Wembley to win the European Championship.

16 December 1996   The MP Vera Lengsfeld and a further six former members of the East German civil rights group leave Bündnis 90/The

Greens and join the CDU. They accuse their former party of "drifting towards the PDS".

1997

14 February 1997   More than 200,000 people form a 10-kilometre-long human chain through the Ruhr area to demonstrate in favour of retaining the threatened industry of hard-coal mining.

30 May 1997   The Berlin regional superior court (*Landgericht*) condemns four former GDR generals to lengthy prison sentences on account of their co-responsibility for shootings on the internal German border.

17 July 1997   Thousands of people have to leave their homes when the River Oder bursts its banks. The Bundeswehr sends troops to the crisis-hit region and it is two weeks before water levels sink. People in both the East and West of Germany show enormous willingness to lend assistance, donating over 40 million DM in relief money.

27 July 1997   Jan Ullrich wins the Tour de France, the first German to do so.

25 August 1997   The GDR's last head of the State Council, Egon Krenz, is condemned to six and a half years in prison for his involvement in the killing of would-be refugees fleeing the GDR. The Federal Court of Jusftice upheld the judgement in November 1999. His co-defendants, Politbüro members Günter Schabowski and Günther Kleiber, receive sentences of three years each, which they begin to serve in January 2000. At the beginning of October 2000, both are pardoned by the Mayor of Berlin, Eberhard Deipgen (CDU). Krenz regards himself as "the victim of victor's justice". Because there is a judicial review of the case, Krenz will only begin his prison sentence on the 13th of January 2000. Meanwhile, he is offered an indeterminate stay of execution and enters a complaint of unconstitutionality at the European Court for Human Rights in Strasbourg. In March 2001 his complaint was unanimously rejected by the court.

1998

5 February 1998   Unemployment reaches its highest level in the history of the Federal Republic at 4.82 million. In East Germany, the jobless rate exceeds the 20% mark for the first time and is twice as high as in the west.

23 April 1998   The Bundestag votes to introduce the Euro for non-cash transactions, effective from the 1st of January, 1999.

| 24 April 1998 | The left-wing terrorist organisation known as the "Red Army Fraction" (RAF) announces that it has decided to disband. |

| 17 June 1998 | The Chairman of the PDS, Lothar Bisky, apologises for the brutal suppression of the popular revolt on the 17th of June, 1953 by the SED. |

| 10 August 1998 | After a trial lasting nine years, the Federal Supreme Court finally absolves the former GDR negotiator, Wolfgang Vogel, from the charge of blackmailing GDR citizens who wanted to leave their country. This decision quashes a conviction handed down by the Berlin regional court. |

| 2 September 1998 | Federal President Roman Herzog opens Potsdamer Platz in Berlin, a square situated on the former no man's land of the Berlin Wall. |

| 27 September 1998 | The SPD wins the Bundestag election with Gerhard Schröder as their Chancellor candidate, and collecting 40.9% of the vote. The CDU/CSU under Chancellor Kohl wins only 35.2%, its worst result since 1949. The Greens become the third strongest party with 6.7% of the vote, while the FDP wins 6.2% and the PDS 5.1%. A "red–green coalition" is formed under Chancellor Schröder. The CDU Chairman, Kohl, resigns his office in favour of Wolfgang Schäuble. |

| 3 November 1998 | In Mecklenburg-Vorpommern, the PDS participates in government for the first time by joining a coalition with the SPD. |

1999

| 1 January 1999 | The European currency union comes into force with the participation of eleven of the member states comprising a total of 290 million inhabitants. |

| 16 February 1999 | Chancellor Gerhard Schröder and twelve heads of leading companies agree to set up a compensation fund for those employed as forced labour under the Nazi regime. |

| 11 March 1999 | The Chairman of the SPD and Federal Finance Minister, Oskar Lafontaine, resigns all his offices. Chancellor Schröder is elected on the 12th of April to the Chairmanship of the SPD. |

| 24 March 1999 | The Kosovo war begins with NATO attacks on Serb positions. The aim of NATO is to stop Serbian genocide in Kosovo and to bring about the fall of the Serbian President, Slobodan Milosevic. For the first time in 54 years, German soldiers are once again involved in military action. |

1 May 1999	The Amsterdam Treaty concerning the further extension of European integration comes into force.
23 May 1999	The former Prime Minister of Nordrhein-Westfalen, Johannes Rau, is elected Federal President.
25 June 1999	The Bundestag approves the project of a Holocaust Memorial in Berlin in memory of the Jews murdered by the Nazis.
1 July 1999	Final session of the Bundestag in Bonn; henceforth it will meet in the *Reichstagsgebäude* in Berlin.
8 December 1999	The Chairman of the CDU, Wolfgang Schäuble, promises to clear up the contributions scandal surrounding the CDU without fear or favour in respect of any individual. As the affair unravels, former Chancellor Kohl is obliged to resign as honorary chairman of the CDU, when he refuses to supply the names of contributors who had given two million DM in undeclared donations. A few months later (16th of February, 2000), Schäuble is also obliged to resign from his offices as Chairman of the Party and of the Parliamentary fraction of the CDU. Angela Merkel is elected Chairperson of the CDU in April 2000.

2000

11 January 2000	The European Court of Justice decides that women are entitled to bear weapons in the *Bundeswehr* from 2001.
13 January 2000	Egon Krenz, the last GDR head of state and SED Party boss, begins his prison term in Berlin. His sentence of six and a half years for his co-responsibility for killings on the internal German border has been confirmed.
14 June 2000	As part of a reform of the *Bundeswehr*, the *Bundestag* decides on a reduction of its 320,000-man strength, bringing the total of men in uniform down to just 280,000 soldiers.
15 June 2000	The Federal Government agrees a "road map" with industry "for exiting from nuclear energy".
1 December 2000	The Bundestag passes the budget for 2001 (477 billion DM). The President of the Parliament, Thierse, declares: "This is the final budget that will be expressed in D-Marks. It is surely permissible to feel a little melancholy about this."
11 December 2000	The EU summit in Nice agrees an EU charter on basic rights and smooths the way for EU enlargement to the East.

Bibliography

The following titles represent only a small selection from the relevant literature which I have relied upon in constructing the present survey of German history since 1945. The bibliography is conceived as an aid for interested readers, who may wish to deepen their knowledge of the issues covered. Considerations of space have meant that recent publications have been given pride of place. Most of the books mentioned below should be seen as amplifying important earlier works, especially those dealing with specialised topics relating to the period here described. These may be topics arising in social history and the history of everyday life, or in memoirs and biographies, or in source books and documentation; or finally topics relating to controversies that have emerged in the wake of research. Using these topics as a base, it should be easy to access related articles appearing in study volumes and journals.

NOTE: In the following bibliography, the German abbreviation *Hrsg.* stands for "*Herausgeber*", in English, "*Editor(s)*". The abbreviation "*u.a.*" stands for "*und andere*", in English, "*and others*".

CHRONICLES

AUSWÄRTIGES AMT (Hrsg.): *Aussenpolitik der Bundesrepublik Deutschland. Dokumente von 1949 bis 1994* (Foreign Policy of the Federal Republic of Germany from 1949 to 1994), Köln 1995.

WOLF-RÜDIGER BAUMANN / WIELAND ESCHENHAGEN u.a.: *Die Fischer Chronik Deutschland 1949–1999. Ereignisse, Personen, Daten* (The Fischer Chronicle of Germany, 1949–1999. Events, Significant People and Dates), Frankfurt am Main 1999.

WOLFGANG BENZ: *Deutschland seit 1945. Chronik und Bilder* (Germany since 1945. An Illustrated Chronicle), München 1999.

HARTWIG BÖGEHOLZ: *Die Deutschen nach dem Krieg. Eine Chronik. Befreit, geteilt, vereint: Deutschland 1945 bis 1995* (The Germans after the War. A Chronicle. Liberated, Divided, Reunited: Germany from 1945 to 1995), Reinbek bei Hamburg 1995.

WERNER CONZE / VOLKER HENTSCHEL (Hrsg.): *Ploetz Deutsche Geschichte. Epochen und Daten* (Ploetz's German History. Periods and Dates), 6. aktualisierte Auflage (revised 6th edition), Freiburg 1998.

GEBHARD DIEMER: *Kurze Chronik der Deutschen Frage* (Short Chronicle of the German Question), München 1990.

ECKHARD FUHR u.a.: *Geschichte der Deutschen 1949–1990. Eine Chronik zu Politik, Wirtschaft und Kultur* (History of the Germans 1949–1990. A Chronicle of Politics, Economy and Culture), Frankfurt am Main 1990.

HANS GEORG LEHMANN: *Deutschland-Chronik 1945 bis 1995* (Chronicle of Germany 1945 to 1995), Bonn 1995.

HELMUT M. MÜLLER: *Brockhaus 1949–1999. 50 Jahre Deutsche Geschichte. Ereignisse, Personen, Entwicklungen* (Brockhaus 1949–1999. 50 Years of German History. Events, Significant People, Developments), Leipzig / Mannheim 1999.

HERMANN SCHÄFER (Hrsg.): *50 Jahre Deutschland Ploetz. Ereignisse und Entwicklungen. Deutsch-deutsche Bilanz in Daten und Analysen* (Ploetz's 50 Years of Germany. Events and Developments. A Stocktaking of the Two Germanies in Dates and Analyses), Freiburg 1999.

WALTER SÜSS: *Ende und Aufbruch—Von der DDR zur neuen Bundesrepublik Deutschland* (An End and a Beginning: From the GDR to the New Federal Republic of Germany), 2. Auflage (2nd Edition), Frankfurt am Main 1997.

ACCOUNTS AND INDIVIDUAL STUDIES

RALF ALTENHOF / ECKHARD JESSE (Hrsg.): *Das wiedervereinigte Deutschland. Zwischenbilanz und Perspektiven* (Reunited Germany. An Interim Report with Future Perspectives), München 1995.

KARL OTMAR FREIHERR VON ARETIN u.a. (Hrsg.): *Das deutsche Problem in der neueren Geschichte* (The German Problem in Recent History), München 1997.

EGON BAHR: *Zu meiner Zeit* (In my Time), München 1996.

ARND BAUERKÄMPER / MARTIN SABROW / BERND STÖVER (Hrsg.): *Doppelte Zeitgeschichte. Deutsch-deutsche Beziehungen 1945–1990* (Contemporary History in a Double Focus: Intra-German Relations 1945–1990), Bonn 1998.

PETER BENDER: *Die "Neue Ostpolitik" und ihre Folgen. Vom Mauerbau bis zur Vereinigung* (The "New Ostpolitik" and its Consequences. From the Building of the Wall to Unification), 4. Auflage (4th Edition), München 1996.

WOLFGANG BENZ: *Potsdam 1945. Besatzungsherrschaft und Neuaufbau im Vier-Zonen-Deutschland* (Potsdam 1945. Occupation and Renewal in the Germany of the Four zones), 3. Auflage (3rd Edition), München 1994.

WOLFGANG BENZ: *Die Gründung der Bundesrepublik. Von der Bizone zum souveränen Staat* (The Founding of the Federal Republic. From *"Bizone"* to Sovereign State), 5. Auflage (5th Edition), München 1999.

WOLFGANG BENZ (Hrsg.): *Die Geschichte der Bundesrepublik Deutschland.*
Band 1: *Politik*, Band 2: *Wirtschaft*, Band 3: *Gesellschaft*, Band 4: *Kultur* (The History of the Federal Republic of Germany. Volume 1: Politics, Volume 2: Economy, Volume 3: Society, Volume 4: Culture), Frankfurt am Main 1989.

PETER BOROWSKY: *Deutschland 1969–1982* (Germany 1969–1982), Hannover 1987.

WERNER BÜHRER (Hrsg.): *Die Adenauer-Ära. Die Bundesrepublik Deutschland 1949–1963* (The Adenauer Era: The Federal Republic of Germany 1949–1963), München 1993.

ECKART CONZE / GABRIELE METZLER (Hrsg.): *50 Jahre Bundesrepublik Deutschland. Daten und Diskussionen* (50 Years of the Federal Republic of Germany. Dates and Debates), Stuttgart 1999.

ROLAND CZADA / HELLMUT WOLLMANN (Hrsg.): *Von der Bonner zur Berliner Republik. 10 Jahre Deutsche Einheit* (From the Bonn to the Berlin Republic. Ten Years of German Unity), (Leviathan-Sonderheft 19), Wiesbaden 2000.

DEUTSCHER BUNDESTAG (Hrsg.): *Materialien der Enquete-Kommission "Aufarbeitung von Geschichte und Folgen der SED-Diktatur in Deutschland"* (Materials of the Commission of Enquiry into "Dealing with the History and Consequences of the SED Dictatorship in Germany"), 18 Volumes, Baden-Baden 1995.

DEUTSCHER BUNDESTAG (Hrsg.): *Materialien der Enquete-Kommission "Überwindung der Folgen der SED-Diktatur im Prozess der deutschen Einheit"* (Materials of the Commission of Enquiry into "Overcoming the Consequences of the SED Dictatorship in the German Unification Process"), 14 Volumes, Baden-Baden 1999.

MARION GRÄFIN DÖNHOFF: *Deutschland deine Kanzler. Die Geschichte der Bundesrepublik vom Grundgesetz zum Einigungsvertrag* (Germany, your Chancellors: The History of the Federal Republic from the Basic Law to the Unification Treaty), München 1992.

KLAUS DREHER: *Helmut Kohl. Leben und Macht* (Helmut Kohl: Life and Power), Stuttgart 1998.

JOST DÜLFFER: *Jalta, 4. Februar 1945. Der Zweite Weltkrieg und die Entstehung der bipolaren Welt* (Yalta, 4th of February, 1945. The Second World War and the Rise of the Bipolar World), 2. Auflage (2nd Edition), München 1999.

THOMAS ELLWEIN / EVERHARD HOLTMANN (Hrsg.): *50 Jahre Bundesrepublik Deutschland. Rahmenbedingungen, Entwicklungen, Perspektiven* (50 Years of the Federal Republic of Germany: the Rules of the Game, Developments, Perspectives), (PVS-Sonderheft 30), Opladen / Wiesbaden 1999.

HELMUT MÜLLER-ENBERGS (Hrsg.): *Inoffizielle Mitarbeiter des Ministeriums für Staatssicherheit. Richtlinien und Durchführungsbestimmungen* ("Unofficial Assistants" Working for the Ministry of State Security. Guidelines and Rules of Engagement), Berlin 1996.

RAINER EPPELMANN u.a. (Hrsg.): *Lexikon des Sozialismus. Das Staats- und Gesellschaftssystem der Deutschen Demokratischen Republik* (The Lexicon of Socialism. The GDR's System of State and Society), Paderborn 1996.

MICHAEL F. FELDKAMP: *Der Parlamentarische Rat 1948–1949* (The Parliamentary Council, 1948–1949), Göttingen 1998.

MARIO FRANK: *Walter Ulbricht. Eine deutsche Biografie* (Walter Ulbricht: A German Biography), Berlin 2001.

NORBERT FREI: *Vergangenheitspolitik* (The Politics of the Past), München 1999.

KARL WILHELM FRICKE: *MfS intern. Macht, Strukturen, Auflösung der DDR-Staatssicherheit* (The Ministry for State Security's Internal Power, Its Structure and the Dissolution of the GDR's State Security System), Köln 1991.

KARL WILHELM FRICKE: *Der Wahrheit verpflichtet. Texte aus fünf Jahrzehnten zur Geschichte der DDR* (The Debt to Truth: Texts from five Decades in the History of the GDR), Berlin 2000.

Geschichte der Bundesrepublik Deutschland in fünf Bänden (History of the Federal Republic of Germany in Five Volumes):
Band 1: THEODOR ESCHENBURG: *Jahre der Besatzung 1945–1949* (Volume 1: The Years of Occupation, 1945–1949), Stuttgart / Wiesbaden 1983.
Band 2: HANS-PETER SCHWARZ: *Die Ära Adenauer 1949–1957* (Volume 2: The Adenauer Era, 1949–1957), Stuttgart / Wiesbaden 1981.
Band 3: HANS-PETER SCHWARZ: *Die Ära Adenauer 1957–1963* (Volume 3: The Adenauer Era, 1957–1963), Stuttgart / Wiesbaden 1983.
Band 4: KLAUS HILDEBRAND: *Von Erhard zur Großen Koalition 1963–1967* (Volume 4: From Erhard to the Grand Coalition), Stuttgart / Wiesbaden 1984.
Band 5/I: KARL DIETRICH BRACHER / WOLFGANG JÄGER / WERNER LINK: *Republik im*

Wandel 1969–1974. Die Ära Brandt (Volume 5/I: The Changing Republic, 1969–1974: the Willy Brandt Era), Stuttgart / Wiesbaden 1986.

Band 5/II: WOLFGANG JÄGER / WERNER LINK: *Republik im Wandel 1974–1982. Die Ära Schmidt* (Volume 5/II: The Changing Republic, 1974–1982: the Helmut Schmidt Era), Stuttgart / Wiesbaden 1987.

Geschichte der deutschen Einheit (History of German Unification):

Band 1: KARL-RUDOLF KORTE: *Deutschlandpolitik in Helmut Kohls Kanzlerschaft. Regierungsstil und Entscheidungen 1982–1989* (Volume 1: Policy towards the German Question during Helmut Kohl's Chancellorship. The Style of Government and Decisions Taken, 1982–1989), Stuttgart 1998).

Band 2: DIETER GROSSER: *Das Wagnis der Währungs-,Wirtschafts- und Sozialunion. Politische Zwänge im Konflikt mit ökonomischen Regeln* (Volume 2: Taking the Risk of Currency, Economic and Social Union. Political Necessities in Conflict with Economic Rules), Stuttgart 1998.

Band 3: WOLFGANG JÄGER: *Die Überwindung der Teilung. Der innerdeutsche Prozess der Vereinigung 1989–90* (Volume 3: Overcoming the Division [of Germany]. The Intra-German Process of Unification 1989–90), Stuttgart 1988.

Band 4: WERNER WEIDENFELD: *Außenpolitik für die deutsche Einheit. Die Entscheidungsjahre 1989–90* (Volume 4: Foreign Policy in Support of German Unity. The Decisive Years, 1989–90), Stuttgart 1998.

HANS-DIETRICH GENSCHER: *Erinnerungen* (Memoirs), Berlin 1999.

JENS GIESEKE: *Die DDR-Staatssicherheit. Schild und Schwert der Partei* (The GDR's System of State Security: The Shield and Sword of the Party), Bonn 2000.

JENS GIESEKE: *Mielke-Konzern. Die Geschichte der Stasi 1945–1990* (Mielke's Firm: The History of the Stasi, 1945–1990), Stuttgart 2001.

MANFRED GÖRTEMAKER: *Geschichte der Bundesrepublik Deutschland. Von der Gründung bis zur Gegenwart* (History of the Federal Republic of Germany from Its Foundation up to the Present), München 1999.

MICHAIL GORBATSCHOW: *Erinnerungen* (Memoirs), Berlin 1995.

MICHAIL GORBATSCHOW: *Wie es war. Die deutsche Wiedervereinigung* (How It Was: German Reunification), Berlin 1999.

HERMANN GRAML: *Die Alliierten und die Teilung Deutschlands. Konflikte und Entscheidungen 1941–1948* (The Allies and the Division of Germany: Conflicts and Decisions, 1941–1948), Frankfurt am Main 1985.

CHRISTIAN HACKE: *Die Außenpolitik der Bundesrepublik Deutschland. Weltmacht wider Willen?* (The Foreign Policy of the Federal Republic of Germany. A World Power Against its Will?), Berlin 1997.

PETER HAMPE (Hrsg.): *Währungsreform und Soziale Marktwirtschaft. Rückblicke und Ausblicke* (Currency Reform and the Social Market Economy. Looking Back and to the Future), München 1989.

PETER HAMPE / JÜRGEN WEBER (Hrsg.): *50 Jahre Soziale Mark(t)wirtschaft. Eine Erfolgsstory vor dem Ende?* (Fifty Years of the Social Market Based on the Deutschmark: A Success Story Nearing its End?), München 1999.

WOLFRAM F. HANRIEDER: *Deutschland, Europa, Amerika. Die Außenpolitik der Bundesrepublik Deutschland 1949–1994* (Germany, Europe, America. The Foreign Policy of the Federal Republic of Germany, 1949–1994), 2. Auflage (2nd Edition), Paderborn 1995.

A. B. Hegedüs / Manfred Wilke (Hrsg.): *Satelliten nach Stalins Tod. Der "neue Kurs" 17.6.1953 in der DDR. Ungarische Revolutuon 1956* (Satellite States after Stalin's Death. The New Course from 17.6.1953 in the GDR. The Hungarian Revolution, 1956), Berlin 2000.

Klaus-Dietmar Henke / Roger Engelmann (Hrsg.): *Aktenlage. Die Bedeutung der Unterlagen des Staatssicherheitsdienstes für die Zeitgeschichteforschung* (The Archive. The Significance of the Documents of the State Security System for Contemporary Historical Research), Berlin 1995.

Volker Hentschel: *Ludwig Erhard. Ein Politikerleben* (Ludwig Erhard: The Life of a Politician), München / Landsberg am Lech 1996.

Ludolf Herbst: *Option für den Westen. Vom Marshallplan bis zum deutsch–französischen Vertrag* (Opting for the West: From the Marshall Plan to the Franco–German Treaty), 2. Auflage (2nd Edition), München 1996.

Jeffrey Herf: *Zweierlei Erinnering. Die NS-Vergangenheit im geteilten Deutschland* (Two Kinds of Memory: The Nazi Past in the Context of a Divided Germany), Berlin 1998.

Hans-Hermann Hertle: *Chronik des Mauerfalls. Die dramatischen Ereignisse um den 9. November 1989* (Chronicle of the Fall of the Wall. The Dramatic Events of the 9th of November, 1989), 3. Auflage (3rd Edition), Berlin 1996.

Klaus Hildebrand: *Integration und Souveränität. Die Außenpolitik der Bundesrepublik Deutschland 1949–1982* (Integration and Sovereignity: Foreign Policy of the Federal Republic of Germany, 1949–1982), Bonn 1991.

Hans Günter Hockerts (Hrsg.): *Drei Wege deutscher Sozialstaatlichkeit. NS-Diktatur, Bundesrepublik und DDR im Vergleich* (Three Ways to a German Social State: The Nazi Dictatorship, the Federal Republic and the GDR Compared), München 1998.

Robert L. Hutchings: *Als der Kalte Krieg zu Ende war. Ein bericht aus dem Innern der Macht* (As the Cold War Came to an End: A Report from the Innermost Circles of Power), Berlin 1999.

Jeremy Isaacs / Taylor Downing: *Der Kalte Krieg. Eine illustrierte Geschichte, 1945–1991* (The Cold War: An Illustrated History, 1945–1991), München / Zürich 1999.

Konrad Jarausch / Hannes Siegrist (Hrsg.): *Amerikanisierung und Sowjetisierung in Deutschland 1945–1970* (Americanisation and Sovietisation in Germany, 1945–1970), Frankfurt am Main 1997.

Konrad H. Jarausch / Martin Sabrow (Hrsg.): *Weg in den Untergang. Der innere Zerfall der DDR* (The Path to Destruction: The Inner Decline of the GDR), Göttingen 1999.

Konrad H. Jarausch: *Die unverhoffte Einheit 1989–1990* (The Unexpected Unification, 1989–1990), Frankfurt am Main 1995.

Eckhard Jesse / Armin Mitter (Hrsg.): *Die Gestaltung der deutschen Einheit. Geschichte, Politik, Gesellschaft* (The Formation of German Unity: History, Politics and Society), Bonn 1992.

Eckhard Jesse / Steffen Kailitz (Hrsg.): *Prägerkräfte des 20. Jahrhunderts. Demokratie, Extremismus, Totalitarismus* (The Dominant Forces of the Twentieth Century: Democracy, Extremism, Totalitarianism), München 1997.

Matthias Judt (Hrsg.): *DDR-Geschichte in Dokumenten. Beschlüsse, Berichte, interne Materialien und Alltagszeugnisse* (The History of the GDR in Documents: Resolutions, Reports, Internal Documents and the Testimony of Everday Life), Bonn 1998.

DETLEF JUNKER (Hrsg.): *Die USA und Deutschland im Zeitalter des Kalten Krieges 1945–1990* (The USA and Germany during the Cold War, 1945–1990), 2 Bände (2 Volumes), Stuttgart / München 2001.

MAX KAASE / GÜNTHER SCHMID (Hrsg.): *Eine lernende Demokratie. 50 Jahre Bundesrepublik Deutschland* (Democracy on a Steep Learning Curve: Fifity Years of the Federal Republic of Germany), (WZB-Jahrbuch 1999), Berlin 1999.

KARL KAISER: *Deutschlands Vereinigung. Die internationalen Aspekte. Mit den wichtigen Dokumenten* (Germany's Reunification. The International Aspects. Accompanied by the Significant Documents), Bergisch Gladbach 1991.

WOLFGANG KENNTEMICH u.a. (Hrsg.): *Das war die DDR. Eine Geschichte des anderen Deutschland* (That Was the GDR. A History of the Other Germany), Berlin 2000.

PETER GRAF KIELMANSEGG: *Nach der Katastrophe. Eine Geschichte des geteilten Deutschland* (After the Catastrophe: A History of Divided Germany), Berlin 2000.

CHRISTOPH KLESSMANN: *Die doppelte Staatsgründung. Deutsche Geschichte 1945–1970* (The Dual Founding of States: German History 1945–1955), 5. Auflage (5th Edition), Bonn 1997.

CHRISTOPH KLESSMANN: *Zwei Staaten, eine Nation. Deutsche Geschichte 1955–1970* (Two States, One Nation: German History, 1955–1970), 2. Auflage (2nd Edition), Bonn 1997.

CHRISTOPH KLESSMANN u.a. (Hrsg.): *Deutsche Vergangenheiten – eine gemeinsame Herausforderung. Der schwierige Umgang mit der doppelten Nachkriegsgeschichte* (German Pasts: a Joint Challenge. The Difficult Process of Coming to Terms with a Dual Post-War History), Berlin 1999.

MICHAEL KLONOVSKY / JAN VON FLOCKEN: *Stalins Lager in Deutschland. Dokumentation, Zeugenberichte* (The Stalinist Camp in Germany: Documentation, Eyewitness Accounts), München 1993.

HUBERTUS KNABE: *Die unterwanderte Republik. Stasi im Westen* (The Infiltrated Republic: The Stasi in the West), Berlin 1999.

GUIDO KNOPP u.a.: *Kanzler. Die Mächtigen der Republik* (Chancellors: The Powerful Men of the Republic), München 1999.

HELMUT KOHL: *"Ich wollte Deutschlands Einheit". Dargestellt von Kai Diekmann und Ralf Georg Reuth* (*"I wanted the unification of Germany"*. Presented by Kai Diekmann and Ralf Georg Reuth), Belin 1996.

HANNS JÜRGEN KÜSTERS / DANIEL HOFMANN (Hrsg.): *Deutsche Einheit. Sonderedition aus den Akten des Bundeskanzleramtes 1989–90* (German Unity: A Special Edition Drawing on the Documentation of the Bundeskanzleramt, 1989–90), Dokumente zur Deutschlandpolitik (Documents on Policy Regarding the German Question), München 1998.

EKKEHARD KUHN: *"Wir sind das Volk!" Die friedliche Revolution in Leipzig, 9. Oktober 1989* (*"We are the people!"* The Peaceful Revolution in Leipzig on the 9th of October, 1989), Berlin 1999.

EBERHARD KUHRT u.a. (Hrsg.): *Am Ende des realen Sozialismus. Beiträge zu einer Bestandsaufnahme der DDR—Wirklichkeit in den 89er Jahren—vier Bände* (At the End of Real Socialism. Contributions to a Stocktaking of the GDR: Reality in the 1980's) (Four Volumes):
Band 1: *Die SED-Herrschaft und ihr Zusammenbruch* (Volume 1: The SED Regime and its Collapse), Opladen 1996.

Band 2: *Die wirtschaftliche und ökologische Situation der DDR in den achtziger Jahren* (Volume 2: The Economic and and Environmental Situation of the GDR in the 1980's), Opladen 1996.

Band 3: *Opposition in der DDR von den 70er Jahren bis zum Zusammenbruch der SED-Herrschaft* (Volume 3: Opposition in the GDR from the 1970's to the Collapse of the SED Regime), Opladen 1999.

Band 4: *Die Endzeit der DDR-Wirtschaft. Analysen zur Wirtschafts-, Sozial-, und Umweltpolitik* (Volume 4: The Last days of the GDR Economy: Analyses of Economic, Social and Environmental Policy), Opladen 1999.

THOMAS KUNZE: *Staatschef a D. Die letzten Jahre des Erich Honecker* (A Former Head of State: The Last Years of Erich Honecker), Berlin 2001.

ULRICH LAPPENKÜPER / DANIEL KOSTHORST: *Bundesrepublik Deutschland. Ein halbes Jahrhundert im Bild* (The Federal Republic of Germany: Half a Century in Pictures), Köln 1999

BERND LINDNER: *Die demokratische Revolution in der DDR 1989–90* (The Democratic Revolution on the GDR, 1989–90), Bonn 1998.

JAN N. LORENZEN: *Erich Honecker. Eine Biographie* (Erich Honecker: A Biography), Reinbeck bei Hamburg 2001.

WILFRIED LOTH: *Helsinki, 1. August 1975. Entspannung und Abrüstung* (Helsinki, the 1st of August, 1975. Détente and Disarmament), München 1998.

WILFRIED LOTH: *Die Teilung der Welt. Geschichte des Kalten Krieges 1941–1955* (The Division of the World: A History of the Cold War, 1941–1955), 9. Auflage (9th Edition), München 1999.

ULRICH MÄHLERT: *Kleine Geschichte der DDR* (A Pocket History of the GDR), 2. Auflage (2nd Edition), München 1999.

PETER MÄRZ (Hrsg.): *40 Jahre Zweistaatlichkeit in Deutschland. Eine Bilanz* (Forty years of Two States in Germany: An Assessment), München 1999.

PETER MÄRZ (Hrsg.): *Dokumente zu Deutschland 1944–1994* (Documents Concerning Germany, 1944–1994), 2. Auflage (2nd Edition), München 2000.

PETER MÄRZ / HEINRICH OBERREUTER (Hrsg.): *Weichenstellung für Deutschland. Der Verfassungskonvent von Herrenchiemsee* (Setting a Course for Germany: The Constitutional Conference at Herrenchiemsee), München 1999.

WERNER MAIBAUM: *Geschichte der Deutschlandpolitik* (History of Policy Regarding the German Question), Bonn 1998.

CHARLES S. MAIER: *Das Verschwinden der DDR und der Untergang des Kommunismus* (The Disappearance of the GDR and the Decline of Communism), Frankfurt am Main 1999.

ARMIN MITTER / STEFAN WOLLE: *Untergang auf Raten. Unbekannte Kapitel der DDR-Geschichte* (Decline by Instalments: Unknown Chapters of the History of the GDR), München 1993.

RUDOLF MORSEY: *Die Bundesrepublik Deutschland. Entstehung und Entwicklung bis 1969* (The Federal Republic of Germany: Its Creation and Development up to 1969), 4. Auflage (4th Edition), München 2000.

HELMUT MÜLLER-ENBERGS u.a. (Hrsg.): *Wer war wer in der DDR? Ein biographisches Lexikon* (Who was Who in the GDR? A Biographical Lexicon), Berlin 2001.

NORMAN M. NAIMARK: *Die Russen in Deutschland. Die sowjetische Besatzungszone 1945 bis 1949* (The Russians in Germany: The Soviet Occupation Zone from 1945 to 1949), Berlin 1997.

HEINRICH OBERREUTER / JÜRGEN WEBER (Hrsg.): *Freundliche Feinde? Die Alliierten und die Demokratiegründung in Deutschland* (Friendly Foes? The Allies and the Establishment of Democracy in Germany), München / Landsberg am Lech 1996.

TORSTEN OPPELLAND (Hrsg.): *Deutsche Politiker 1949–1969* (German Politicians, 1949–1969), 2 Bände (2 Volumes), Darmstadt 1999.

WILFRIEDE OTTO: *Erich Mielke—Biographie. Aufstieg und Fall eines Tschekisten* (Erich Mielke—A Biography: The Rise and Fall of a Cheka Operative), Berlin 2000.

ALEXANDER VON PLATO / ALMUT LEH: *"Ein unglaublicher Frühling". Erfahrene Geschichte im Nachkriegsdeutschland 1945–1948* ("An unbelievable springtime": History at First Hand in Post-War Germany, 1945–1948), Bonn 1997.

MICHAEL PLOETZ: *Wie die Sowjetunion den Kalten Krieg verlor. Von der Nachrüstung zum Mauerfall* (How the Soviet Union Lost the Cold War: From the Arms Race to the Fall of the Wall), Berlin / München 2000.

HORST PÖTZSCH: *Deutsche Geschichte von 1945 bis zur Gegenwart. Die Entwicklung der beiden deutschen Staaten* (German History from 1945 to the Present: the Development of the Two German States), München 1998.

HEINRICH POTTHOFF: *Die "Koalition der Vernunft". Deutschlandpolitik in den 80er Jahren* (The "Coalition of Good Sense": Policy Regarding the German Question in the 1980's), München 1995.

HEINRICH POTTHOFF: *Bonn und Ost-Berlin 1969–1982. Dialog auf höchster Ebene und vertrauliche Kanäle. Darstellung und Dokumente* (Bonn and East Berlin, 1969–1982: Dialogue at the Highest Level of State and Confidential Channels of Communication. Presentation and Documents), Bonn 1997.

HEINRICH POTTHOFF: *Im Schatten der Mauer. Deutschlandpolitik 1961 bis 1990* (In the Shadow of the Wall: Policy on the German Question from 1961 to 1990), Berlin 1999.

PETER PRZYBYLSKI: *Tatort Politbüro. Die Akte Honecker* (The Politbüro Scene of the Crime: The Honecker File), Berlin 1991.

PETER PRZYBYLSKI: *Tatort Politbüro.* Band 2: *Honecker, Mittag* and *Schalck-Golodkowski* (The Politbüro Scene of the Crime. Volume 2: Honecker, Mittag and Schalck-Golodkowski), Berlin 1992.

GERHARD A. RITTER: *Über Deutschland. Die Bundesrepublik in der deutschen Geschichte* (On Germany: The Federal Republic in German History), München 1998.

HEIDI ROTH: *Der 17. Juni 1953 in Sachsen. Mit einem einleitenden Kapitel von Karl Wilhelm Fricke* (The 17th of June, 1953 in Saxony. With an Introductory Chapter by Karl Wilhelm Fricke), Köln 1999.

GÜNTER SCHABOWSKI: *Der Absturz* (The Crash), Berlin 1991.

WOLFGANG SCHÄUBLE: *Der Vertrag. Wie ich über die deutsche Einheit verhandelte* (The Treaty: How I Negotiated German Unification), München 1993.

AXEL SCHILDT u.a. (Hrsg.): *Dynamische Zeiten. Die 60er Jahre in den beiden deutschen Gesellschaften* (Dynamic Times: The 1960's in the Two German Societies), Hamburg 2000.

GREGOR SCHÖLLGEN: *Die Außenpolitik der Bundesrepublik Deutschland. Von den Anfängen bis zur Gegenwart* (The Foreign Policy of the Federal Republic of Germany: From the Beginnings up to the Present), Bonn 1999.

GREGOR SCHÖLLGEN: *Willy Brandt. Die Biographie* (Willy Brandt: The Biography), Stuttgart 2001.

KLAUS SCHROEDER: *Der SED-Staat. Geschichte und Strukturen der DDR* (The SED State: History and Structures of the GDR), München 1998.

KLAUS SCHROEDER: Der *Preis der Einheit. Eine Bilanz* (The Price of Reunification: An Assessment), München 2000.

HANS-PETER SCHWARZ: *Adenauer. Der Aufstieg: 1876–1952* (Adenauer: His Rise to Power, 1876–1952), 3. Auflage (3rd Edition), Stuttgart 1991.

HANS-PETER SCHWARZ: *Adenauer: Der Staatsmann: 1952–1967* (Adenauer: The Statesman, 1952–1967), Stuttgart 1991.

HANS-PETER SCHWARZ: *Das Gesicht des Jahrhunderts. Monster, Retter und Mediokritäten* (The Face of the Century: Monsters, Saviours and Mediocrities), Berlin 1998.

KURT SONTHEIMER: *So war Deutschland nie. Anmerkungen zur politischen Kultur der Bundesrepublik* (Germany was Never like This: Notes on the Political Culture of the Federal Republic), München 1999.

DIETRICH STARITZ: *Geschichte der DDR 1949–1990* (History of the GDR, 1949–1990), Frankfurt am Main 1996.

ROLF STEININGER / JÜRGEN WEBER u.a. (Hrsg.): *Die doppelte Eindämmung. Europäische Sicherheit und die deutsche Frage in den Fünfzigern* (The Double Containment: European Security and the German Question in the 1950's), Mainz 1993.

ROLF STEININGER: *Deutsche Geschichte seit 1945. Darstellung und Dokumente in vier Bänden* (German History since 1945: Presentation and Documents in Four Volumes), Frankfurt am Main 2002:
Band 1 (Volume 1): *1945–1947.*
Band 2 (Volume 2): *1948–1955.*
Band 3 (Volume 3): *1955–1969.*
Band 4 (Volume 4): *1969–2002.*

ROLF STEININGER: *Der Mauerbau. Die Westmächte und Adenauer in der Berlinkrise 1958–1963* (The Building of the Wall: The Western Powers and Adenauer in the Berlin Crisis, 1958–1963), München 2001.

ANGELA STENT: *Rivalen des Jahrhunderts. Deutschland und Rußland im neuen Europa* (The Rivals of the Century: Germany and Russia in the New Europe), München 2000.

Stiftung Haus der Geschichte der Bundesrepublik Deutschland. Zeitgeschichtliches Forum Leipzig (Hrsg.): *Einsichten. Diktatur und Widerstand in der DDR* (Insights into Dictatorship and Resistance in the GDR), Leipzig 2001.

GERHARD STOLTENBERG: *Wendepunkte. Stationen deutscher Politik 1947 bis 1990* (Turning Points: Significant Moments in German Politics from 1947 to 1990), Berlin 1997.

SIEGFRIED SUCKUT / WALTER SÜSS (Hrsg.): *Staatspartei und Staatssicherheit. Zum Verhältnis von SED und MfS* (The State Party and State Security: On the relationship between the SED and the Ministry for State Security), Berlin 1997.

HORST TELTSCHIK: *329 Tage. Innenansichten der Einigung* (329 Days: An Inside View of Reunification), Berlin 1991.

WOLFGANG THIERSE u.a. (Hrsg.): *Zehn Jahre Deutsche Einheit. Eine Bilanz* (Ten Years of German Unification: An Assessment), Opladen 2000.

BRUNO THOSS / WOLFGANG SCHMIDT (Hrsg.): *Vom Kalten Krieg zur deutschen Einheit. Analysen und Zeitzeugenberichte zur deutschen Militärgeschichte 1945 bis 1995* (From the Cold War to German Unification: Analyses and Contemporary Accounts of German Military History from 1945 to 1995), München 1995.

DIETRICH THRÄNHARDT: *Geschichte der Bundesrepublik Deutschland* (History of the Federal Republic of Germany), Frankfurt am Main 1996.

GERD R. UEBERSCHÄR (Hrsg.): *Der Nationalsozialismus vor Gericht. Die alliierten Prozesse gegen Kriegsverbrecher und Soldaten 1943–1952* (Nazism in Court: The Allied Trials of War Criminals and Soldiers, 1943–1952), Frankfurt am Main 1999.

JUTTA VERGAU: *Aufarbeitung von Vergangenheit vor und nach 1989. Eine Analyse des Umgangs mit dem historischen Hypotheken totalitärer Diktaturen in Deutschland* (Dealing with the Past before and after 1989. An Analysis of how Germany came to Terms with the Burden of its Totalitarian Dictatorships), Marburg 2000.

HANS-JOCHEN VOGEL: *Meine Bonner und Berliner Jahre* (My Years in Bonn and Berlin), München/ Zürich 1996.

CLEMENS VOLLNHALS (Hrsg.): *Der Fall Havemann. Ein Lehrstück politischer Justiz* (The Havemann Case: An Instructive Example of Political Justice), Berlin 1998.

CLEMENS VOLLNHALS / JÜRGEN WEBER (Hrsg.): *Der Schein der Normalität. Alltag und Herrschaft in der SED-Diktatur* (The Apperance of Normality: Everyday Life and Domination in the SED Dictatorship), München 2001.

HERMANN WEBER: *Aufbau und Fall einer Diktatur. Kritische Beiträge zur Geschichte der DDR* (The Rise and Fall of a Dictatorship: Critical Contributions to the History of the GDR), Köln 1991.

HERMANN WEBER: *Die DDR 1945–1990* (The GDR, 1945–1990), 3. Auflage (3rd Edition), München 1999.

HERMANN WEBER: *Geschichte der DDR* (History of the GDR), 5. Auflage (5th Edition), München 2000.

JÜRGEN WEBER / PETER STEINBACH (Hrsg.): *Vergangenheitsbewältigung durch Strafverfahren? NS-Prozesse in der Bundesrepublik Deutschland* (Are Criminal Proceedings an Effective Way of Coming to Terms with the Past? Nazi Trials in the Federal Republic of Germany), München 1984.

JÜRGEN WEBER (Hrsg.): *Die Republik der fünfziger Jahre. Adenauers Deutschlandpolitik auf dem Prüfstand* (The Republic in the 1950's: Adenauer's Policy on the German Question is Put to the Test), München 1989.

JÜRGEN WEBER (Hrsg.): *Geschichte der Bundesrepublik Deutschland 1945/49–1963*) (History of the Federal Republic of Germany 1945/49–1963), 5 Bände (Neuauflagen), (5 Volumes [New Editions]), München 1993/98.

JÜRGEN WEBER (Hrsg.): *Der SED-Staat. Neues über eine vergangene Diktatur* (The SED State: New Light on a Vanished Dictatorship), München 1994.

JÜRGEN WEBER / MICHAEL PIAZOLO (Hrsg.): *Eine Diktatur vor Gericht. Aufarbeitung von SED-Unrecht durch die Justiz* (A Dictatorship is Brought before the Courts: Dealing with the SED Criminality by Judicial Means), Landsberg am Lech 1995.

JÜRGEN WEBER (Hrsg.): *Der Bauplan für die Republik. Das Jahr 1948 in der deutschen Nachkriegsgeschichte* (Laying Plans for the Republic: The Year 1948 in German Post-war History), München / Landsberg am Lech 1996.

JÜRGEN WEBER (Hrsg.): *Das Jahr 1949 in der deutschen Geschichte. Die doppelte Staatsgründung* (The Year 1949 in German History: The Foundation of Two German States), Landsberg am Lech 1997.

JÜRGEN WEBER (Hrsg.): *Aufbau und Neuorientierung. Die Geschichte der Bundesrepublik 1950–1955* (Renewal and Reorientation: The History of the Federal Republic, 1950–1955), Landsberg 1998.

JÜRGEN WEBER / MICHAEL PIAZOLO (Hrsg.): *Justiz im Zwielicht. Ihre Rolle in Diktaturen und die Antwort des Rechtsstaates* (The Judiciary in a Dubious Light: Its Role in Dictatorships and the Response of the Rule of Law), München 1998.

WERNER WEIDENFELD / KARL-RUDOLF KORTE (Hrsg.): *Handbuch zur deutschen Einheit* (Handbook to German Unification), 3. Auflage (3rd Edition), Bonn 1999.

FALCO WERKENTIN: *Politische Strafjustiz in der Ära Ulbricht* (Politically Motivated Legal Punishment in the Ulbricht Era), Berlin 1995.

FALCO WERKENTIN: *Recht und Justiz im SED-Staat* (Law and Justice in the SED State), Bonn 1998.

GERHARD WETTIG: *Bereitschaft zu Einheit und Freiheit? Die Sowjetische Deutschlandpolitik 1945–1955* (Readiness for Reunification and Freedom? The Soviet Policy on the German Question, 1945–1955), München 1999.

HEINRICH AUGUST WINKLER: *Der lange Weg nach Westen. Zweiter Band: Deutsche Geschichte vom "Dritten reich" bis zur Wiedervereinigung* (The Long Road to the West. Volume Two: German History from the "Third Reich" to Reunification), München 2000.

STEFAN WOLLE: *Die heile Welt der Diktatur. Alltag und Herrschaft in der DDR 1971–1989* (The Self-Contained World of Dictatorship: Everday Life and the Ruling Power in the GDR, 1971–1989), Bonn 1998.

PHILIP ZELIKOW / CONDOLEEZZA RICE: *Sternstunden der Diplomatie. Die deutsche Einheit und das Ende der Spaltung Europas* (Great Moments in Diplomacy: The Reunification of Germany and the End of the Division of Europe), 2. Auflage (2nd Edition), Berlin 1997.